SOFT SURFACES

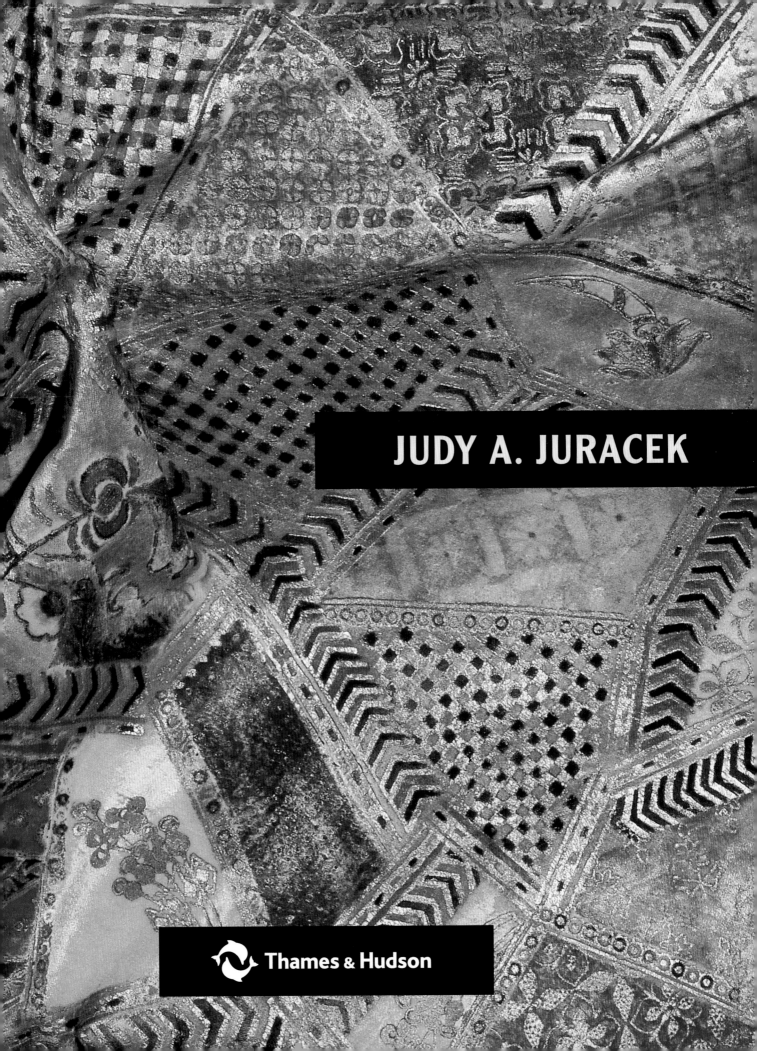

JUDY A. JURACEK

Thames & Hudson

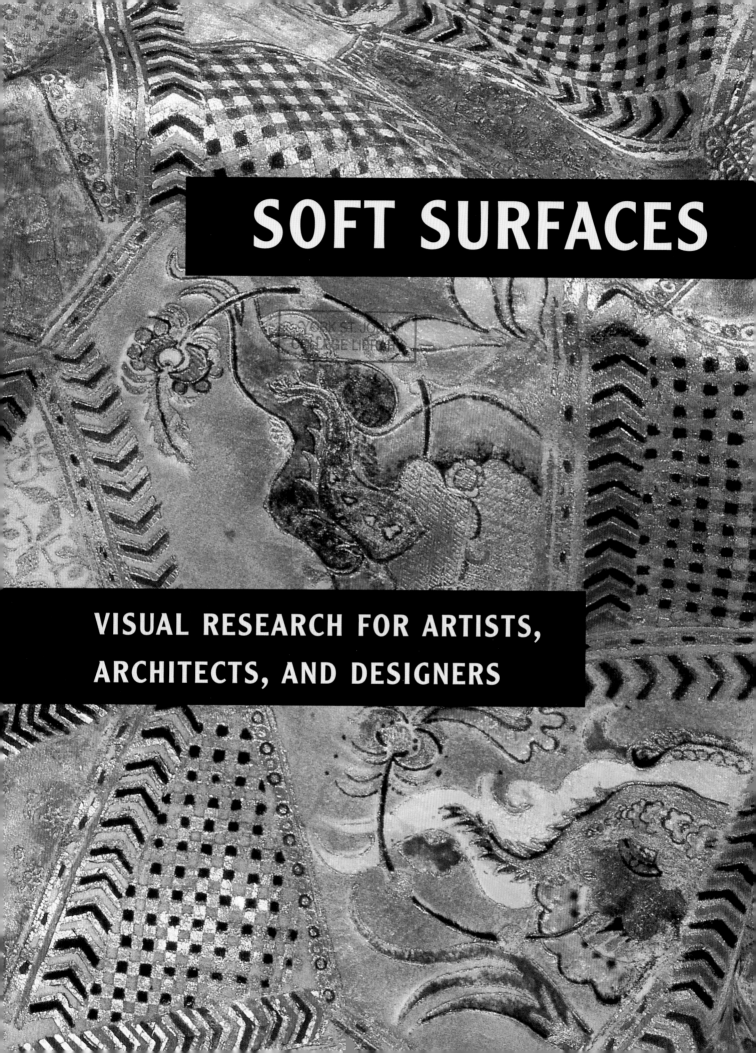

SOFT SURFACES

VISUAL RESEARCH FOR ARTISTS, ARCHITECTS, AND DESIGNERS

page 1. Top: Silver and gold lamé (Sommers Plastics). Bottom: Woven tubing,
fiberglass (white), aramid (yellow) (© Tech in Tex)
pages 2-3. Paint and graufage on velvet (Entree Libre/Sabina Fay Braxton, artist)
page 5. Bird on silk *fukusa*, Japan, Edo period (Orientations)

First published in the United Kingdom in 1999 by Thames & Hudson Ltd,
181A High Holborn, London WC1V 7QX

British Library Cataloguing-in-Publication Data

A catalogue record for this book is available from the British Library

ISBN 0-500-01969-X

Printed and bound in Hong Kong

Technical consultant: Marypaul Yates

The text of this book is composed in Clearface
Manufacturing by Colorprint Offset
Drawings by Dawn Peterson
Book design by Gilda Hannah

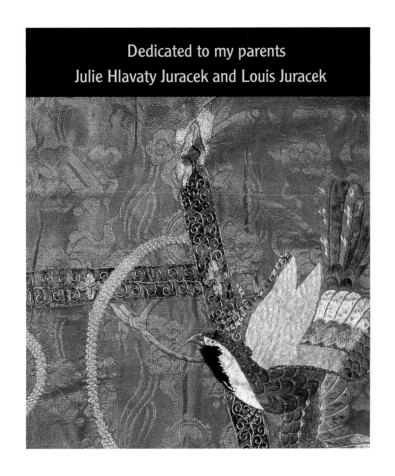

Dedicated to my parents
Julie Hlavaty Juracek and Louis Juracek

CONTENTS

BASIC WEAVES

PRINTED, PAINTED, DYED FABRIC

BROCADE, DAMASK DOUBLE CLOTH

NEEDLEWORK

PILE WEAVES

LACE, KNITS CROCHET, TRIM

RUGS & CARPETS

NONWOVENS

FURNISHINGS & STRUCTURES

WORKING PAPERS

ACKNOWLEDGMENTS

Most books are somewhat indebted to people other than the author. In the case of *Soft Surfaces,* it can truly be said that without the advice and generosity of those mentioned here and listed in the source section, this book simply would not have happened. Since I am a scenic artist by profession, my knowledge of fabric was that of an educated consumer who had researched and used it, not that of a textile professional. My personal network of sources and information was limited. To compile a photo-research collection requires access to a wide range of materials: this access was provided by individuals within the fabric industry and by those with historical collections who allowed me to photograph their materials, shared their knowledge and love of fabrics, and in many cases took the time to give information for the captions.

Early on in this project, Marypaul Yates agreed to advise me, giving this book a dimension that would otherwise not have been possible. Not only did she guide me in photographing her fabric library and help me in organizing the images, but she has generally lent the point of view of a professional in the textile business. Her expertise and fluency in it has been an invaluable contribution, particularly in compiling the glossary.

Various companies have been exceptionally gracious in opening their archives, collections, and showrooms to me. In particular, my gratitude goes to Robert Bitter at Scalamandré for the time he gave to this project, to Andrea Donaldson and Karen Rogers at Lee Jofa, Murray Douglas at Brunschwig & Fils, Christina Diechman at Grey Watkins, Ellen Lanahan at Randolph & Hein, Inge Lano at Manuel Canovas, Lloyd Jackson at Donghia, Maryanne Solensky at Pollack & Associates, Enriko Horiki at Shimus, Mizue Okada at Nuno, Fred Schecter at Sommers Plastics, Teddy Edelman at Edelman Leather, and to Suzanne Tick.

I also thank all the individuals, dealers, and collectors who allowed me to photograph their wonderful antique textiles, especially Rigo Carden, Elizabeth Enfield, Buik Fardin, Peter Davies, Mary O'Reilly, and Renate Halpern, who guided me through her collection. Special appreciation goes to Paul Miller and The Preservation Society of Newport for once again providing the opportunity to photograph decorative arts in beautiful settings, to the Royal College of Art, Bruce Museum of Greenwich, Wilton Historical Society, and Props for Today for their cooperation. Kathy Craughwell-Varda was immensely helpful with general information and for sections of the needlework and print captions. For help with the lace captions I relied on Marianna Klaiman, and Peter Davies helped with identification of Oriental rugs. The drawings are the work of Dawn Peterson.

My gratitude goes to those who shared their knowledge of fabrics and design in the interviews.

This section would not be complete without words of appreciation to Nancy Green, for a degree of encouragement and guidance rare in any editor, to Gilda Hannah, who turns a group of pictures into a book, and to the careful eye of Leeann Graham. I am most grateful to Barbara Braun. And I can never adequately thank Guy Gurney for his constant support.

INTRODUCTION

Fabric is a primary element of our tactile world, and plays a substantial part in the visual education of most designers. But fabric shapes everyone's visual reflexes because the fabrics of everyday life—clothing and furnishings—surround us from childhood on. Even our vocabulary is peppered with images that refer to fabrics. "Smooth as satin" is as succinct a metaphor as one can find, and comparing life to a tapestry has become a cliché because the imagery is so universally understood—even by those who have never heard of "warp" or "weft."

Artists and designers readily associate certain patterns and types of textiles with specific styles and historical periods, but this recognition is not limited to designers: our audiences and clients usually have similar reactions. The visual language that these materials generate is so rich that most people immediately have a very specific picture of time and place when they see a Navaho rug, gingham curtains, or voluminous swags of richly brocaded silk drapery.

The connections we have with fabric go deeper than the association of, say, orange Naugahyde with the 1960s. Many of the earliest efforts of people to control their environment involved turning materials like bark or raw silk filament into things that provided protection and beauty. Oriental carpets fulfilled an important religious function. Embroidery samplers were a major element in the education of young women in the eighteenth century. Later, immigrants who could only carry what would fit in a suitcase gave space to pieces of lace and weavings done by their grandmothers. African patterns and palettes were incorporated into quilts sewn in American slave quarters. Balinese double-ikat cloths, whose intricate patterns are still said to have magical and protective powers, are primary to that culture's ritual and daily life.

Textiles are flexible and portable, and in that respect a natural for something to carry along when people move. The amazing thing about textiles is that objects used on a daily basis have commanded enough respect to enable this basically fragile product to endure centuries. Even when the actual fabric has not survived, designs and construction techniques have been passed on, and continue to be recycled by modern designers and craftsmen. Some processes and patterns have been with us for hundreds, even thousands, of years, and today designers combine those fabrics of the past with the styles and technology of the contemporary world to create modern materials.

Where do designers find fabrics to use as research? For historical fabrics, museum textile collections, of course, are the most obvious place. In addition to extensive exhibits, many have collections intended for hands-on study. (Collections are usually accessible by appointment.) Antique fairs and flea markets are interesting on a broad level because they offer diversity: vintage fabric still on the bolt, period furniture clad in its original upholstery, Victorian beaded pillows, Venetian lace, and American hooked rugs can often be found all at one show. Markets are held in cities and small towns all over the world. There is also an international circuit of shows dedicated to historic and ethnographic textiles, offering not only an opportunity to purchase but also to encounter an extraordinary range of types and periods of textiles that otherwise are easily available only to serious collectors and academicians. (Schedules of established markets and shows are available in decorator periodicals and travel publications.)

Collectors and curators are not the only ones who frequent these marketplaces. Interior decorators may look for specific articles requested by a client, or use period carpets and fabrics as a visual theme. Textile designers look for vintage fabrics to reproduce or use as inspiration for a contemporary line. Set decorators working on period films and plays are highly dependent on flea markets and antique and secondhand stores for set dressings—without those inventories they could not create the authentic period movies we have come to expect. An interesting thing to note is that "period" can mean anything more than a few years old, and often the textile research library will include a seventeenth-century brocade, swatch books from the 1840s, remnants from the 1970s, and everything in between.

Extensive collections also exist within the fabric industry. Many individual designers and companies maintain archives of vintage textiles, ethnographic pieces, and a general sampling of fabrics of various constructions, fiber content, and print patterns that may be of use in future designs. Also included are archival samples of their past product lines with the design documents (renderings and technical specifications), and research for current projects. The more traditional research materials of art and design books, picture files, industry-related periodicals, and technical texts are also sources for designers.

Another part of the working textile library is innovative fabrics and new materials. Modern industry has provided a staggering array of products and processes waiting to be used directly, combined with traditional materials, modified for specific purposes, or used as sources of inspiration. Companies that began as manufacturers of boating sails develop light, strong fabrics from materials originally researched by NASA for the space program. Those products may find their way into the hands of architects who design membrane tensile structures, furniture designers looking for highly durable upholstery, or scenic designers and artists searching for the right material for a certain effect. An exciting liaison between artists, designers, and manufacturing has resulted in libraries of materials found in most architectural and interior design firms. Similar collections are now being established for the general public to give new materials a broader audience.

A collection of fabric can be organized in any number of ways: material content, construction techniques, pattern, or motif. The manner of organization depends on the usage. Museum collections may be organized chronologically, ethnologically, or by application of fabric, such as a costume or furnishing collection. Textile designers may file one fabric in several different categories. Decorators may organize files based on the end use —drapery, upholstery, or wall coverings—with other files dedicated to color palettes.

In this book, pictures are arranged in several ways. Some of the fabrics are grouped by construction because that best describes them—brocade, damask, double cloth, pile weaves, nonwoven. Fabrics that are a combination of constructions, such as brocaded velvet, may be placed in either category; they are indexed both ways. With some fabrics, the manner of decoration forms the common bond—for example, printed fabric and applied needlework. Lace, crochet, and knitting are constructions in which the fabric is made with needles, rather than a loom, and are grouped separately from needlework that is applied. Rugs and carpets are classed for the most part by usage, although blankets and wall hangings that are ruglike are included. The section Furnishings and Structures focuses not on specific fabrics but on the applications to which they are put—for example, curtains and draperies, upholstery, umbrellas, tents.

Within each section the images are broken down into subgroups. For example, the fabrics in Printed, Painted, Dyed Fabric are grouped by motif (floral, geometric, pictorial) and by technique (e.g., ikats). Examples of metallics, sheers, pleated fabrics, and moirés that are effects generated from plain-weave manipulation are in the Basic Weaves section. For convenience, jacquards that did not fit into a more specific subcategory are also included in Basic Weaves.

The vocabulary used here will be familiar to those in industries centered on furnishing fabrics, but note that specific termi-

nology varies from generation to generation, from country to country, and even between related fields in the same city. So the following section, Notes on Fabric, outlines nomenclature used in this book. Consult the glossary for helpful definitions of specialized terms, but for authoritative information on technical aspects of specific materials, seek the expert advice of the publications and organizations listed at the back of the book.

A textile designer discussing a weaving technique with a manufacturer must be concerned about textile terminology because the product depends on the mutual understanding of specific terms. For many professionals who work with fabric, however, the important thing is not a construction definition but rather what is visually conjured up by a name. For example, the "tapestry" upholstery described by a client to an interior designer may not be a tapestry at all. It only resembles the fabric produced by that traditional weaving technique. Its "look" has come to mean tapestry just as surely as a textile loomed as a true tapestry. The pictures in this book were assembled with such visual needs in mind. They constitute an eclectic collection of historical pieces, modern techno-textiles, nonwovens, and other soft materials used for decorative and structural purposes. *Soft Surfaces* is not intended as an academic study or comprehensive view of fabrics but rather as a visual reference for artists and designers who either work directly with these materials, or use the patterns and weaves as a source of imagery, or just need a picture of curtains in a window.

NOTES ON THE CAPTIONS

The captions that accompany the photographs in *Soft Surfaces* are not solely for identification but also as an aid in organizing the visual information. They facilitate the use of the book as a picture file of the fabrics, motifs, and objects. The information given in the captions varies depending on the subject and what is known: the date and country or area of origin of historical pieces is given when possible; the fiber content, when the fabric is used as an example of a material or when the material is of particular interest. Other useful information is included—for example, the key word "lettering" refers to words or text, so everything with lettering, whether on embroidery or awnings, is indexed under that heading as well as by construction or motif. Motifs that appear in different formats are treated in the same way, so a "geometric" pattern will be indexed also as a figured weave, print, quilt, drapery.

The information found in the captions was compiled from a variety of sources, and any inaccuracies are the responsibility of the author.

Copyright notices appear with images at the request of the source, and the names of designers are given when this information was supplied. Assume that all designs and processes credited to manufacturers or individuals are their property and may not be used for any commercial application without permission; their addresses are listed in Fabric Sources on page 324.

NOTES ON FABRIC
BY MARYPAUL YATES

When Judy Juracek first asked me to help categorize and organize the materials for *Soft Surfaces,* she already had a substantial photographic archive. She had confronted the inconsistent and sometimes contradictory terminology of textiles, meeting herself coming and going through the references. She needed an organizational structure that would accurately label the materials and be as useful to readers as the format of the companion volume, *Surfaces.*

My colleagues in the textile field have all grown up using mostly the same vocabulary to define the materials with which we work. Unfortunately, however, we often find that we do not always use them to mean the same thing. The global marketplace, communication network, and accessibility of information have brought together designers trained on different continents, along with textile curators, conservators, historians, and interested parties from other fields like the theater. Moreover, textiles is a field that is learned less through academia than through experience, so the rifts that naturally occur in any living language seem to speed through a world full of dialect. Yet we all want and need to learn from one another, and the hectic pace of our lives decreases our patience for translation. When we specify a particular material, we want to call, order it, and receive what we expected.

All disciplines seem to have two languages: one in which professionals can speak more precisely among themselves, and one in which those professionals can communicate with everyone else. Because *Soft Surfaces* is intended primarily as a pictorial reference for those who use the materials and secondarily for those who might make the materials, it must be clear and accurate to both categories of potential users. We have eschewed technical terminology when a simple, descriptive label that most people can understand will serve just as well.

For starters, what is a textile? Fabric? Cloth? *Textile* is generally accepted to mean woven material of any content, while *cloth* is a fiber-based pliable material of any construction. *Fabric* is a broader term yet, and may include such materials as film, vinyl, wire mesh, and even carpet or rugs. Nonetheless, these terms are frequently interchanged; in particular, *textile* is often used imprecisely as an inclusive term.

Fabrics of the same construction can likewise vary considerably because of the patterns in which they are rendered, material of which they are made, and finishes or aftertreatments that are applied to them. Within the field, fabrics are categorized by construction, appearance, and origin. The terminology has evolved over centuries, and any material can be grouped under several headings. Because *Soft Surfaces* is organized mainly by construction, each category inevitably includes a great variety. Since the book is intended for visual research, the categories are based on how most people consider the fabrics most of the time, but the images are cross-referenced in the index so that they can be located under as many headings as seem practical, including fiber content, motif, origin, or technique. For example, fabrics of wool content could all be grouped together: felt, tweed, suiting, flannel, venetian. Or fabrics of "fuzzy" finish, like felt and flannel, could be grouped with velours and velvets. The venetian, of satin weave, could be grouped with damasks.

Conversely, a particular fabric might fall under several categories. Many fabric terms have come to represent different aspects of fabric, so fabrics that are very different in appearance are sometimes grouped under one heading. Damask is a case in point. Although the damask section includes certain fabrics that are of damask structure but would probably be classified as a damask only by a textile designer or technician, it also includes fabrics with the general look and feel of damask. A type of construction that utilizes two weaves and can be executed in any pattern, damask is also widely used to describe the kinds of patterns that are traditionally executed in this construction. These are usually two-color designs that feature stylized leaf, floral, vase and urn motifs in symmetrical layouts. Most people would still call such a pattern a "damask" whether woven or printed, even with a third or fourth weave added to achieve shading, and even when a third accent color is introduced. For the purposes of *Soft Surfaces,* if a piece walks, talks, and acts like a damask, then that is what we call it, whether it is truly of damask construction or simply a design that resembles damask.

Lampas and brocatelle began, like damask, as terms of construction, but never caught on as broad, descriptive names for all fabrics made of those weave and structure combinations.

Rather, each became largely attached to the types of designs that were executed in its early days, either at a time in history when the technique was developed or when it became attached to a particular name. Today, *lampas* could be used to describe all fabrics woven with filling yarns of two different colors in which each fill can be separately brought to the surface so that it is "isolated" through the weave structure. But this term would not be widely understood in such a context; rather, a traditional pattern that looks like a simplified brocade would more likely come to the minds of professionals who mostly use the term lampas. Although "a brocade-like design" seems a straightforward way to describe many fabrics of lampas construction, such specific terminology is included here because an artist or designer doing research might encounter certain terms that are closely linked to period textiles. We have applied such labels in this historical context rather than categorize fabrics by a construction technique that only an expert could confirm.

Most of the categories here are self-evident. Precise definitions can be found in the glossary: pile fabrics of varying sorts, all manner of printed fabrics (even those such as warp prints in which only one element has been printed), and needlework are all logical and popular categories for any design archive. Two of the section titles bear a brief explanation: Basic Weaves and Nonwovens. Each is used here as a broad descriptive category, not in a narrow technical sense. True nonwovens are assemblies of textile fiber that are held together in a random net by some bonding process; the basic weaves are plain weave, twill, and satin, the three weave combinations upon which all other weave structures are based. For our purposes, however, nonwovens includes true nonwovens as well as certain similar filmlike materials that are not woven and have a character similar to true nonwovens. Basic weaves include many of the derivatives of the three basic weaves, and treatments that are applied to them. *Jacquard* describes an attachment that allows a loom to weave large-scale patterns in fabrics of any construction. Because silk velvet and airplane seat covers are both jacquards, the term is unsuitable as a main heading for our purposes. Yet many vastly popular fabrics are large-scale-patterned wovens of no particular pedigree that can readily be described only as "jacquards" or by their motif or fiber content. Such jacquard patterns are grouped in the Basic Weaves section. (After all, all textiles are made up of three basic weaves.)

A colleague responded to my inquiry about the connotation of a particular term: "First let me think back to the 1960s when I last heard it used." We immediately determined that we could surely find a better way to classify the fabric in question. Dictionary definitions become outdated or simply unpopular. Other terms pick up meanings as they go along; a new material becomes popular and looks similar to an old material, so the old definition is broadened. For example, moleskin has always been a fine woven cotton with a softly sanded finish. Currently, microfiber polyesters of similar construction are popular, and cotton fabrics of this type are rare. Perhaps eventually, moleskin will refer only to microfiber polyester.

Opposite: BW-0 Woven paper filling with an undulating beater (Juraku Co.)

Basic Weaves

BW-1 Sheer lamé curtains

BW-2 Gauze bunting with printed stars

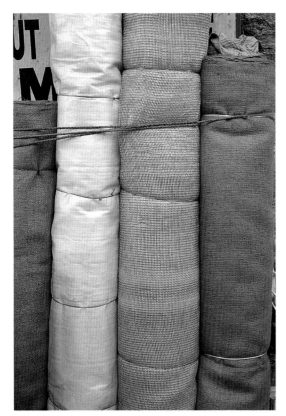

BW-3 Rolls of burlap and synthetic sacking

BW-4 Worn cotton cloth in factory window

BW-5 Satin table skirt with scalloped linen tablecloth

BW-6 Jacquard coverlet with braided fringe and fleur-de-lis motif

The Preservation Society of Newport

BW-7 Satin stripe swag with ball fringe over chiffon table skirt

BW-8 Flags hanging in windows

BW-9 Stacks of spice sacks in warehouse

Jeffery Myers, Primitive and Fine Arts

BW-10 Chilkat ceremonial blanket, Alaska, ca.1875

BW-11 Canvas patio umbrella

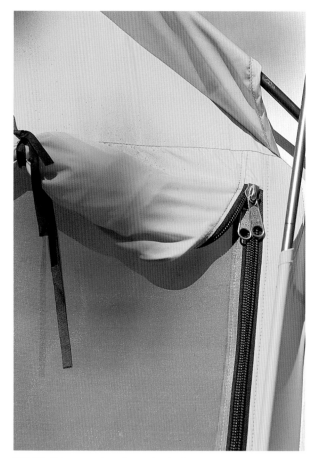

BW-12 Zipper opening of camping tent

BW-13 Canvas striped awning with lettering

BW-14 Canvas striped awning, showing worn seam

Synthetic Industries, Inc.

BW-15 Waffle weave, geosynthetic erosion control material

Doblin Fabrics

BW-16 Waffle weave, diamond repeat with interlaced ground pattern

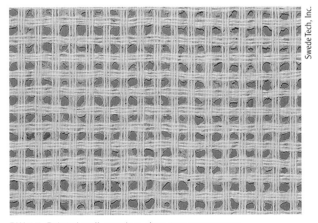

Swede Tech, Inc.

BW-17 Painted wall covering, glass yarn open weave

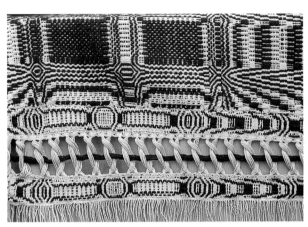

BW-18 Overshot design with border and fringe

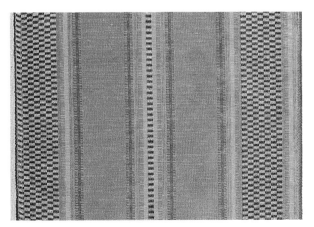

BW-19 Multicolored and checked stripes

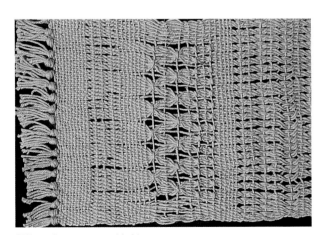

BW-20 Leno weave with fringe

Groundworks–Lee Jofa

BW-21 Diamond motif cut in cotton attached to polyester net

© Swiss Net

BW-22 Metallic stripe in sheer fabric

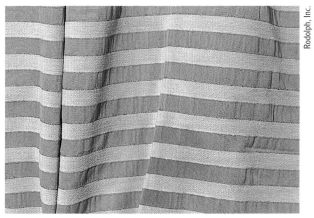

Rodolph, Inc.

BW-23 Seersucker and tight plain weave stripes

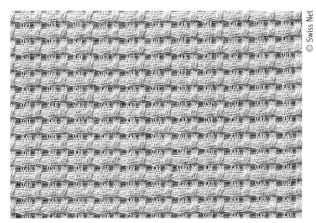

© Swiss Net

BW-24 Mock leno, basket weave

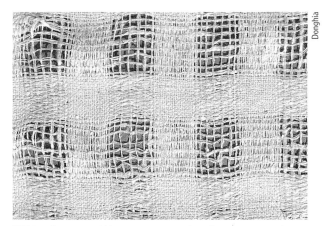

Donghia

BW-25 Square motif in open weave on loosely woven ground

Rodolph, Inc./Marypaul Yates, designer

BW-26 Dash motif repeated in chenille yarn on a silk rib ground

Rodolph, Inc./Marypaul Yates, designer

BW-27 Plaid in plain weave, silk

BW-28 Draped silk; contrasting colored border with metallic stripe

Thomas Dare

BW-29 Draped silk with striae

© Maverick Group/Marypaul Yates, designer

BW-30 Striped dobby weave

Rodolph, Inc./Marypaul Yates, designer

BW-3I Plaid in plain weave, silk

Grey Watkins, Ltd.

BW-32 Multicolored stripe, silk

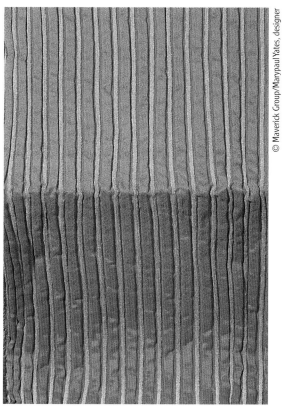

© Maverick Group/Marypaul Yates, designer

BW-33 Irregular stripe resulting from corded effect

BW-34 Multicolored nylon sail material

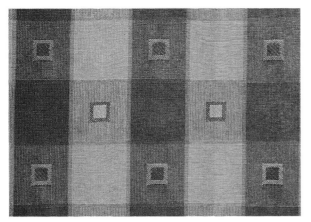

BW-35 Square pattern on stripe, cotton

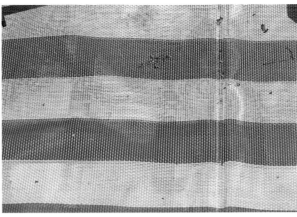

BW-36 Open plain weave stripe, outdoor upholstery, vinyl yarn

BW-37 Ombré stripes woven in taffeta

BW-38 Plaid in chenille yarn

© GA Peach Designs/Marypaul Yates

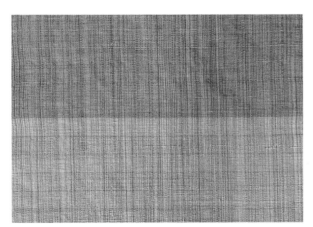

BW-39 Handwoven silk with striae

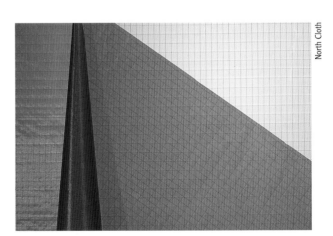

BW-40 Nylon rip stop spinnaker (sail) cloth

North Cloth

Crezana

BW-41 Draped iridescent polyester chiffon

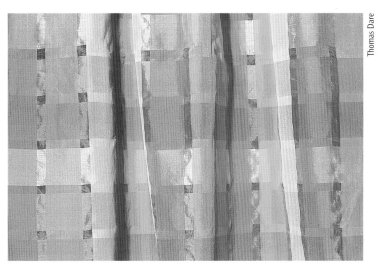

Thomas Dare

BW-42 Balanced plaid, silk

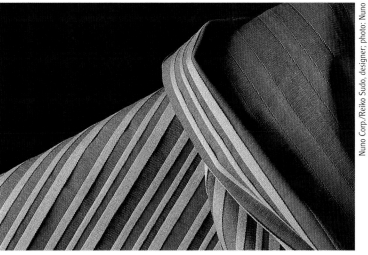

Nuno Corp./Reiko Sudo, designer; photo: Nuno

BW-43 Dimensional stripe created by varying warp tension

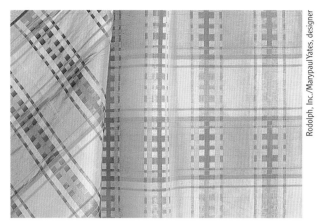

Rodolph, Inc./Marypaul Yates, designer

BW-44 Plaid woven in satin and plain weaves, silk

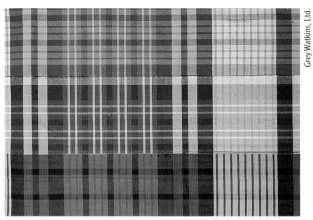

Grey Watkins, Ltd.

BW-45 Plaid shown in different colorways

Courtesy of Calico Corners

BW-46 True check, plain weave, cotton

Lee Jofa

BW-47 True check, plain weave

Grey Watkins, Ltd.

BW-48 Plaid, plain weave, cotton

Grey Watkins, Ltd.

BW-49 Plaid, plain weave, silk

BW-50 Dobby pattern in bouclé yarn

Groundworks-Lee Jofa/Suzanne Tick, designer

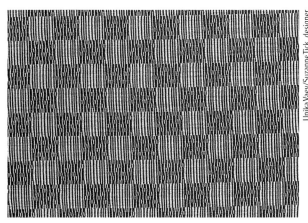

BW-51 Stylized check pattern, dobby weave

Unika Vaev/Suzanne Tick, designer

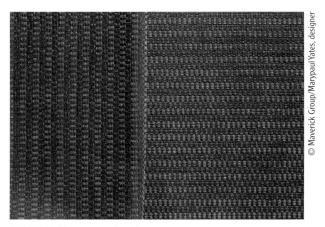

BW-52 Dobby weave, chenille yarn

© Maverick Group/Marypaul Yates, designer

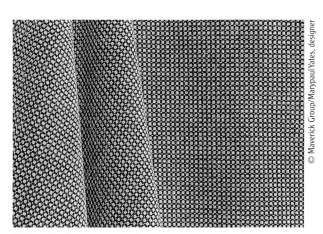

BW-53 Dobby weave, chenille yarn

© Maverick Group/Marypaul Yates, designer

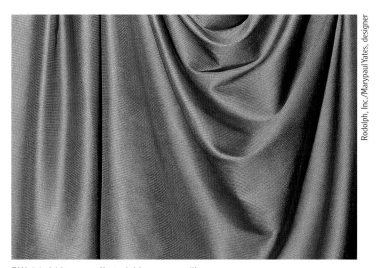

BW-54 Iridescent effect, dobby weave, silk

Rodolph, Inc./Marypaul Yates, designer

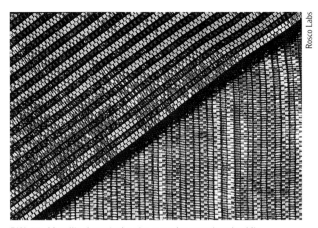

Rosco Labs

BW-55 Metallic theatrical scrim, translucent when backlit

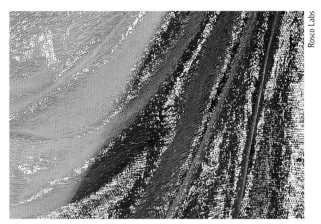

Rosco Labs

BW-56 Draped iridescent clear and colored woven fabric, slit-film yarn, PVC

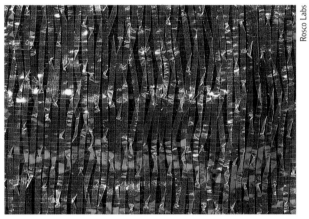

Rosco Labs

BW-57 Iridescent woven fabric, slit-film yarn, PVC

Rosco Labs

BW-58 Draped metallic shot with multicolored stripes, slit-film yarn, PVC

Sommers Plastics

BW-59 Draped silver and gold lamé

Groundworks–Lee Jofa

BW-60 Draped sheer silver lamé

Rosco Labs

BW-61 Draped iridescent woven fabric, slit-film yarn, PVC

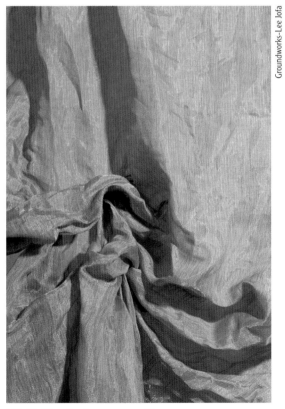

Groundworks–Lee Jofa

BW-62 Metallic sheer, woven with copper yarn

Nuno Corp./Keiji Otani, designer

BW-63 Applied metallic with random arcs of polyester, nylon base fabric

Turkana Gallery

BW-64 Tribal weaving, Anatolian Turkey, 19th c.

BW-65 Circle and curve pattern with leaf scrollwork

BW-66 Ethnic motif in stripe layout, Eastern Europe, 19th c.

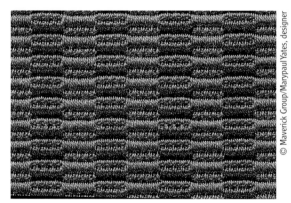

© Maverick Group/Marypaul Yates, designer

BW-67 Repp in dobby pattern, wool blend

Manuel Canovas, Inc.

BW-68 Stripes with repeated irregular spiral motifs

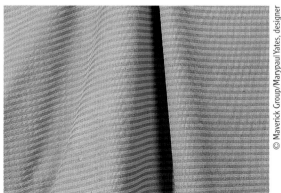

© Maverick Group/Marypaul Yates, designer

BW-69 Chenille rib weave

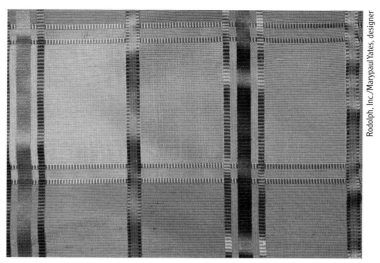

Rodolph, Inc./Marypaul Yates, designer

BW-70 Satin stripes in multicolored rib ground, silk

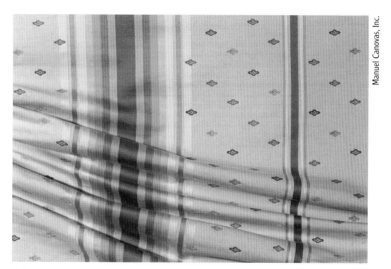

Manuel Canovas, Inc.

BW-71 Ombré satin stripes in rib ground, cotton blend

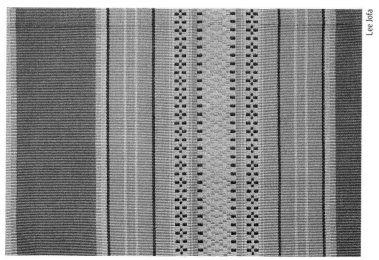

Lee Jofa

BW-72 Multicolored stripes with diamond and cross motifs

Country Curtains

BW-73 Dotted Swiss curtains

Donghia

BW-74 Irregular open weave in cotton/linen blend

Lee Jofa

BW-75 Windowpane check in open weave

BW-76 Sheer ruffled curtain with lace trim

Monkwell Limited

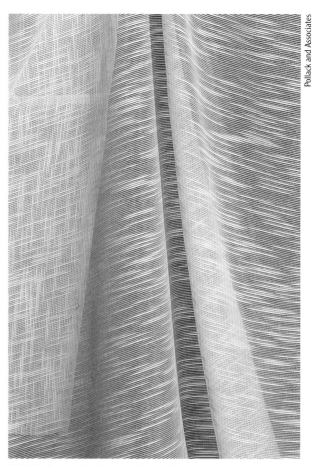

Pollack and Associates

BW-77 Floral scrollwork on sheer ground, burn-out process

BW-78 Sheer with slub yarn ribbed effect

Lee Jofa

BW-79 Lion and foliage motif on sheer ground, burn-out process

Crezana

BW-80 Permanently pleated polyester

Crezana

BW-81 Permanently pleated sheer polyester

Nuno Corp./photo: Nuno

BW-82 Sheer polyester pleated and stitched into wave patterns

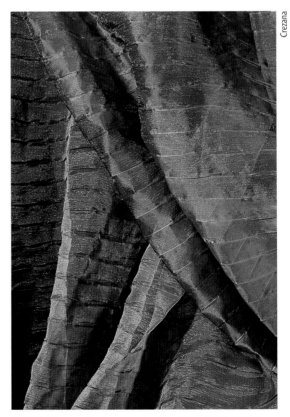

Crezana

BW-83 Sheer polyester permanently pleated into stripes

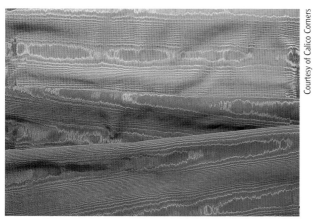

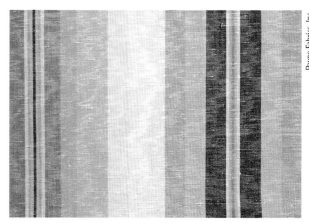

BW-84 Moiré finished taffeta

Courtesy of Calico Corners

BW-85 Moiré finish on multicolored stripe, rib weave

Payne Fabrics, Inc.

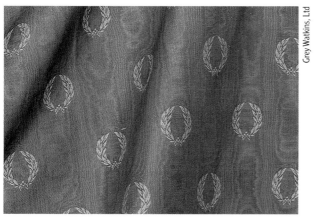

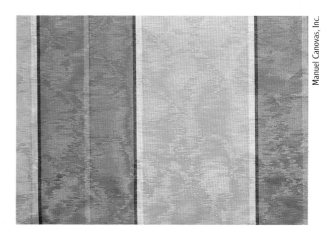

BW-86 Moiré finished ground with laurel wreath motif

Grey Watkins, Ltd

BW-87 Moiré finish on multicolored stripe

Manuel Canovas, Inc.

Patricia Lea

BW-88 Chenille embroidered flowers on moiré ground, ca. 1920

Charles Wibell

BW-89 Peacock and floral vine on chenille bedspread

BW-90 Decorative tufting on striped homespun fabric

BW-91 Wavy stripes on chenille bedspread

BW-92 Floral motif on chenille bedspread

BW-93 Frontier scene with bear on chenille bedspread

BW-94 Grid pattern on plain-weave cotton ground, chenille bedspread

Craftex Mills, Inc.

BW-95 Foliage pattern, tapestry weave

Sunbury Textile Mills, Inc.

BW-96 Medallion pattern, tapestry weave

© Maverick Group/Marypaul Yates, designer

BW-97 Scale pattern, tapestry weave

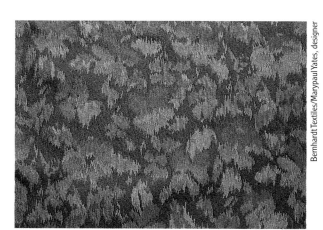

Bernhardt Textiles/Marypaul Yates, designer

BW-98 Floral motif, tapestry weave

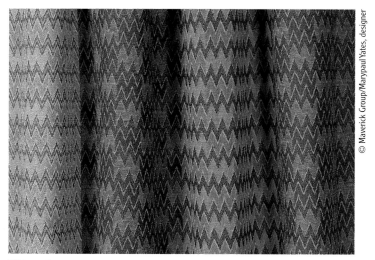

© Maverick Group/Marypaul Yates, designer

BW-99 Zigzag stripe in colorways, tapestry weave

Grey Watkins, Ltd.

BW-100 Stylized leaf diaper pattern, tapestry weave

Craftex Mills, Inc.

BW-101 Abstract mosaic pattern, tapestry weave

Craftex Mills, Inc.

BW-102 Harlequin motif, tapestry weave

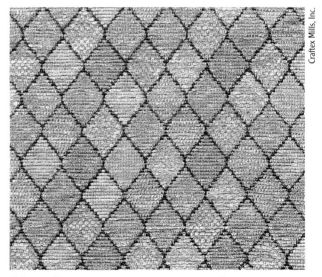

Craftex Mills, Inc.

BW-103 Harlequin motif, tapestry weave, chenille yarn

BW-104 Ethnic motifs, slit-weave tapestry, pre-Columbian Peru, ca. 1000–1400

BW-105 Circle within border, slit-weave tapestry, Coptic, 6th c. or later

BW-106 Landscape, slit-weave tapestry

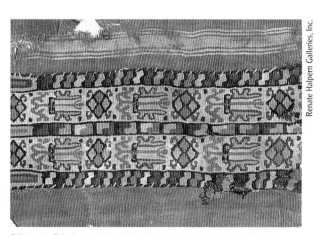

BW-107 Ethnic motifs with border, slit-weave tapestry, Coptic, 6th–8th c.

BW-108 Floral motifs and scrollwork, *k'ossu* tapestry, China, 19th c.

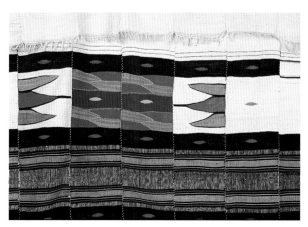

BW-109 Ethnic motifs and banding, eccentric tapestry, Africa

The Preservation Society of Newport

BW-110 Medieval scene based on 15th c. tapestry, "Dame à la Licorne"

Myrna Meyers, Arts d'Extrême Orient

BW-111 Male figure from *kesi* tapestry, China, 17th c.

Sheryl Sachs, Antique Textiles

BW-112 Dragon and wave border, *k'ossu* tapestry, China, 19th c.

The Preservation Society of Newport

BW-113 Floral scrollwork on framed Beauvais tapestry firescreen, 18th c.

BW-114 Mythical scene in silk and metal wrapped yarn, tapestry, Brussels, 17th c.

BW-115 Gothic court scene, tapestry, Tournai or Brussels, ca. 1520

BW-116 Peasant country scene, tapestry, Lille, France, ca. 1738

BW-117 Wavy stripes, twill pocket weave, cotton/polyester/acrylic

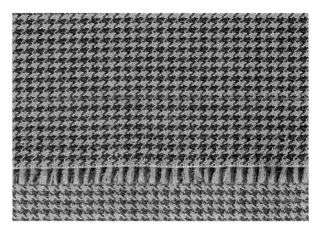

BW-118 Houndstooth, wool

BW-119 Detail of twill weave in neoclassical acanthus leaf motif, 19th c.

BW-120 Squares with motifs in basket weave pattern

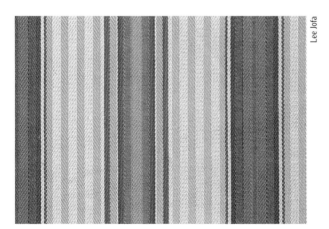

BW-121 Multicolored stripes, cotton

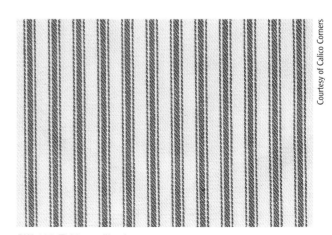

BW-122 Ticking twill stripe, cotton

BW-123 Tartan plaid, twill weave

BW-124 Multicolored squares and stripes

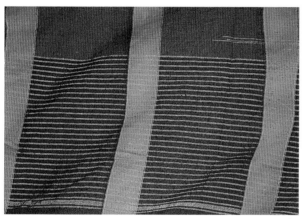

BW-125 Vertical and horizontal stripes

BW-126 Multicolored plaid

BW-127 Large-scale stripe

BW-128 Herringbone

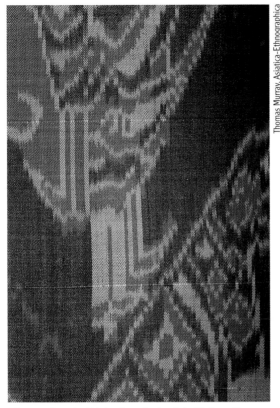

BW-129 Detail of *Pidan* (temple ritual cloth), ikat silk, Cambodia, 19th c.

BW-130 Plaid blanket

BW-131 Coverlet with fringe

BW-132 Paisley center surrounded by *boteh* border and border of diamond motifs, cotton, India

Textile Artifacts

BW-133 Flowers embroidered on satin ground, Continental, ca. 1900

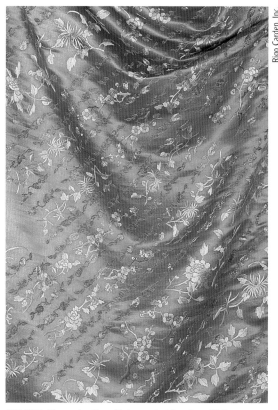

Rigo Carden, Inc.

BW-134 Draped satin with brocaded floral motif, Japan, ca. 1920–30

Rigo Carden, Inc.

BW-135 Draped satin with printed floral motif

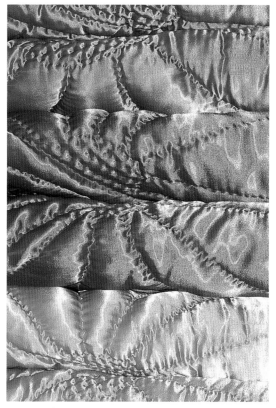

BW-136 Quilted satin bedspreads

Scalamandré Archives

BW-137 Neoclassical motif on satin border

Sherryl Sachs, Antique Textiles

BW-138 Dragon and man embroidered on satin, China, 19th c.

BW-139 Medallion motifs on draped satin

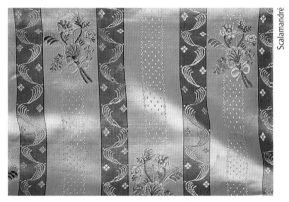

Scalamandré

BW-140 Stripe and floral motif brocaded on satin

Rigo Carden, Inc.

BW-141 Lozenge with fowl motif, rosette pattern, and diamond border on satin

Susan Simon, Antique Textiles

BW-142 Embroidered blazon (family crest) on satin, France, 19th c.

BW-143 Crib quilt with pieced satin squares, ca. 1880

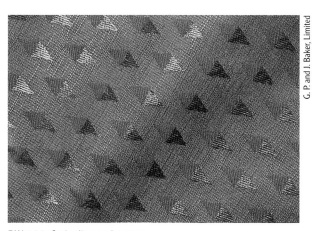

BW-144 Satin diamond pattern

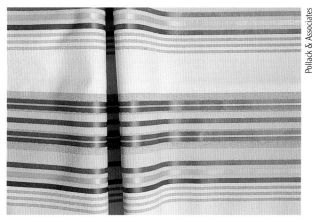

BW-145 Multicolored satin stripes

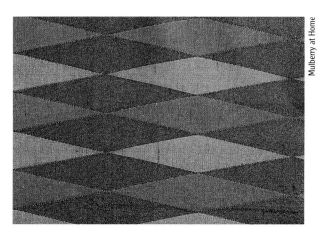

BW-146 Satin harlequin pattern

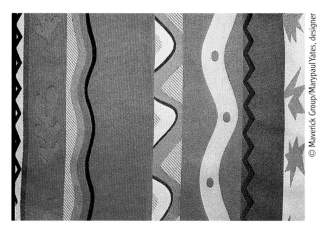

BW-147 Abstract design

BW-148 Rectangle pattern in satin weave

Donghia

BW-149 Basket weave motif, silk

Pollack & Associates

BW-150 Fleur-de-lis pattern

Textillery

BW-151 Square motifs in chenille yarn

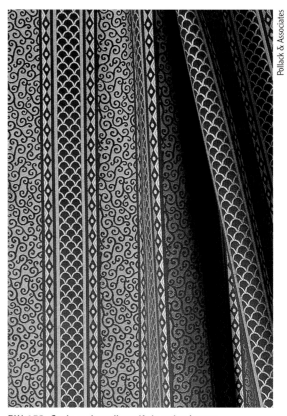

Pollack & Associates

BW-152 Scale and scroll motifs in stripe layout

Manuel Canovas, Inc.

BW-153 Iris floral motif

Renate Halpern Galleries, Inc.

BW-154 Stylized feather pattern in vertical layout, rayon, ca. 1920

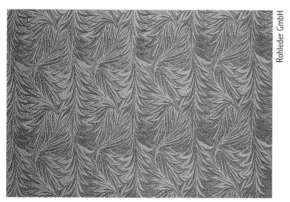

Rohleder GmbH

BW-155 Stylized leaf or feather pattern

Lee Jofa

BW-156 Scroll and rosette motif, jacquard damask, chenille

Pollack & Associates

BW-157 Metallic lotus floral pattern

Groundworks-Lee Jofa/Suzanne Tick, designer

BW-158 Multicolored geometric repeat, jacquard tapestry, (left) face, (right) back

Bernhardt Textiles/Suzanne Tick, designer

BW-159 Multicolored warp stripe

Bernhardt Textiles/Jennifer Eno, designer

BW-160 Leaf pattern, on ribbed ground

Manuel Canovas, Inc.

BW-161 Stylized floral motif, reversible, jacquard

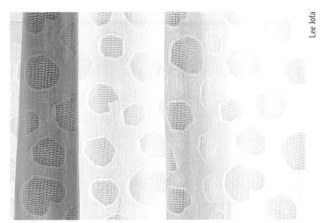

Lee Jofa

BW-162 Irregular circle in open weave on tight weave ground

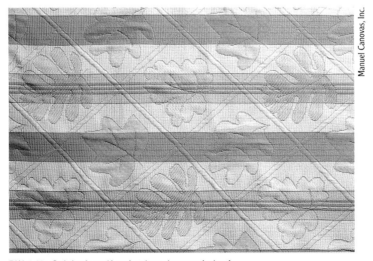

Manuel Canovas, Inc.

BW-163 Oak leaf motif and stripes, jacquard piqué

JACQUARD PATTERNS

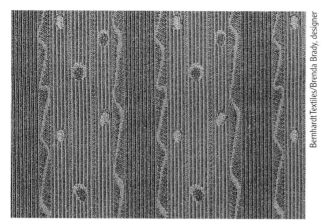

BW-164 Zigzag stripe, ribbed jacquard

Bernhardt Textiles/Brenda Brady, designer

BW-165 Multicolored twill stripes, jacquard

Pollack & Associates

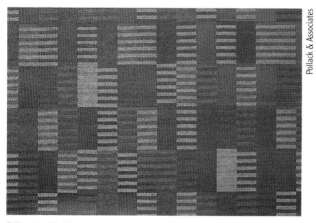

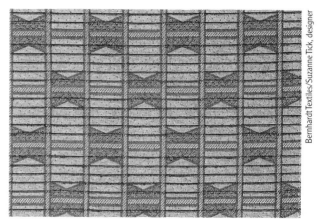

BW-166 Multicolored interlocking geometric pattern

Pollack & Associates

BW-167 Interlocking geometric pattern

Bernhardt Textiles/Suzanne Tick, designer

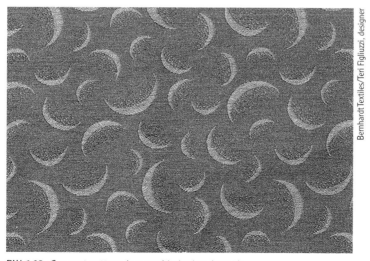

BW-168 Crescent pattern, jacquard imitation damask

Bernhardt Textiles/Teri Figliuzzi, designer

Lee Jofa

BW-169 Trailing leaf motif with stripes

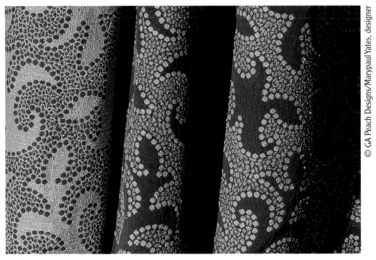

© GA Peach Designs/Marypaul Yates, designer

BW-170 Reversible jacquard

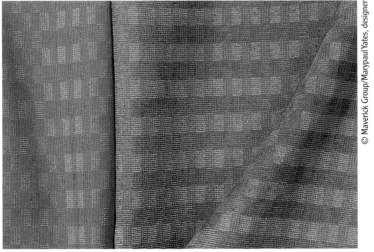

© Maverick Group/Marypaul Yates, designer

BW-171 Plaid pattern

Opposite: BD-0 Brocatelle, floral scroll pattern, silk and linen (Scalamandré)

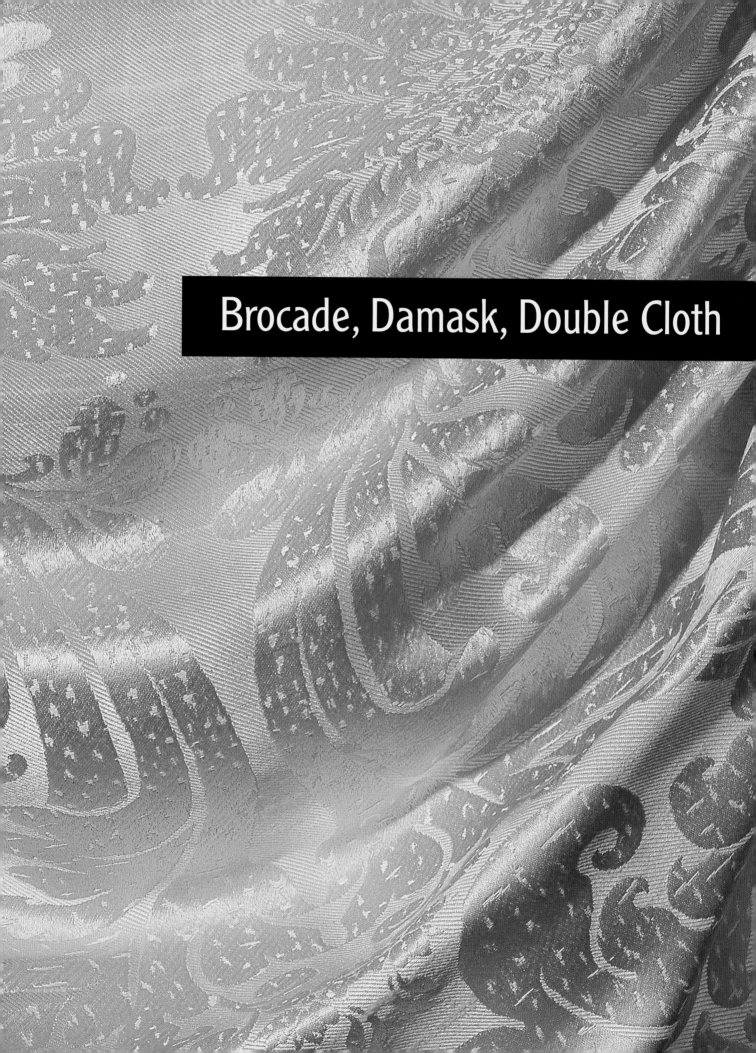

Brocade, Damask, Double Cloth

Teresa Coleman, Fine Arts, Ltd.

BD-1 Clawed dragon in gold wrapped silk thread, brocade, China, 17th c.

Rigo Carden, Inc.

BD-2 Floral bouquet pattern, silk brocade

P. M. Vintage

BD-3 Outer-space-motif bedspread, damask

BD-4 Temple pennant, pieced damask and brocade, Tibet, 18th or 19th c.

BD-5 Swag with macaroon and tassels tieback, silk damask

BD-6 Picture frame covered with floral brocade on metallic ground, ca. 1890

BD-7 Multicolored ombré chevron motif, silk brocade, Japan, 19th c.

Sherryl Sachs, Antique Textiles

BD-8 Damask patterns, obi, Japan, 19th c.

Scalamandré Archives

BD-9 Medallion, laurel, and cherub on damask chair seat

Scalamandré Archives

BD-10 Scenic pattern, reproduction of Italian Renaissance lampas in brocaded taffeta

BD-11 Detail of *kesa*, patchwork of brocades, Japan, 19th c.

Sheryl Sachs, Antique Textiles

BD-12 Floral and leaf motif with bird, silk damask wall covering

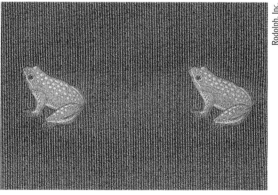

BD-13 Frog motif in metallic yarn on striae ground, brocade

Rodolph, Inc.

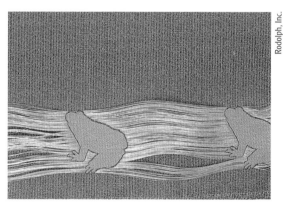

BD-14 Metallic float on back of brocade

Rodolph, Inc.

BD-15 Altar cover from patchwork of Chinese silk brocades, Tibet

Zee Stone Gallery

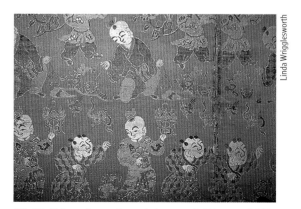

BD-16 Chinese figures brocaded on panel, China, ca. 1460

Linda Wrigglesworth

BROCADE, DAMASK, DOUBLE CLOTH

Groundworks-Lee Jofa

BD-17 Shaggy stripe effect in raffia

Scalamandré

BD-18 Abstract tapestry effect

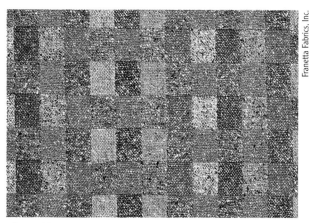

Franetta Fabrics, Inc.

BD-19 Multicolored check in heather mixture yarn

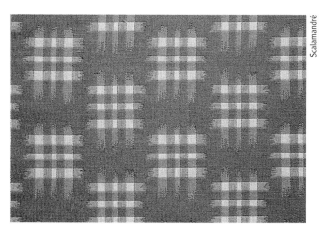

Scalamandré

BD-20 Woven ikat effect

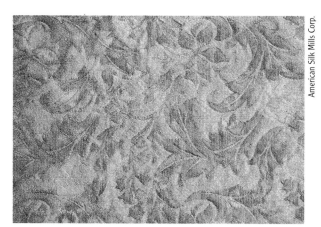

American Silk Mills Corp.

BD-21 Floral raised pattern

Groundworks-Lee Jofa/Suzanne Tick, designer

BD-22 Squares and rectangles, jacquard double cloth

Groundworks-Lee Jofa/Suzanne Tick, designer

BD-23 Draped double cloth with square motif (both sides)

Groundworks-Lee Jofa/Suzanne Tick, designer

BD-24 Horizontal stripes, cotton slub floats between sheer layers of double cloth

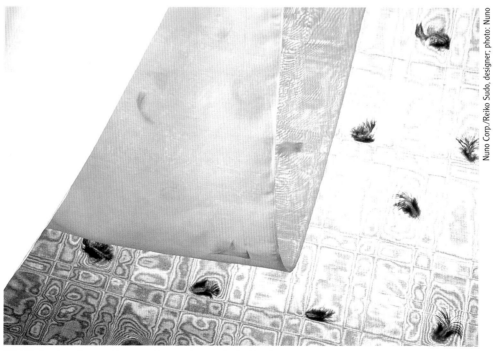

Nuno Corp./Reiko Sudo, designer; photo: Nuno

BD-25 Feathers inserted between layers of organdy double cloth

BD-26 Patriotic American motif on coverlet

BD-27 Star and rosette motifs with border

BD-28 Horse and floral pattern, chenille double cloth (both sides), ca. 1929

BD-29 Ethnic geometric motifs repeated in stripes, with fringe

Renate Halpern Galleries, Inc.

BD-30 Arabic lettering

BD-31 Interlocked geometric motifs on check ground, with fringe

BD-32 Rosette motif in box layout

Scalamandré

© Maverick Group/Marypaul Yates, designer

BD-33 Arabesque motif

Renate Halpern Galleries, Inc.

BD-34 Animal motifs on double cloth (both sides), England, 19th c.

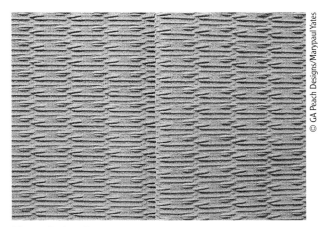

Lee JofaCredit

BD-35 Quilted effect with dot pattern

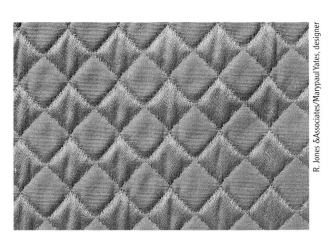

© GA Peach Designs/Marypaul Yates

BD-36 Puckered texture

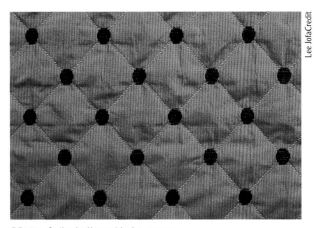

BD-37 Bird's eye pattern

Groundworks-Lee Jofa/Suzanne Tick, designer

BD-38 Interlocking circle pattern, silk blend

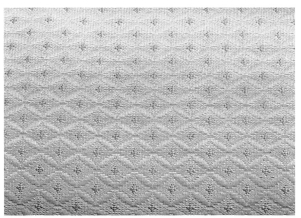

Scalamandré

BD-39 Basket weave pattern with center crosses

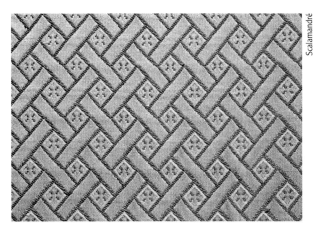

R. Jones &Associates/Marypaul Yates, designer

BD-40 Diamond pattern in satin

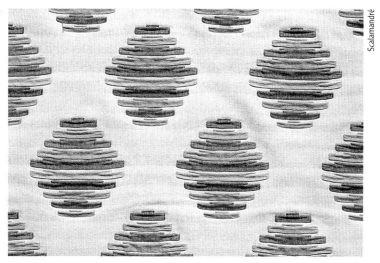

Scalamandré

BD-41 Multicolored diamond pattern, cotton

Robert Allen Fabrics

BD-42 Floral motif on crepe

Doblin Fabrics

BD-43 Floral scroll pattern with chenille yarn

BROCADE, DAMASK, DOUBLE CLOTH

BD-44 Floral motif, jacquard damask, early 19th c.

BD-45 Raised metallic leaf motif, variation on damask

BD-46 Floral scrollwork, variation on damask

BD-47 Striped damask with grapevine and floral motifs

BD-48 Leaf and arabesque pattern

BD-49 Damask floral motif with striped, moiré ground

BD-50 Leaf motif in cotton and silk

BD-51 Floral motif with stripes in imberline pattern

BD-52 Leaf pattern in colorways

BD-53 Draped damask with acanthus leaf pattern

BD-54 Variety of botanical motifs

Kay Mertens, Vintage Textiles

Rigo Carden, Inc.

BD-55 Colonial couple in cameo, stripe layout, pictorial damask

BD-56 Floral motif in novelty yarn

Rigo Carden, Inc.

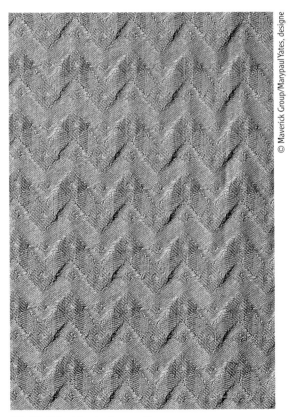

© Maverick Group/Marypaul Yates, designe

BD-57 Lotus floral and scrollwork, cotton and silk.

BD-58 Raised herringbone pattern

BD-59 Fleur-de-lis diaper pattern

Valdese Weavers

BD-60 Check, silk damask brocaded with metallic, Japan, 19th c.

Renate Halpern Galleries, Inc.

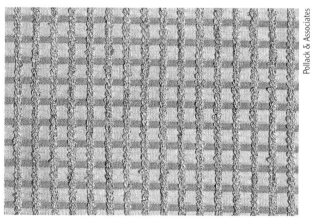

BD-61 Grid motif, damask with bouclé accent stripe

Pollack & Associates

BD-62 Draped damask with stripe

Bernhardt Textiles/Marypaul Yates, designer

BD-63 Check and stripe motif, silk

Rodolph, Inc./Marypaul Yates, designer

BD-64 Leaf diaper pattern

© Maverick Group/Marypaul Yates, designer

BD-65 Star and geometric diaper patterns with border

Jon Eric Riis, Antique Textiles

BD-66 Square diaper pattern with stripes

Scalamandré Archives

BD-67 Rosette motif on basket weave pattern, brocaded damask

Country Repeats

BD-68 Flower and vine border with fringe on tea towel

Mt. Vernon Antiques

BD-69 East Indian elephant in floral wreath on tea towel, ca.1900

Diana de Mori

BD-70 Animal motif and floral scrollwork on tablecloth border

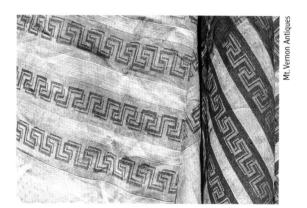

Mt. Vernon Antiques

BD-71 Greek key motif in bands on jacquard tablecloth, England

Diana de Mori

BD-72 Peacock and tree border on tablecloth

BD-73 Leaf pattern on napkin border

Pollack & Associates

BD-74 Chinoiserie scene

Kay Mertens, Vintage Textiles

BD-75 Heraldic lion pattern with border on curtain panel

Scalamandré Archives

BD-76 Chinese figures on pictorial damask, China

BD-77 Geometric "American Indian" motif on blanket

BD-78 Rosettes and stripes and border with wheel motif on blanket

BD-79 Geometric border and plaid ground on blanket

BD-80 "Indian chief" motif on blanket

BD-81 Rosettes brocaded in silk and metal thread, India, 17th c.

BD-82 Rope motif stripe

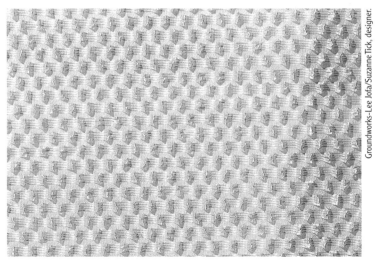

BD-83 Pucker effect in diaper pattern, raffia on polyester ground

BD-84 Multicolored flame pattern

Scalamandré

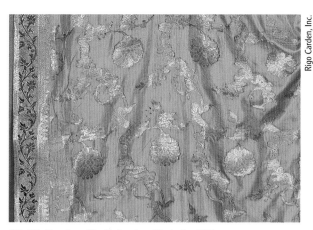

BD-85 Floral motif with border, silk, India, 19th c.

Rigo Carden, Inc.

BD-86 Ethnic motif with rosettes and border, metallic on cotton

BD-87 Leaves and scrollwork brocaded in bouclé, silk and metallic, Spain, 16th c.

Renate Halpern Galleries, Inc.

BD-88 Leaf and flower pattern, lisere brocade, silk

Scalamandré

BD-89 Floral motif in chenille on jacquard-woven brocaded lampas

Scalamandré Archives

Charles Wibel

BD-90 Scroll motif with butterfly border

Exquisite Kimono

BD-91 Butterfly and rosette medallions on shell motif ground, silk and metallic obi, Japan

Renate Halpern Galleries, Inc.

BD-92 Fan and flower pattern with bands, silk and metallic

Rigo Carden, Inc.

BD-93 Meandering rose vine and scrollwork stripes, silk, copy of 18th c. French design

BROCADE, DAMASK, DOUBLE CLOTH

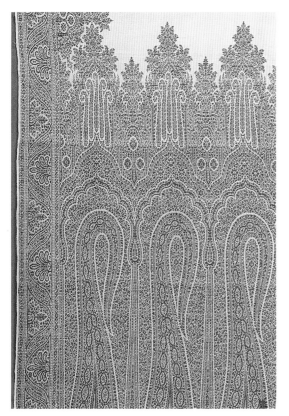

BD-94 Paisley with border, wool

BD-95 Shell pattern, simulated brocade

BD-96 Meadering flowers and lace motif stripe, lisere, style of 18th c.

BD-97 Flowers and leaves on satin ground, lampas

Scalamandré Archives

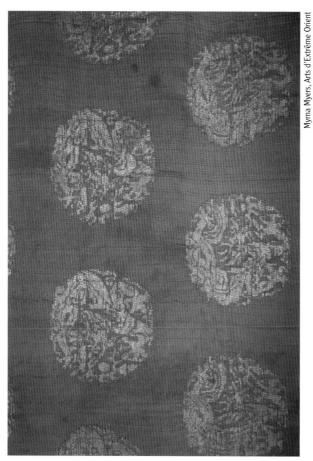

Myrna Myers, Arts d'Extrême Orient

BD-98 Circular motif repeat in leather on silk, China, Jin Dynasty, 12th–13th c.

Renate Halpern Galleries, Inc.

BD-99 Draped brocade with floral pattern, metallic and silk, 18th c.

Renate Halpern Galleries, Inc.

BD-100 Spiral and zigzag stripe pattern, metallic and silk, Japan, 20th c.

Scalamandré

BD-101 Botanical pattern, hand-brocaded silk

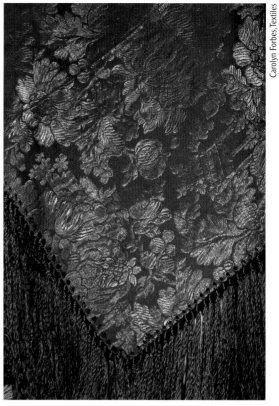

Carolyn Forbes, Textiles

BD-102 Piano shawl, floral pattern, with fringe, silk

Rigo Carden, Inc.

BD-103 Floral serpentine pattern

Renate Halpern Galleries, Inc.

BD-104 Palmettes in medallion on diamond pattern, silk and metallic, Japan, 20th c.

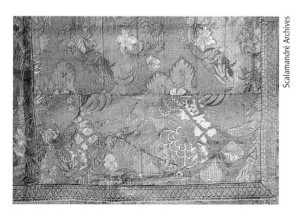

Scalamandré Archives

BD-105 Brocaded lampas, Spain, late 17th–early 18th c.

Scalamandré

BD-106 Floral motif, brocaded damask, silk

Renate Halpern Galleries, Inc.

BD-107 Water scene with cranes, silk and metallic, Japan, 20th c.

Scalamandré Archives

BD-108 Medallion with birds and garland

P. M. Vintage

BD-109 Rodeo scene, bedspread

Exquisite Kimono

BD-110 Flying cranes on scenic background, Japan

BD-111 Geometric motifs on sheer ground, clipped cloth

© Swiss Net

BD-112 Squares on clear woven slit-plastic ground, clipped cloth

Nuno Corp./Reiko Sudo, designer; photo: Nuno

BD-113 Diagonal stripes of washi paper woven into organdy
ground and clipped

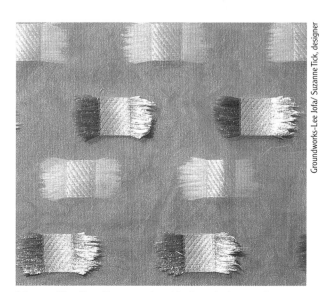

Groundworks-Lee Jofa/ Suzanne Tick, designer

BD-114 Metallic raffia rectangles with clipped edges on sheer
polyester ground

BD-115 Animal and ethnic motifs in wool on cotton ground, Sardinia, 19th c.

Renate Halpern Galleries, Inc.

BD-116 Figure and animal ethnic motifs in bands, supplementary weft, Mexico, ca. 1900

Renate Halpern Galleries, Inc.

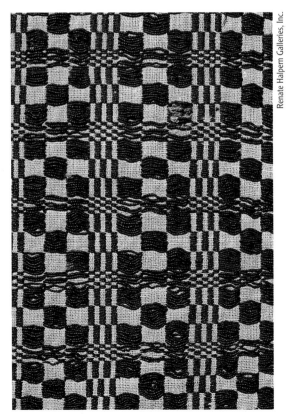

BD-117 Boxed check motif, wool brocade on cotton, Sardinia, 19th c.

Renate Halpern Galleries, Inc.

BD-118 Ethnic motif with border

Textile Arts

Scalamandré Archives

BD-119 Floral motif lampas, silk, from Royal Palace in Naples, 19th c.

Scalamandré Archives

BD-120 Serpentine floral motif, brocaded lampas, silk, France, mid-18th c.

Scalamandré Archives

BD-121 Chinoiserie with garland, brocaded lampas, silk, Italy, 18th c.

Scalamandré

BD-122 Meandering flowers and vine on stripe, lampas, silk

BROCADE, DAMASK, DOUBLE CLOTH

Scalamandré Archives

Scalamandré

BD-123 Butterfly and flowers on satin ground, lampas, silk

BD-124 Lampas, revival of rococo design

Scalamandré Archives

Scalamandré

BD-125 Arch motif in metallic and silk, brocaded lampas

BD-126 Meandering flower and vines, lampas

Scalamandré Archives

Scalamandré

BD-127 Floral portal on lace pattern, 20th c. reproduction
of Italian baroque lampas

BD-128 Floral motif on striped ground, revival of 19th c.
French lampas, silk

Rigo Carden, Inc.

BD-129 Floral and scroll motif, lampas, France, 19th c.

Renate Halpern Galleries, Inc.

BD-130 "Bizarre silk" lampas, silk and metallic, France, 18th c.

Scalamandré Archives

BD-131 Acanthus leaf scrollwork, brocatelle, Italy, 19th c.

Scalamandré Archives

BD-132 Acanthus leaf motif, reproduction of Italian baroque brocatelle

Scalamandré

BD-133 Floral motif, lampas, revival of 18th c. French design

Scalamandré Archives

BD-134 "Bizarre silk" lampas, floral motif, 18th c. style

BROCADE, DAMASK, DOUBLE CLOTH

BD-135 Leaf motif in vertical repeat on striae ground, brocatelle

BD-136 Lampas, stars and rosette pattern, reproduction of 19th c. design

BD-137 Hybrid lampas, arabesque and rosette in lozenge (outer border) and diaper pattern

Opposite: P-0 Velvet upholstery on chair back with diamond tufting

Scalamandré Archives

Scalamandré

Scalamandré

Pile Weaves

Props for Today

P-1 Moquette or frisé upholstery, floral pattern, and channel trim

Groundworks–Lee Jofa/Suzanne Tick, designer

P-2 Draped mohair velvet

P-3 Polygon in box pattern on velvet upholstered chair, ca. 1960

Rigo Carden, Inc.

P-4 Silk velvet curtain panel with scrollwork border and ball fringe

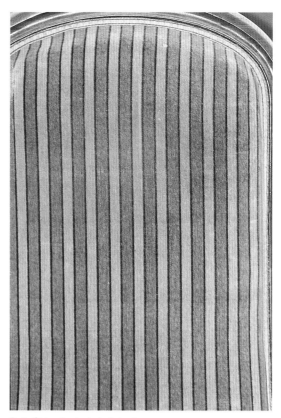

P-5 *Onshak* carpet valance over silk velvet draperies

P-6 Striped velvet chair back

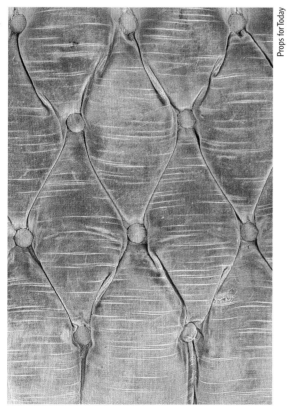

P-7 Velvet chair back, diamond tufted, showing wear

P-8 Draped silk velvet with satin lining

P-9 Velvet screen, embroidered religious scene, applied metallic scrollwork, Italy, 19th c.

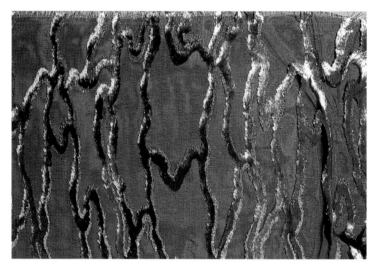

P-10 Multicolored velvet, abstract motif on sheer ground, burn-out process

P-11 Silk velvet lap robe trimmed with ermine, satin, and lace

PILE WEAVES

P-12 Cut velvet with metallic, medallion pattern, Turkey, 16th c.

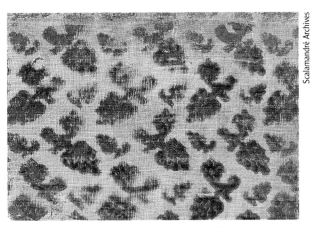

P-13 Cut and voided velvet, leaf pattern, Italy, 16th c.

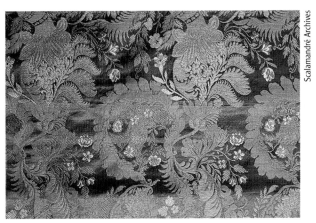

P-14 Brocaded velvet, floral pattern

P-15 Voided velvet, floral pattern, France, 19th c.

P-16 Lion and pillar pattern, voided velvet, copy of Byzantine fabric

P-17 Cut and voided velvet, serpentine floral stripe

Scalamandré Archives

Renate Halpern Galleries, Inc.

P-18 Cut and voided velvet, bats and lotus motifs, China, Manchu Dynasty

P-19 Cut and voided velvet, lotus motif with scrollwork, China, 19th c.

Scalamandré

Rigo Carden, Inc.

P-20 Cut and voided velvet, floral scrollwork with striae

P-21 Cut and voided velvet on metallic ground, flower bouquet in frame

Renate Halpern Galleries, Inc.

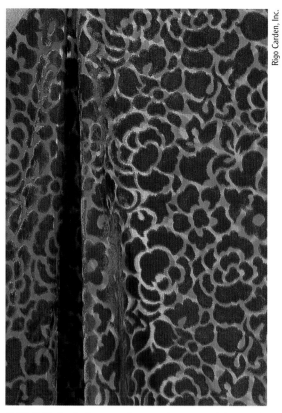

Rigo Carden, Inc.

P-22 Draped cut and voided velvet, floral pattern on sheer ground, ca. 1930

P-23 Voided velvet, rose pattern on sheer ground, burn-out process, ca. 1930

Lee Jofa

Renate Halpern Galleries, Inc.

P-24 Voided velvet, lotus in vase pattern

P-25 Cut and voided velvet, Persian scene in medallion, Continental, 19th c.

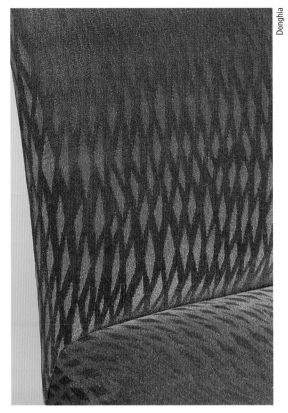

Donghia

P-26 Jacquard velvet on chair upholstery, diamond pattern, mohair pile

P-27 Velvet chair upholstery, biscuit tufted back, printed floral and scroll pattern

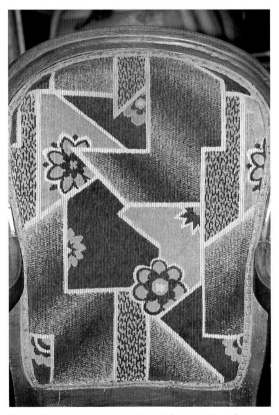

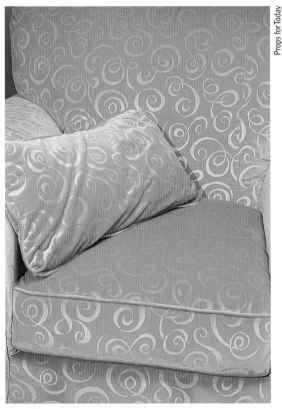

Props for Today

P-28 Chair upholstery, printed ombré geometric and rosette motifs

P-29 Upholstered chair, arabesque pattern

Renate Halpem Galleries, Inc.

P-30 Cut and voided velvet stripes, Middle East, 18th–19th c.

Malden Mills Industries, Inc.

P-3I Cut and voided velvet check pattern

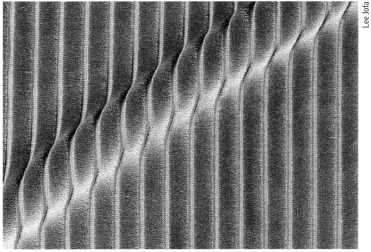

Lee Jofa

P-32 Cut and voided velvet stripes

P-33 *Kuba* textile, geometric pattern, raffia

P-34 *Kuba* textile, geometric motif, raffia

P-35 *Kuba* textile, basket weave pattern, raffia

P-36 Multicolored basket weave pattern

Lee Jofa

P-37 Interlocking geometric motif with stripe, mohair moquette

P-38 Boxed geometric motifs, mohair moquette

P-39 Triangle and geometric pattern, mohair moquette

CUT PILE

P-40 Floral motif on chenille velvet, France, ca. 1920–30

P-41 Roses printed on mohair pile

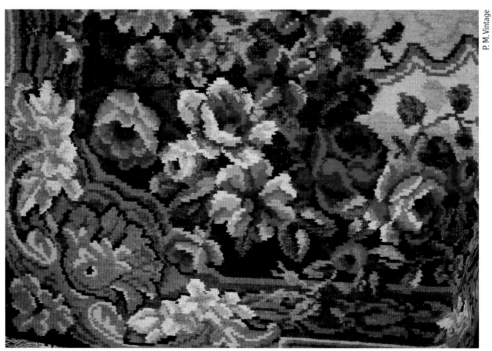

P-42 Floral and scrollwork border on chenille velvet

LOOPED PILE

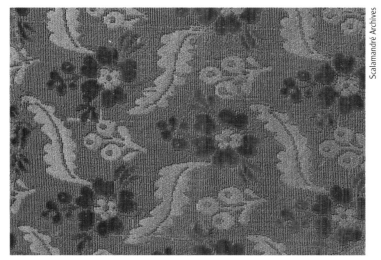

P-43 Cut and voided velvet, leaf, flower, and berry pattern

P-44 Cut, looped, and voided velvet, floral motif

P-45 Voided velvet with bouclé brocade, arabesque and medallions, Spain, 16th c.

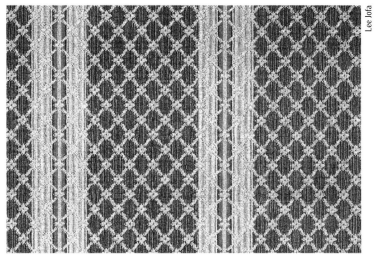

Lee Jofa

P-46 Epingle, stripe and diaper pattern with crosses

Lee Jofa

P-47 Epingle, true plaid

P-48 Jacquard-woven looped pile, tapestry effect

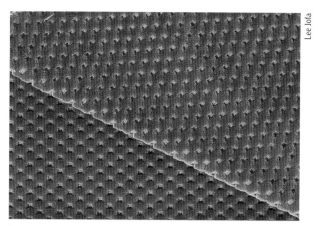

Lee Jofa

P-49 Cut and looped pile, pin-dot pattern

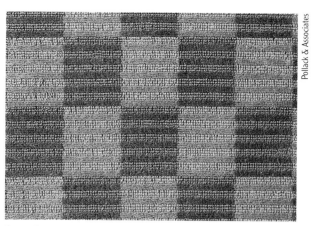

Pollack & Associates

P-50 Cut and looped pile, rectangular check pattern

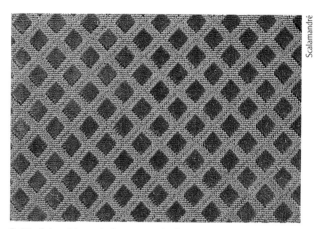

Scalamandré

P-51 Cut and looped pile, geometric diaper pattern

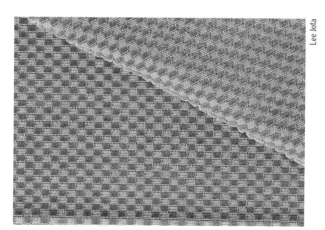

Lee Jofa

P-52 Cut and looped pile, rectangular check pattern

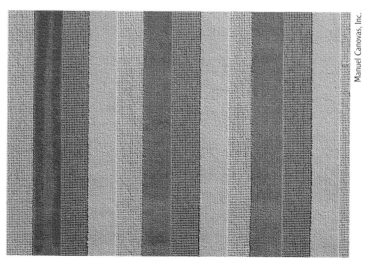

Manuel Canovas, Inc.

P-53 Cut and looped pile, multicolored stripes

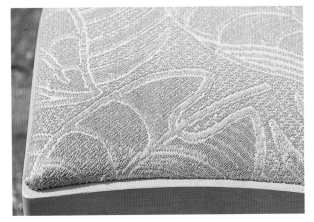

P-54 Moquette or frisé upholstered chair seat

P-55 Swag pattern, moquette or frisé

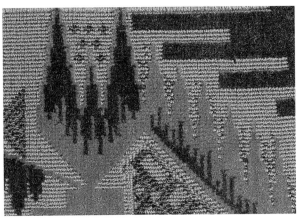

P-56 Abstract motif, moquette or frisé

P-57 Arabesque pattern, moquette or frisé upholstery

P-58 Scale motif in diaper pattern, moquette or frisé upholstery

Renate Halpern Galleries, Inc.

P-59 Oval art deco pattern, metallic on velvet, France, ca. 1920

Joh. Backhausen & Son, GmbH.

P-60 Spirals, ovals, and mosaic motifs on velvet

P-61 Zigzag and ovals on terry cloth, ca. 1970

Patricia Lea

P-62 Paisley and flower pattern on velvet valance, ca. 1930

Renate Halpern Galleries, Inc.

P-63 Multiflower pattern on drapery panel, U.S., ca.1950

Rigo Carden, Inc.

P-64 Egyptian motif on velvet, U.S., ca. 1920

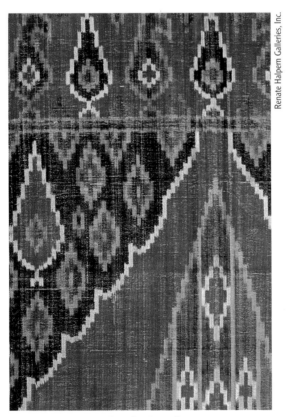

Renate Halpern Galleries, Inc.

P-65 Ikat-dyed silk velvet, Persia, 19th c.

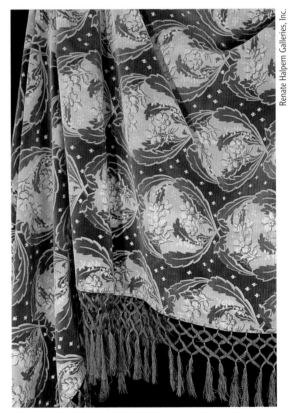

Renate Halpern Galleries, Inc.

P-66 Flower and circle pattern on draped velvet shawl, with fringe

Scalamandré Archives

P-67 Flower and acanthus leaf pattern on velvet

P-68 Floral patterns printed on synthetic pile blankets

Lee Jofa

P-69 Floral and fruit printed on corduroy

P-70 Floral damask motif, metallic graufage on velvet

Entree Libre/Sabina Fay Braxton, artist

P-71 Draped velvet with graufage in damask pattern

Scalamandré Archives

P-72 Floral scrollwork pattern embossed and printed on velvet

Entree Libre/Sabina Fay Braxton, artist

P-73 Check and square patterns, metallic graufage on velvet

Opposite: PP-0 Print on jacquard ground (Pollack & Associates)

Printed, Painted, Dyed Fabric

PP-1 Printed vinyl (flannel-backed) tablecloth material

PP-2 Tobacco premiums, roller-printed with flags, cotton flannel, ca. 1900

PP-3 Calico fabric used for ikat lining, ca. 1900

PP-4 Calligraphy painted on silk damask, China, 19th c.

Sherryl Sachs, Antique Textiles

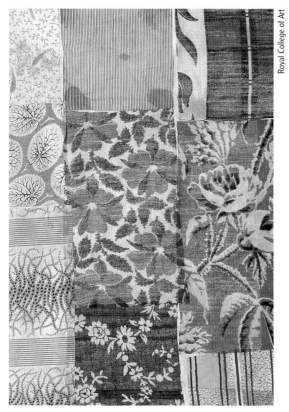

Royal College of Art

PP-5 Prints from sample book, England, 19th or 20th c.

PP-6 Printed burlap feed bag

Diana de Mori

PP-7 Stripes of wave pattern, hand-printed, linen

PP-8 Floral motifs in box pattern printed on linen, adhered to table, 20th c.

Rigo Carden, Inc.

PP-9 Fortuny print, drapery and upholstery, cotton, Italy, ca. 1930

Thomas Murray, Asiatica-Ethnographica

PP-10 *Pidan* (temple ritual cloth), detail, ikat, silk, Cambodia, 19th c.

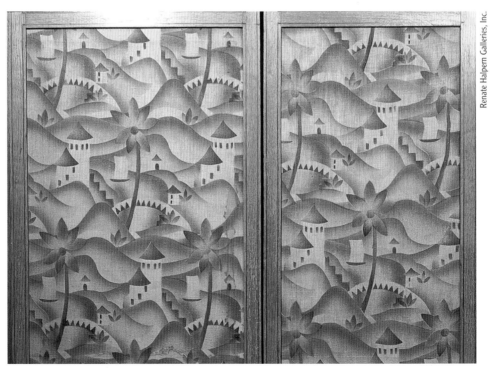

Renate Halpern Galleries, Inc.

PP-11 Palm tree and castle pattern, cotton on framed screen, ca. 1900

Lee Jofa

PP-12 Floral bouquet, glazed cotton

Snow Leopard Antiques

PP-13 Roses in stripe layout, drapery panel, cotton, ca. 1950

Rigo Carden, Inc.

PP-14 Stripes of figurative, floral, and vegetable motifs, cotton, Portugal, 19th c.

PP-15 Trailing flowers and leaves pattern, 20th c.

Pollack & Associates

PP-16 Leaf motif printed on woven ottoman ground

Sivasli Istanbul Yazmacisi

PP-17 Floral motifs in stripe layout, cotton

Manuel Canovas, Inc.

P-18 Tulip motif, cotton

Grey Watkins, Ltd.

PP-19 Floral pattern, hand-silk-screened, cotton

Grey Watkins, Ltd.

PP-20 Botanical print, hand-silk-screened, cotton

Stock in Trade

PP-21 Serpentine grape vine pattern, cotton, 20th c.

Susan E. Oostdyk, Antiques

PP-22 Floral bouquets and serpentine vine pattern, crepe bark cloth, ca. 1930

Lee Jofa

PP-23 Lotus flowers on branch, linen

Lee Jofa

PP-24 Trailing leaves and berries pattern, linen-cotton blend

Lee Jofa

PP-25 Floral bouquets with serpentine garland pattern, cotton

PP-26 Rosette pattern, batik, cotton, Japan, 19th c.

PP-27 Rosette pattern with contrasting border, cotton

PP-28 Flowers in scrollwork cameo pattern, glazed chintz, 19th c.

Textile Artifacts

PP-29 Floral "Kyoto" pattern, cotton, Liberty of London, ca. 1910

G. P. & J. Baker, Limited

PP-30 Pomegranate pattern with border, linen and cotton

Snow Leopard Antiques

PP-31 Serpentine floral pattern, drapery panel, crepe bark cloth, U.S., ca. 1930

Scalamandré Archives

PP-32 Butterfly and floral resist or discharge print on cotton, Chinese, 20th c.

Textile Artifacts

Lee Jofa

PP-33 Floral motif, drapery panel, cotton, England, c. 1910

PP-34 Basket of flowers on specialty weave imitation gros-point

Lee Jofa

PP-35 Floral motif on cotton (left) and on linen (right)

PP-36 Floral and geometric patterns in metallic ink on sheer ground

PP-37 Gold-leaf geometric and diaper patterns on dyed silk

PP-38 Trailing floral pattern with rosette border, block-printed cotton, India, 18th c.

PP-39 Chrysanthemum pattern resist print, cotton, Japanese, 19th–20th c.

PP-40 Grape vine pattern with border, hand-printed cotton

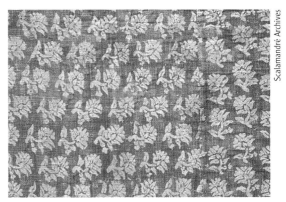

PP-41 Monotone flower pattern, resist print, 18th–19th c.

Lee Jofa

PP-42 Acanthus leaf ornamental pattern, cotton

Fonthill, Ltd.

PP-43 Scrollwork with rose border in two colorways

Renate Halpern Galleries, Inc.

PP-44 Fortuny design, detail, hand-printed linen, Italy, ca. 1930

G. P. & J. Baker, Limited

PP-45 Floral arabesque motif, linen-cotton blend

Scalamandré Archives

PP-46 Serpentine floral stripe discharge print, 18th–19th c.

Renate Halpern Galleries, Inc.

PP-47 Fortuny print, detail, cotton, Italy, ca. 1930

Scalamandré Archives

PP-48 Floral bouquets and serpentine stripes, indigo resist print, France, 18th c.

Lee Jofa

PP-49 Grapes and pomegranates pattern, cotton

Susan E. Oostdyk, Antiques

PP-50 Floral bouquets, crepe bark cloth, ca. 1950

Snow Leopard Antiques

PP-51 Alternating floral and leaf stripes, cotton

Snow Leopard Antiques

PP-52 Rhododendron pattern on "patio print" drapery, ca. 1940

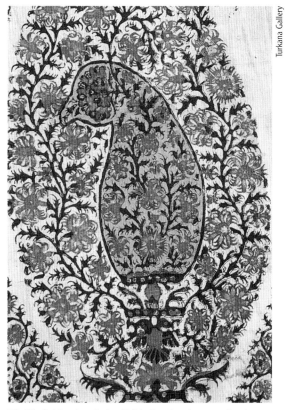

PP-53 Paisley *boteh*, detail, block-printed cotton, Persia, 19th c.

PP-54 Floral motif with border, block-printed cotton, Persia, 19th c.

PP-55 Printed and painted "Indiennes" design, 19th c.

PP-56 Summer carpet, detail, with floral motifs, stenciled, resist-painted, dyed cotton, India, 1640–45

Grey Watkins, Ltd.

PP-57 Paisley repeat, hand-screened cotton

Grey Watkins, Ltd.

PP-58 Paisley and floral motif in stripe layout, hand-screened cotton

Royal College of Art

PP-59 Paisley *boteh* and border, roller-printed wool, 19th c.

Grey Watkins, Ltd.

PP-60 Draped paisley pattern, silk

PP-61 Monkeys in fantasy figurative design, hand-screened cotton

PP-62 Persian scene, roller engraving, 19th c.

PP-63 "The Arts," toile copperplate, cotton, ca. 1815

PP-64 Floral wreath with eagle, polychromatic roller engraving, 19th c.

PP-65 Egyptian motif, copperplate, cotton, France, 19th c.

PP-66 "Folly Cove" pictorial print, cotton, U.S., ca. 1930

PP-67 Persian scene, cotton

PP-68 Pastoral village scene, crepe bark cloth, 20th c.

PP-69 Farm scene, vinyl kitchen chair upholstery

PP-70 Oriental boat scene, crepe bark cloth, 1940

G. P. & J. Baker, Limited

Scalamandré Archives

PP-71 Toile with figures and medallions, copperplate or roller print, cotton, 19th c.

PP-72 Toile-inspired pastoral scene, cotton

PP-73 Toile pastoral scene, cotton

PP-74 Toile copperplate print, linen, French, late 18th c.

PP-75 Seashell motif, hand-screened on jacquard-woven-seashell cotton ground

PP-76 Knights on horses pattern, cotton or linen, 20th c.

PP-77 Fortuny print, lion pattern, cotton, Italy, ca. 1930

PP-78 Ethnic and animal motifs, cotton

PP-79 Flying birds pattern, screen print, probably 20th c.

PP-80 Crocodile and skull pattern, warp ikat, cotton, Indonesia

Lee Jofa

PP-81 Deer and hound motif, cotton

Sivasli Istanbul Yazmacisi

PP-82 Animal and ethnic motifs with border, resist or discharge print, cotton

Scalamandré Archives

PP-83 Fish motif, discharge print, Associated Artists, U.S., 19th c.

Passamameria Valmar

PP-84 Imitation tapestry with unicorn, screen-printed on rough linen

Scalamandré

PP-85 Bird in bush, pillar print, engraved roller or block print on glazed chintz, 19th c.

Renate Halpern Galleries, Inc.

PP-86 Animal motif in box layout, block-printed, cotton, U.S., ca. 1930

PP-87 Animal and ethnic motifs with border, cotton

Renate Halpern Galleries, Inc.

PP-88 Dancing figures in abstract box layout, cotton, ca. 1950

Scalamandré

PP-89 Chinoiserie with trailing vine, cotton

Scalamandré Archives

PP-90 Pastoral scene, polychromatic toile, engraved roller and block print

Auntie Macassar Ltd.

PP-91 Floral vine with bird

PP-92 Automobile motif

Susan E. Oostdyk, Antiques

PP-93 Moderne pattern, leaf and step motifs, ca. 1950

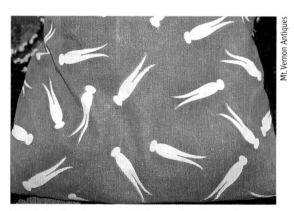

Mt. Vernon Antiques

PP-94 Clothespin pattern, block or resist print, 20th c.

PP-95 Still-life pattern of dishes, cotton, ca. 1940

PP-96 Dutch-inspired motifs in box layout, cotton, ca. 1940

Courtesy of Calico Corners

PP-97 Abstract painting motif, cotton

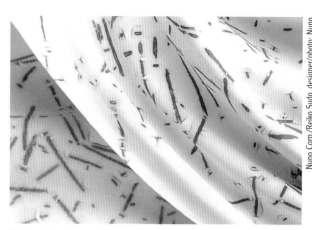

Nuno Corp./Reiko Sudo, designer/photo: Nuno

PP-98 Free-form pattern hand-printed with rusty metal shapes oxidized on rayon

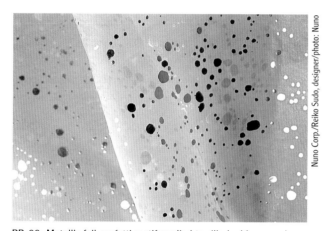

Nuno Corp./Reiko Sudo, designer/photo: Nuno

PP-99 Metallic foil confetti motif applied to silk double organdy

Renate Halpern Galleries, Inc.

PP-100 Abstract motif (Taliesin), hand-printed cotton, Frank Lloyd Wright, U.S., 1951

G. P. & J. Baker, Limited

PP-101 Abstract painting motif, cotton

PP-102 Interlocking geometric pattern, metallic ink on multicolored dyed silk ground

PP-103 Stripe with geometric pattern border hand-screened on silk

PP-104 *Kente* cloth, geometric pattern, cotton

PP-105 Multicolored irregular stripe, printed cotton

PP-106 Leaf pattern border around diaper pattern, cotton

PP-107 Leaf pattern in stripes, cotton, ca. 1920

PP-108 Fowl with flowers in water scene

PP-109 Greek Revival architectural scene, engraved roller print, early 19th c.

PP-110 Pillar print, engraved roller and block print, 19th c.

PP-111 Hibiscus motif, block print or roller engraving and block print, 19th–20th c.

Renate Halpern Galleries, Inc.

PP-112 Painted bird motif on tapestry-woven wool blanket, China, 19th c.

PP-113 Cherubs painted on check damask ground

PP-114 Oriental scene with bird, resist-dyed and painted

Snow Leopard Antiques

PP-115 Pastoral scene, printed with painted details, pillow top, U.S., 1900

PP-116 Resist-dyed and painted African scene

Kay Mertens Vintage Textiles

PP-117 Tibetan *tanka*, painted and dyed, with applied gold leaf

Textile Arts

PP-118 Primitive battle scene painted on linen

Snow Leopard Antiques

PP-119 Gibson Girl, printed with painted details, pillow top, U.S., 1900

Scalamandré Archives

PP-120 Dragon and flowers, resist-dyed and painted
cotton

PP-121 Embroidered and painted ribbon with ivy, cotton
twill

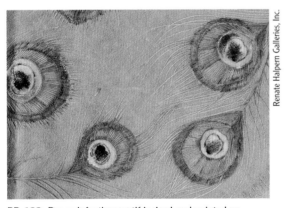

Renate Halpern Galleries, Inc.

PP-122 Peacock feather motif incised and painted on
cotton, ca. 1900

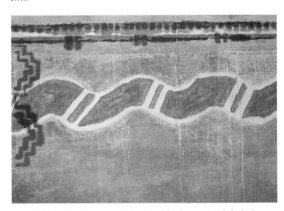

PP-123 Snake design painted on Hopi ceremonial cloth

PP-124 Girl in garden scene, embroidered and painted, ca.
1940

PP-125 Woven flame design with printed and painted
colors, wool, 20th c.

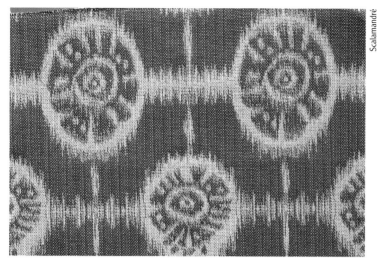

Scalamandré

PP-126 Ikat-inspired woven design

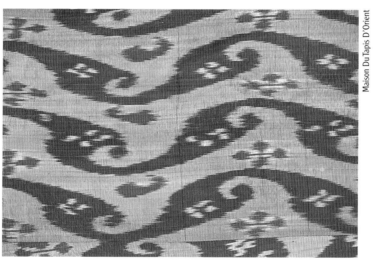

Maison Du Tapis D'Orient

PP-127 Ikat-dyed textile, Central Asia, 19th–20th c.

Maison Du Tapis D'Orient

PP-128 Ikat-dyed textile, Central Asia, 19th–20th c.

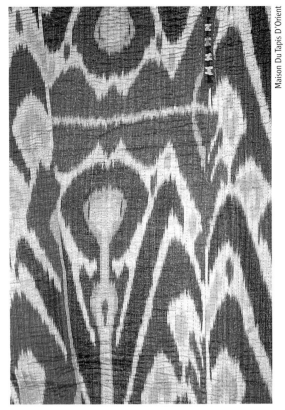

Maison Du Tapis D'Orient

PP-129 Ikat-dyed textile, Central Asia, 19th–20th c.

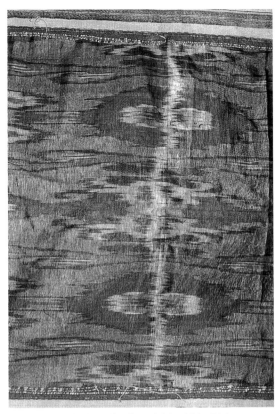

PP-130 Ikat-dyed textile, Central Asia, 19th–20th c.

James W. Blackmon, Antique Textile Art

PP-131 Ikat-dyed textile, Central Asia, 19th–20th c.

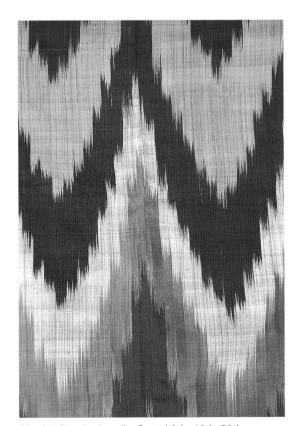

PP-132 Ikat-dyed textile, Central Asia, 19th–20th c.

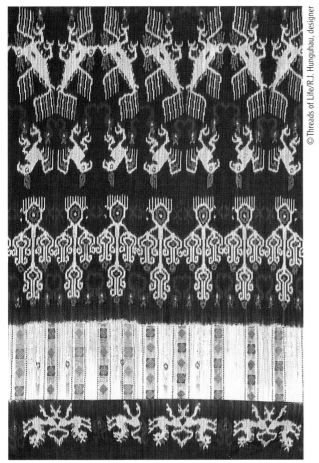

PP-133 Warp ikat with supplementary warp, handspun cotton, Indonesia

PP-134 Geometric double ikat, *geringsing* cloth, handspun cotton, Bali

PP-135 Geometric double ikat, *geringsing* cloth, handspun cotton, Bali

PP-136 Warp ikat, handspun cotton, Indonesia

Thomas Murray, Asiatica-Ethnographica

PP-137 Tie-dyed geometric pattern, detail, wool, Tibet, 17th c.

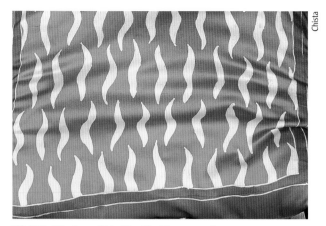

Chista

PP-138 Ethnic motif, batik, silk pillow cover, Java

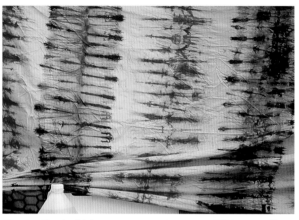

PP-139 Tie-dyed fabric

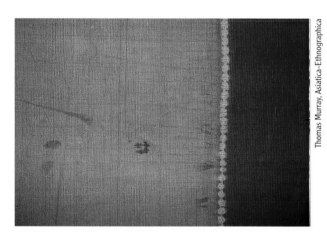

Thomas Murray, Asiatica-Ethnographica

PP-140 *Lawon* ritual cloth, tritik-dyed, silk, Sumatra, 19th c.

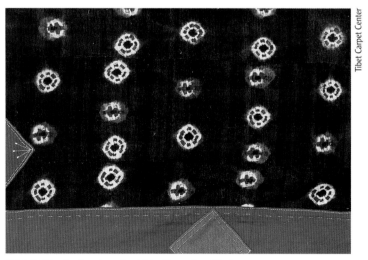

Tibet Carpet Center

PP-141 Tie-dyed and appliquéd textile, cotton, Tibet

Opposite: N-0 Embroidered floral motif, Czechoslovakia (Gillian Hine Antiques)

Needlework

N-1 Unicorn and lion in needlepoint scene, chair back, 19th c.

N-2 *Kuba* textile with appliqué, Kenya

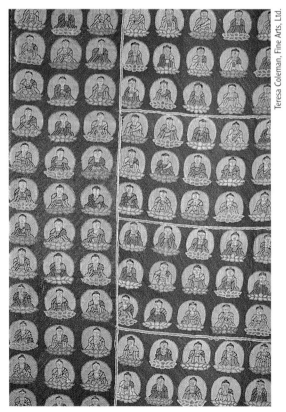

N-3 Figure repeat embroidered on Buddhist panel, China, 15th c.

N-4 Medieval knights appliquéd on net, hanging panel, England, late 19th c.

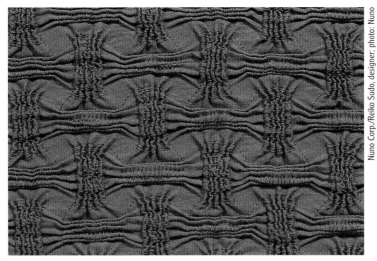

N-5 Schiffli-embroidered pattern inspired by Japanese wickerware fishnets

N-6 Birds and flowers embroidered in silk on linen, Portugal, 18th c.

N-7 Gros-point seat cover, floral pattern, 18th c.

Textile Artifacts

Rigo Carden, Inc.

N-8 Table runner, flame stitch embroidery on linen ground, France, c. 1920

N-9 Floral-geometric motif, pierced and embroidered, India, 19th c.

Renate Halpern Galleries, Inc.

Teresa Coleman, Fine Arts, Ltd.

N-10 Figures and flowers embroidered in silk on cotton, Crete, 18th c.

N-11 Dragon embroidered in couched peacock feathers, silk floss, and metallic thread, China, 17th c.

N-12 Floral scrollwork appliquéd in silk and embroidered on velvet valance, England

N-13 Stylized floral scrollwork, appliqué and couched cord, Spain, 17th c.

N-14 Bird and acanthus-leaf scroll on linen, Continental, c. 1870

N-15 Flowers, cotton cross and running stitch and trellis couching, U.S., 20th c.

The Preservation Society of Newport

N-16 Floral embroidery on silk firescreen, silk satin stitch and french knots, 18th c.

Gillian Hine Antiques

N-17 Corner design on wool, silk chenille satin and buttonhole stitch

Sherryl Sachs, Antique Textiles

N-18 Butterfly on satin, satin and running stitch and french knots, China, 19th c.

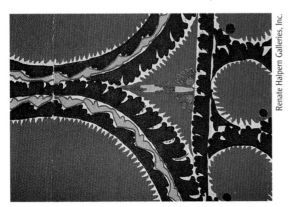

Renate Halpern Galleries, Inc.

N-19 Suzani, detail, silk embroidery on cotton, Central Asia, late 19th c.

N-20 Rose embroidered on silk, silk satin and fishbone stitch

Webb-Deane-Stevens Museum

N-21 Floral embroidery, wool Irish, stem, satin, and filling stitch and french knots, U.S., ca. 1750

Lee Jofa

N-22 Floral pattern, machine crewelwork

Rigo Carden, Inc.

N-23 Floral bouquet pattern, crewelwork on linen, satin, chain, and stem stitch and french knots, England, 18th c.

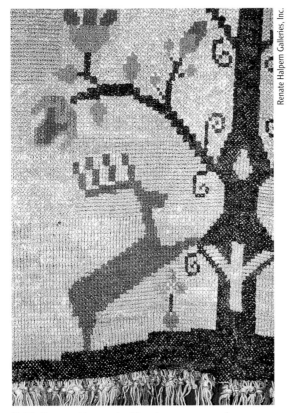

Renate Halpern Galleries, Inc.

N-24 Deer and tree embroidered on canvas, wool,
A. Müller-Helwich, Germany, ca. 1915

Sheryl Sachs, Antique Textiles

N-25 Fowl embroidered on silk, satin and outline stitch and
couched metallic thread, China, 18th c.

N-26 Dog and floral motif, cross, running, and herringbone
stitch

Mt. Vernon Antiques

N-27 Dog and foliage in crewelwork, chair cover, U.S.,
18th c.

Zee Ztone Gallery

N-28 Dragon scene on silk velvet, China

Fardin's Oriental Rugs

N-29 Camel motifs with geometric border, Central Asia

Sherryl Sachs, Antique Textiles

N-30 Dragon and figure on satin, silk and metallic thread, China, 19th c.

Teresa Coleman, Fine Arts, Ltd.

N-31 Canopy with dragons on fabric woven from gold thread, China, 17th c.

Sherryl Sachs, Antique Textiles

N-32 Bird on satin panel, silk floss and couched metallic thread, China, 19th c.

Marie Despres

N-33 Floral embroidery on piano shawl with woven fringe

Sivasli İstanbul Tazmacisi

N-34 Floral motif on cotton, silk chain stitch

N-35 Floral repeat on linen, stem, running, and Roumanian stitch

N-36 Circular floral motif, silk floss, Czechoslovakia, 19th c.

Susan Simon, Antique Textiles

N-37 Floral embroidery on silk ground, silk satin and stem stitch

Maison Du Tapis D'Orient

N-38 Flower and vine repeat on suzani

Rigo Carden, Inc.

N-39 Floral embroidery on velvet, silk satin and stem stitch, 17th c.

N-40 Geometric motif and border, silk satin and chain stitch

N-41 Geometric motif and border, silk on cotton, Caucasus, early 19th c.

N-42 Geometric repeat, silk on cotton, Caucasus, 19th c.

N-43 Geometric motif and border, silk on cotton, Caucasus, 18th c.

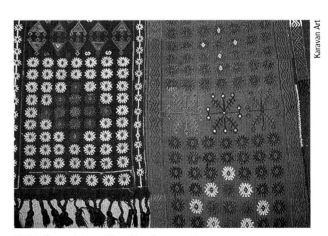

N-44 Geometric motif, chain stitch

N-45 Geometric motif and border on cotton

Sherryl Sachs, Antique Textiles

N-46 Butterfly and flowers with diamond and garland border on satin, China, 19th c.

Renate Halpern Galleries, Inc.

N-47 (top) Horse and figures, 18th c.; (bottom) tapestry-woven geometric motif, Russia, 19th c.

Rigo Carden, Inc.

N-48 Parrot motif in border with floral repeat, India

Sherry Sachs, Antique Textiles

N-49 Peony in vase on satin, silk and metallic thread, China, 19th c.

Courtesy of Spink London

N-50 Altarpiece on silk, silk and metallic thread, Tibet, 16th c.

Susan Bean

N-51 Peacock and plum branches on silk drapery, Japan, 19th c.

The Preservation Society of Newport

N-52 Oriental scene with deer embroidered and painted on silk firescreen, China

N-53 Woman and child, embroidered and appliquéd on pole screen, English, 18th c.

N-54 Grecian figure, Turkey-red outline stitch, U.S., ca. 1880–90

N-55 Domestic scene, Turkey-red outline stitch, Czechoslovakia, 19th c.

N-56 Seated woman, satin and bullion stitch with applied paper cutout, 19th c.

N-57 Floral motif cut work with border, linen

N-58 Cut work scalloped border, linen

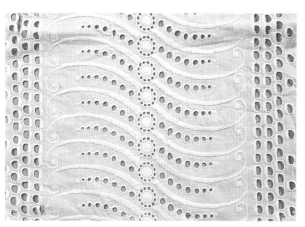

N-59 Scrollwork embroidery and border with cut work circles

N-60 Grape vine motif border on *Pina* cloth, Philippines

La Belle Epoque

N-61 Cut work with needle lace and drawn work

N-62 Cut work with lace animal insets

Joe and Mary KovalCredit

N-63 Dogwood branch and lettering on painted pillow cover

N-64 White-on-white embroidered text and scalloped border

Nea Martin

N-65 Patriotic motto in wool on punched paper, ca. 1860–80

N-66 Islamic text and flowers on linen

Country Repeats

N-67 Letter A on linen towel

Ewa Grabowski

N-68 Sampler, silk cross stitch on cotton, 19th c.

N-69 Corner embroidered on satin, metallic threads and couched metallic bands, Persia, 19th c.

N-70 Paisley *boteh* corner motif, gold metallic thread, India

N-71 Corner design on moiré silk runner, silver, Continental, ca. 1800

N-72 Animal and floral motif appliquéd and embroidered on felt, metallic thread

N-73 Floral motif, colored and metallic thread, Turkey

N-74 Man and tortoise on *fukusa*, Japan, Edo period

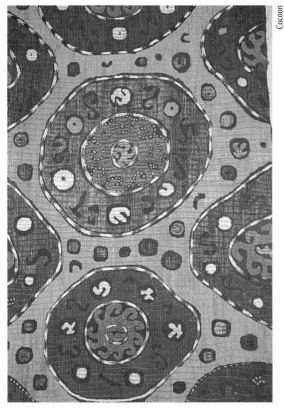

N-75 Kaitag, silk on cotton, Caucasus, 17th–8th c.

N-76 Kaitag, silk on cotton, Caucasus, 17th–18th c.

N-77 Floral motif and border on suzani, Central Asia

N-78 Kaitag, silk on cotton, Caucasus, 17th–18th c.

N-79 Wall hanging with central star, Central Asia

Turkana Gallery

N-80 Wall hanging with paisley and natural motifs, Caucasus, 19th c.

James W. Blackmon, Antique Textile Art

N-81 Wall hanging with floral motif, Central Asia

Turkana Gallery/photo: Turkana

N-82 Abstract appliquéd and embroidered motif, Africa, 20th c.

Photo: Guy Gurney

N-83 Animal and natural motifs, cut out and appliquéd on molas, Panama

N-84 Flower garden design, appliquéd and quilted

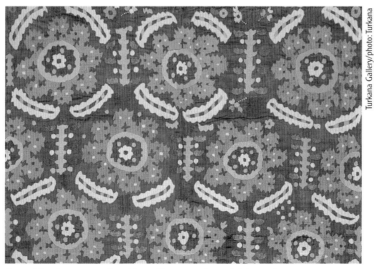

Turkana Gallery/photo: Turkana

N-85 Floral repeat appliquéd on silk suzani, Central Asia, 19th c.

N-86 Yo-yo work appliquéd on backing, ca. 1920–30

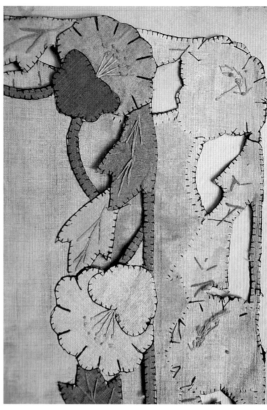

N-87 Floral border appliquéd and embroidered on cut work

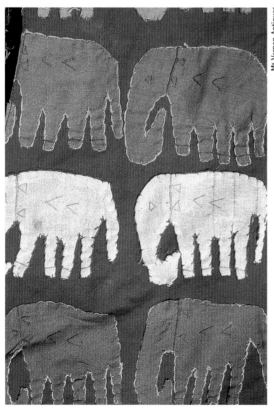

N-88 Elephants appliquéd on cotton, India

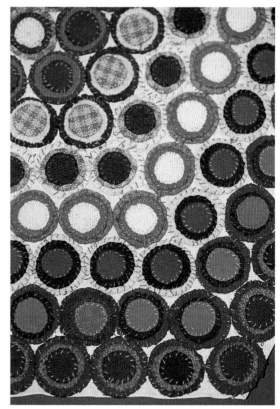

N-89 Penny carpet, felt

Mt. Vernon Antiques

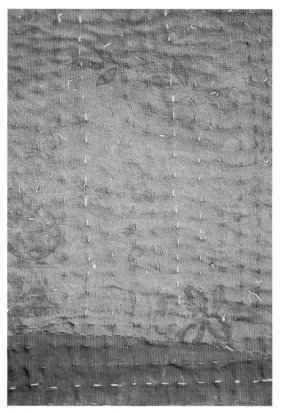

N-90 Hand-stitched quilt backing

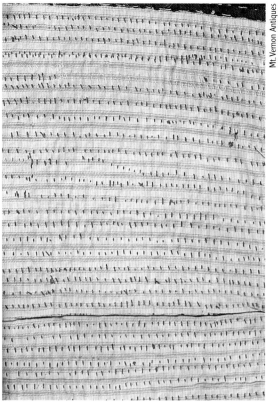

Mt. Vernon Antiques

N-91 Quilted ticking

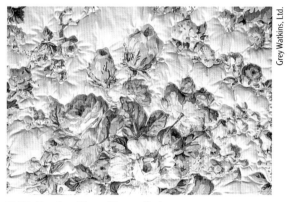

Grey Watkins, Ltd.

N-92 Floral motif, machine-quilted

Historical Offering

N-93 Silk plaid and printed cotton, quilted with running stitch in herringbone pattern

Susan Bean

N-94 Pieced silk quilt, diamond pattern and bars with quilted Art Nouveau printed lining, France, ca. 1900

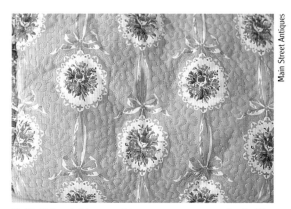

Main Street Antiques

N-95 Printed ribbons and bouquets on cotton, quilted with chain stitch

N-96 Patchwork quilt

N-97 Pinwheel pattern quilt with signatures

Susan Parrish, Antique Quilts

N-98 Signed quilt, detail

Susan Parrish, Antique Quilts

N-99 Appliquéd quilt with animals, stars, and moon

N-100 LeMoyne (lemon) pattern doll quilt, U.S., c. 1880

Mt. Vernon Antiques

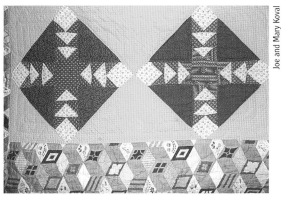

Joe and Mary Koval

N-101 Appliquéd and pieced quilt, Princess Feather border in "cheater cloth" print, U.S., ca. 1830–50

Mt. Vernon Antiques

N-102 Swag border on appliquéd quilt, U.S.

N-103 Cat and flowers appliqué in squares on pieced quilt

N-104 Flowers in basket motif, appliquéd on quilt

N-105 Star of Bethlehem quilt

N-106 Sunburst pattern, ground quilted with running stitch, grid and circle pattern, U.S., 19th c.

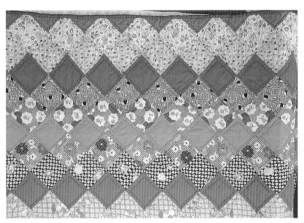

N-107 Pieced quilt with rows of floral and solid-colored squares

N-108 Quilted "cheater cloth" printed squares with pots of flowers

N-109 Star of Bethlehem pieced quilt, ground quilted with running stitch, diamond pattern, U.S., 19th c.

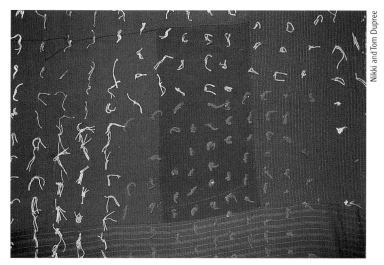

Nikki and Tom Dupree

N-110 String-tufted quilt, possibly African-American, ca. 1900

William and Connie Hayes, Antiques

N-111 Log Cabin (straight furrow variation) pieced quilt with herringbone quilted border

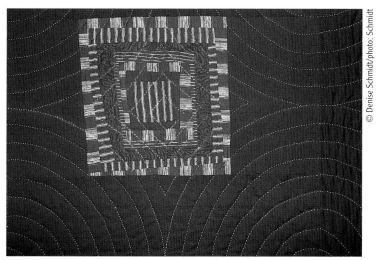

© Denise Schmidt/photo: Schmidt

N-112 Geometric motif quilt, detail, machine-pieced, hand-quilted

Joe and Mary Koval

N-113 Log Cabin (light and dark variation) pieced quilt,
U.S., 19th c.

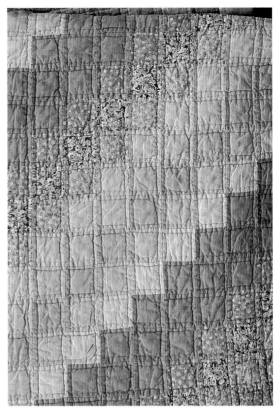

N-114 Squares in pieced quilt with ombré effect

N-115 Log Cabin (straight furrow variation) pieced quilt,
U.S., 19th c.

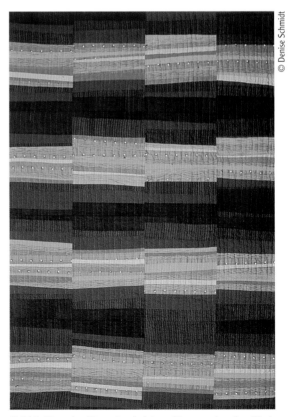

© Denise Schmidt

N-116 Pieced quilt made of vintage kimonos, hand-quilted

N-117 Nine Patch pieced quilt; ground quilted in running stitch arcs, U.S., 19th c.

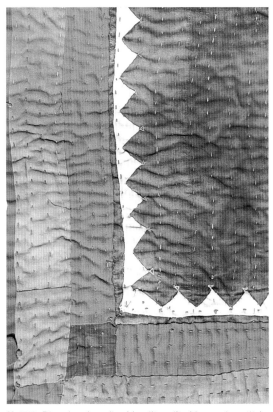

N-118 Pieced and appliquéd quilt, quilted in running stitch

N-119 Pieced quilt, possibly African-American, ca. 1930

N-120 Roman Stripes pieced quilt, border quilted in diamond pattern, U.S., 19th c.

Nikki and Tom Dupree

Wilton Historical Society

N-121 Crazy quilt embroidered with silk herringbone, buttonhole, running, and feather stitch, U.S., 1884

N-122 Paisley embroidered wool squares, India, 19th c.

Textile Artifacts

N-123 Alternating lace and embroidered quilted squares

Wilton Historical Society

N-124 Crib quilt embroidered with silk stem, herringbone, and satin stitch and french knots, U.S., 19th c.

Wilton Historical Society

N-125 Crazy quilt, embroidered with silk feather, satin, stem, outline, and herringbone stitch and french knots, U.S., 1884

N-126 Stylized checkerboard motif, tent stitch

N-127 Geometric motif and border, Spain

N-128 Floral needlepoint, tent stitch and petit-point

N-129 Chair seat, tent stitch ground with cross stitch motifs

The Preservation Society of Newport

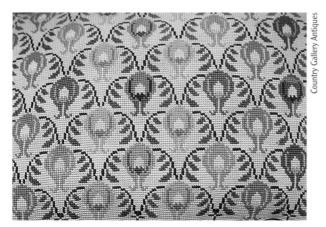

N-130 Chair seat, leaf and bulb motif in scale repeat

Country Gallery Antiques

N-131 Embroidered chair seat, wool, cross stitch, U.S.,19th c.

Norwalk Museum

Stella Rubin

N-132 Floral with scrollwork

Patricia Lea

N-133 Floral with scrollwork and fringe

Textile Artifacts

N-134 Rose bouquet on linen chair cover, petit-point, France, ca. 1920

Trudi Roth, Antique Textiles

N-135 Roses and lily, needlepoint with fringe

Rigo Carden, Inc.

N-136 Woman, satyr, and floral scrollwork

The Preservation Society of Newport

N-137 Persian scene on chair back, England, 19th c.

Robert Coviello

N-138 Scene with Renaissance figures, silk petit-point

Textile Artifacts

N-139 Lion and heraldic motif

Renate Halpern Galleries, Inc.

N-140 Chinese scene, wool and metallic needlepoint and petit-point, France, 18th c.

Lolly Chase, Antiques

N-141 Fox and fowl scene, 19th century copy of earlier design

N-142 Native American quillwork

N-143 Hanging flowers in glass beaded design

N-144 Cowrie shells and beaded motifs, Africa

N-145 Andean featherwork, Bolivia, 18th c.

Turkana Gallery/photo: Turkana

page 171: L-0 Macramé with woven ribbons

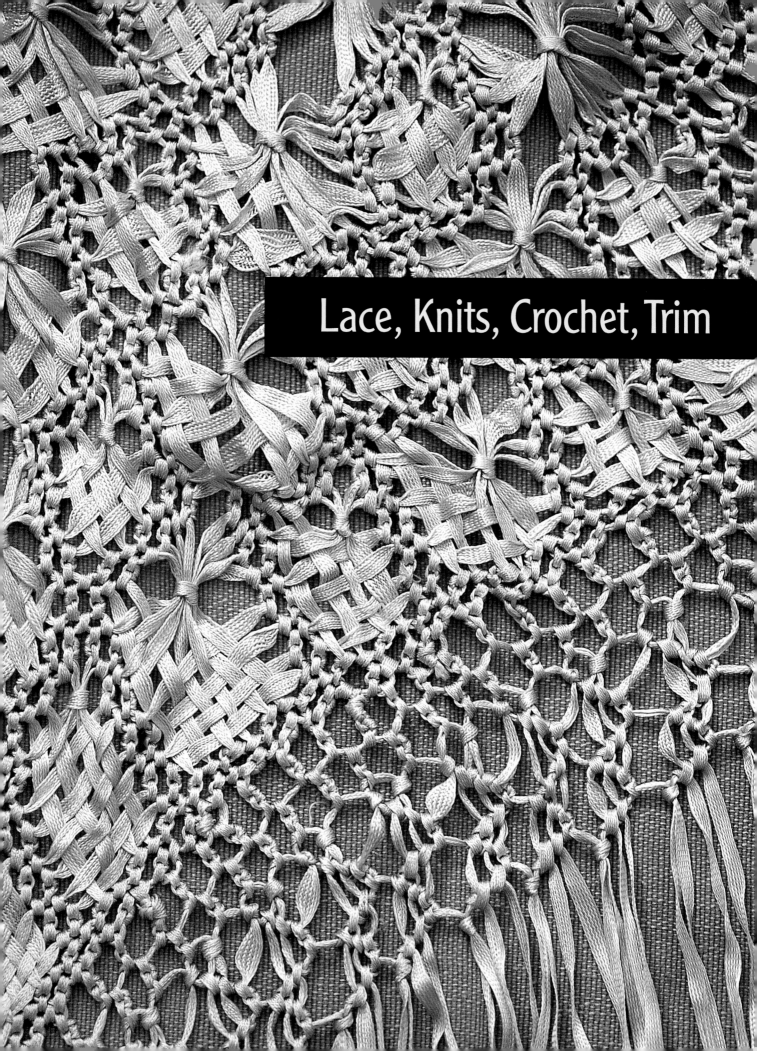

Lace, Knits, Crochet, Trim

Passamameria Valmar

The Preservation Society of Newport

L-1 Striped damask pillows with applied metallic trim and tassels

L-2 Metallic bullion and silk tassels with glass insets

Passamameria Valmar

L-3 Machine-made net from plastic cord

L-4 Cherubs with moiré silk ribbon bows

LACE, KNITS, CROCHET, TRIM

L-5 Plaited border and spiral motifs in cotton cord

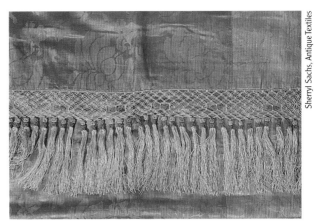

L-6 Silk tassels with knotted net border on damask, China, 19th c.

Sherryl Sachs, Antique Textiles

Ortaasya ve Semertkan

L-7 Ethnic motifs, woven bands, Central Asia

L-8 Striped awning with dagged edge and tassels

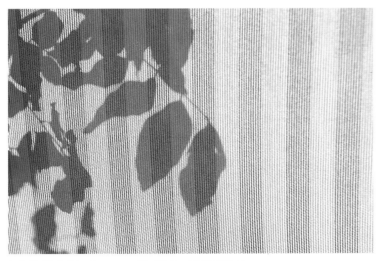

L-9 Knitted striped canopy with shadows from foliage

LACE, KNITS, CROCHET, TRIM

Textile Artifacts

L-10 Embroidered net lace curtain, wheel motif in macramé border, France, ca. 1910

L-11 Geometric and floral pattern with border, needle-embroidered filet lace, 20th c.

Country Curtains

L-12 Rose motif, machine-made lace curtains

Patricia Lea

L-13 Machine-embroidered net dot and scroll pattern with chemical lace floral inset, 20th c.

La Belle Epoque

L-14 Grecian figures in autumn scene, needlepoint lace, 20th c.

L-15 Dancing girls, needlepoint lace, 20th c.

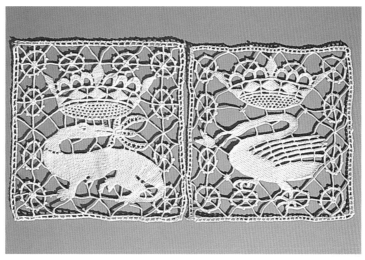

L-16 Heraldic animals, needlepoint lace, 20th c.

L-17 Scalloped floral border, bobbin lace, 20th c.

L-18 Cut work filled with tape lace, 20th c.

La Belle Epoque

L-19 Needle-embroidered filet lace medallion; cut work embroidery (upper right); tape lace (left and bottom), 20th c.

Rigo Carden, Inc.

L-20 Needlepoint lace corner motif, cut and drawn work embroidered scrollwork, 19th c.

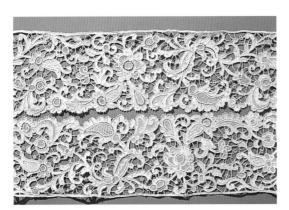

L-21 Floral scrollwork, Venetian needlepoint lace, 19th c.

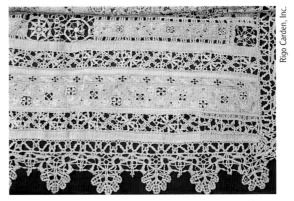

Rigo Carden, Inc.

L-22 Bands of rosette motifs in drawn work, "Reticella" lace bands, style of 17th c.

Rigo Carden, Inc.

L-23 Floral motifs and scrollwork in squares, bobbin lace, "Binche" type, style of 17th c.

L-24 Floral motifs and fringe, Irish crochet lace, 19th c.

L-25 Hanging bunches of grapes, chemical lace, 20th c.

La Belle Epoque

L-26 Cherub in embroidered net medallion and floral motifs in needlepoint lace, 19th c.

La Belle Epoque

L-27 Figurative scene in floral scrollwork frame, tambour appliqué muslin on net, 20th c.

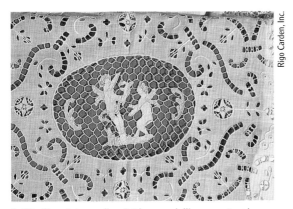

Rigo Carden, Inc.

L-28 Cherub in needlepoint lace medallion on cut and drawn work, 19th c.

L-29 Doves, laurel wreath, and border, drawn thread lace, 20th c.

The Preservation Society of Newport

L-30 Birds, scrollwork, and rosettes, needle-embroidered filet lace, Portugal, 20th c.

La Belle Epoque

L-3I Leaf scrollwork, tambour appliqué muslin on net, 20th c.

Rigo Carden, Inc.

L-32 Dot motif on pieced embroidered net and floral bands of Valencienne insertion lace, Alençon lace edging, 20th c.

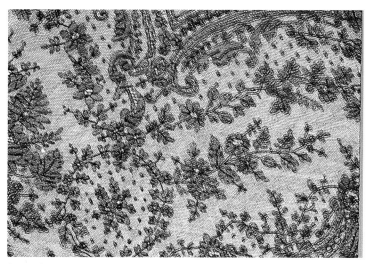

L-33 Chantilly lace, 19th c.

L-34 Brussels mixed needle lace: Point de Gaze and Duchesse, 19th c. copy of 18th c. style

L-35 Geometric motifs with dagged border, needle-embroidered filet lace, 20th c.

L-36 Geometric motifs, needle-embroidered filet lace, 20th c.

L-37 Meandering floral stripe, needle-embroidered filet lace (center), with geometric banding, bobbin lace, 20th c.

L-38 Lozenge motif, needle-embroidered filet lace, 20th c.

L-39 Varied bands with rosette motifs in circular crocheted tablecloth

L-40 Shell motif repeat, crochet coverlet

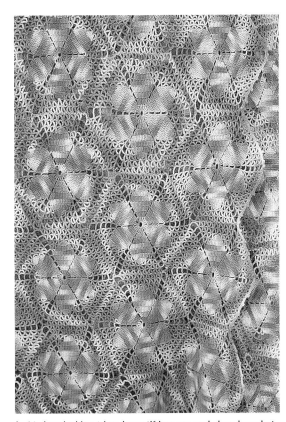

L-41 Interlocking triangle motif in open and closed crochet stitches, mottled effect

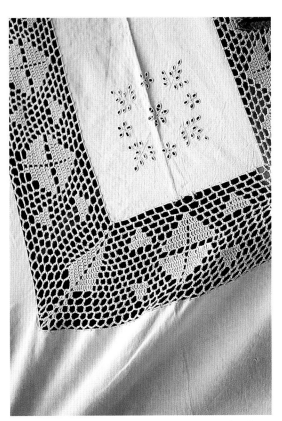

L-42 Geometric motif in crochet lace insets around eyelet embroidery, linen tablecloth

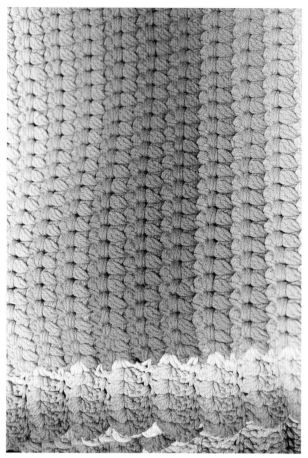

L-43 Raised star and square motifs in machine-made coverlet with tassel fringe

L-44 Ombré and scalloped edge in crocheted coverlet

L-45 Multicolored crochet squares in coverlet

L-46 Bull's-eye motif in tight crochet stitches

L-47 Crochet lace in chevron and square motifs

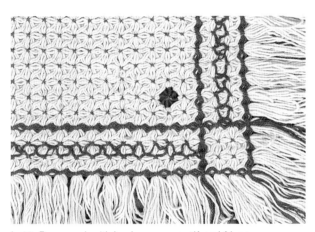

L-48 Frame work with border, corner motif, and fringe

L-49 Crochet throw in chevron pattern with multicolored banding

Rich BeauTique

L-50 Crocheted lace doily with lettering

L-51 Honeycomb pattern, machine-knitted sheer curtain fabric

L-52 Diagonal ribbed effect, machine-knitted sheer curtain fabric

L-53 Machine-knitted chair seat with suede trim

L-54 Metallic leaf fused onto fabric

© Tech in Tex

L-55 Honeycomb effect, industrial fiberglass fabric in machine-fabricated (raschel-crochet) process

© Tech in Tex

L-56 Sheer knitted fabric, tennis court fencing

© Tech in Tex

L-57 Industrial braided tubes: (left to right) fiberglass, copper, carbon fibers

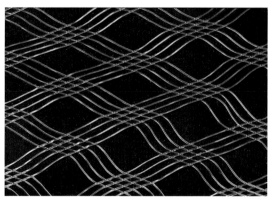

L-58 Clear plastic expandable netting

© Tech in Tex

L-59 Knitted industrial fabric: (left) silver-coated copper; (right) copper

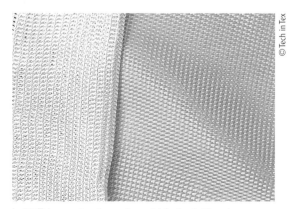

© Tech in Tex

L-60 Tube constructions of aramid (yellow), fiberglass (white)

Scalamandré

L-61 Tassels used as drapery tiebacks

Scalamandré

L-62 Tassels used as drapery tiebacks

Scalamandré

L-63 Tassels with rosette and ribbon drapery tiebacks

Scalamandré

L-64 Multicolor tassels

L-65 Ceremonial "priest's knot," Japan

L-66 Tassel

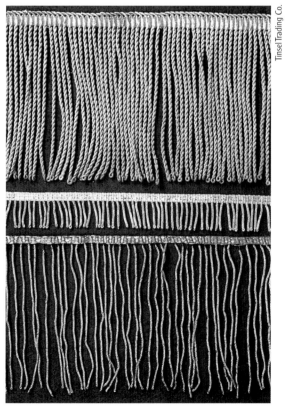

L-67 Metallic bullion fringe

Tinsel Trading Co.

L-68 Tassels used as drapery tiebacks

Scalamandré

M & J Decor

Tinsel Trading Co.

L-69 (top to bottom) French cut fringe, Italian tassel fringe, French tassel fringe

L-70 (top to bottom) French tassel fringe, French ball fringe

Tinsel Trading Co.

Tinsel Trading Co.

L-71 Brass and copper bullion tassels, France, ca. 1920–30

L-72 Silver bullion tassels, France, ca. 1920–30

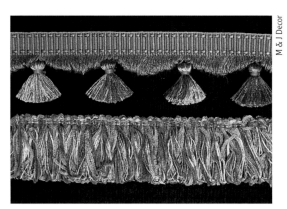

M & J Decor

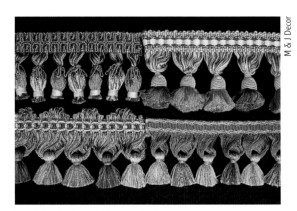

M & J Decor

L-73 (top to bottom) Italian tassel fringe, Italian chenille looped brush fringe

L-74 Italian tassel fringe variations

L-75 Tassels applied to ethnic textile

L-76 Damask and brocade runners with metallic woven trim and tassel fringe

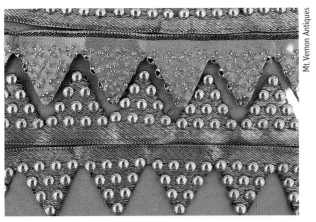

L-77 Brass studs and lamé in triangle motif trim, France, c. 1920

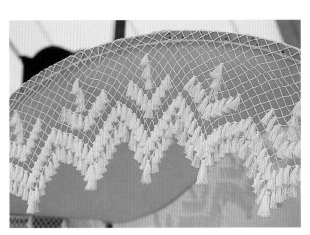

L-78 Tassel fringe on net bed canopy

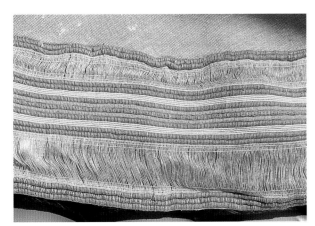

L-79 Woven trim with band of cords and open weave

L-80 Braided and twisted metallic trim

TRIM

L-81 Woven trim with geometric motifs

L-82 Trim, interlaced designs

Scalamandré

Scalamandré

L-83 Woven trim with Greek key, floral, abstract, and eagle motifs, ca. 1920

Tinsel Trading Co.

Opposite: R-0 Pile rug, millefleur design, Persia, 19th c.

LACE, KNITS, CROCHET, TRIM

Rugs & Carpets

Chuck Auerbach

R-1 Unfinished hooked rug on frame, ca.1930

Fardin's Oriental Rugs

R-2 Oriental pile rugs

Fardin's Oriental Rugs

R-3 Laver Kerman pile rug, Arabic lettering, Persia, 1880

Fardin's Oriental Rugs

R-4 Oriental rugs hanging in a courtyard

R-5 Mats woven from vinyl-covered cord

R-6 Aubusson-style rugs, rosette motifs in frame

R-7 Geometric border on worn rug

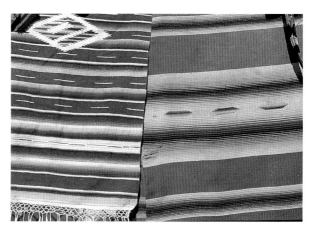

R-8 Southwestern textiles, multicolored stripes

R-9 Yüncü Yorük kilim fragment, Anatolian Turkey, 18th c.

Turkana Gallery/photo: Turkana

R-10 Unfinished hooked rug, square motifs, U.S., ca. 1950

R-11 Mats woven from vinyl-covered cord

R-12 Floral patterns on worn pile rugs

R-13   Aubusson rug, floral scrollwork border

Marcy Burns American Indian Arts

R-14   Navaho pictorial rug, Teec Nos Pos, ca. 1880–1900

Mt. Vernon Antiques

R-15   Arts and Crafts machine-woven rug with geometric motifs, ca. 1900

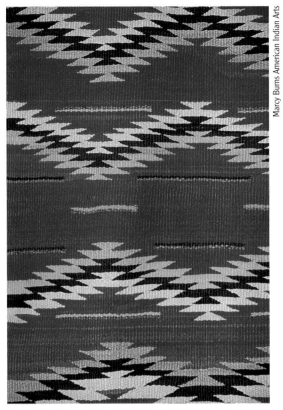

R-16 Navaho transitional blanket, ca. 1880–1900

R-17 Southwestern textile, stripes and square motif

R-18 Southwestern textile, geometric border

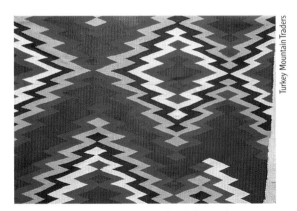

R-19 Southwestern textile, multicolored diamond pattern

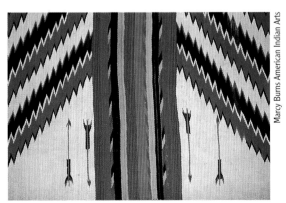

R-20 Navaho transitional blanket, stripes, ca. 1880–1900

R-21 Multicolor striped *Nambu* ikat-dyed rug, Tibet

R-22 Southwestern textile with herringbone border, diamond design, fringe

R-23 Nez Percé textile twined from cornhusk string, hemp, and wool, ca. 1900

R-24 Navaho blanket, diamond motifs, ca. 1880–1900

R-25 Southwestern textile, multicolored check pattern

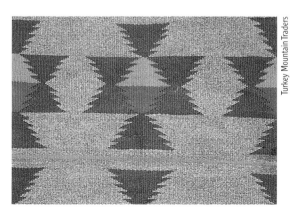

R-26 Southwestern textile, geometric pattern

R-27 Southwestern textile, geometric border

R-28 Tapestry-woven geometric motif and fringe

Louis Lawrence, Fine Artwork/Polly Barton, artist

R-29 Southwestern textile, diamond motif and fringe

Rick Dodge

R-30 Aubusson rug by Jean Picart Le Doux, fish motif, ca. 1948–50

R-31 Southwestern textile, geometric pattern

R-32 Multicolored rag rug, geometric in box layout, with fringe

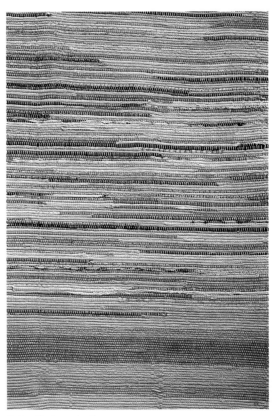

R-33 Horizontal-effect rag rug

Country Gallery Antiques

R-34 Irregular horizontal banded rag rug

Mt. Vernon Antiques

R-35 Multicolored rag rug, U.S., ca. 1940

R-36 Carpeting woven from seagrass

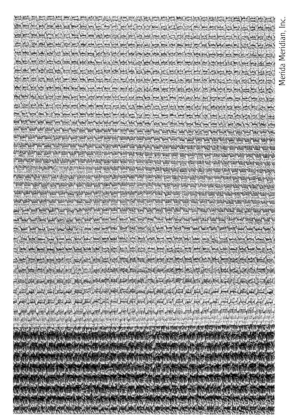

R-37 Carpeting woven from sisal

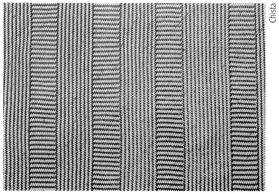

R-38 Rattan matting plaited with stripes, Borneo

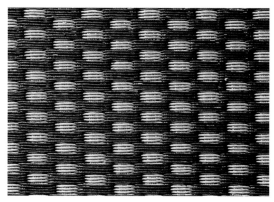

R-39 Carpeting woven from paper cord

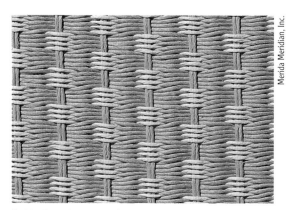

R-40 Carpeting woven from paper cord

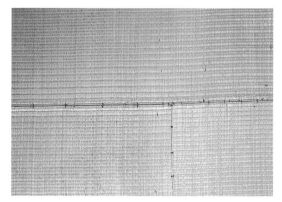

R-41 Rattan matting, summer floor covering, 20th c.

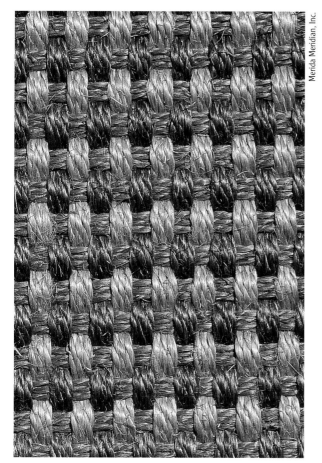

R-42 Carpeting woven from sisal

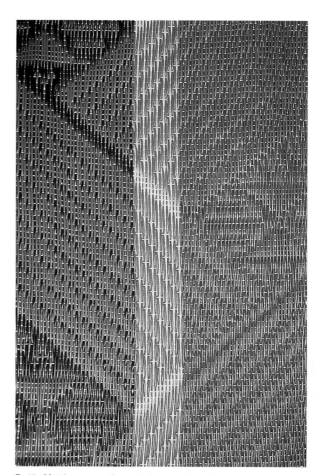

Merida Meridian, Inc.

R-43 Matting woven from vinyl-covered cord

R-44 Matting woven from vinyl-covered cord

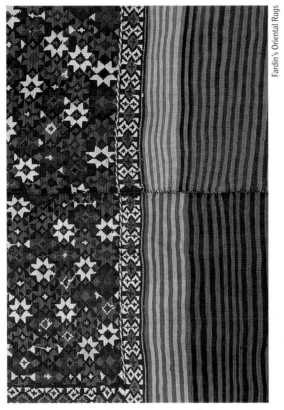

R-45 Kilim, stripes and geometric patterns, Turkey, ca.1920

R-46 *Jajim* kilim, geometric motifs in stripes, Uzbekistan, 1900

R-47 Seccade kilim, corner and border, western Anatolia

R-48 Kilim, alternating multicolored bands

R-49 Prayer kilim, border detail, Turkey, 1843

R-50 Azar Bizan kilim, border detail, 1930

R-51 Konya region kilim, border detail, central Turkey, 19th c.

R-52 Prayer kilim, corner and border detail, Anatolia, 19th c.

R-53 Helvacity kilim, multicolored diamond pattern, Anatolian Turkey

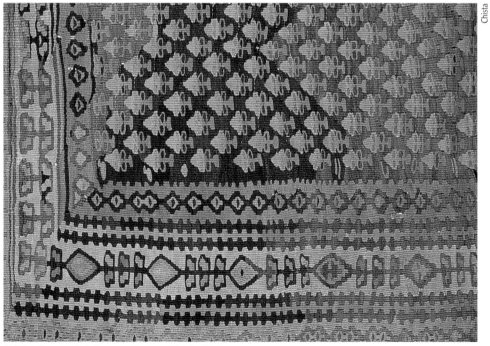

R-54 Kilim, central diaper pattern and border, Turkey

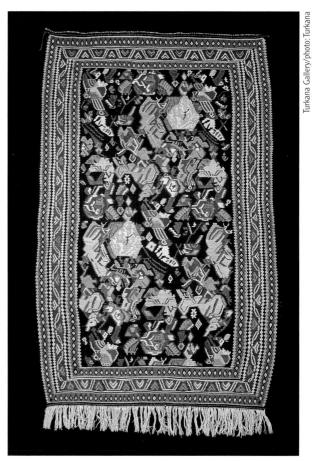

R-55 Kilim, multiple diaper patterns and border, Anatolian Turkey

R-56 Bidjar kilim, floral, animal motifs and border, Persia, 19th c.

R-57 Elmadag prayer kilim, Anatolian, Turkey

Wren & Thistle

R-58 Soumak, geometric motifs, Morocco, 20th c.

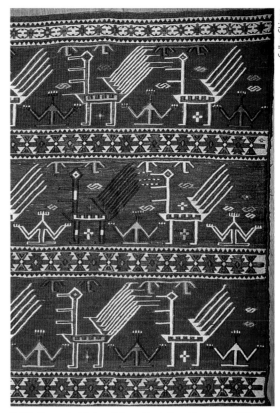

Gallery Shirvan

R-59 Soumak, bird motifs and banding, Caucasus, 19th c.

R-60 Soumak, bird and flower motifs and border, Caucasus, 19th c.

Chista

R-61 Soumak, corner and geometric border

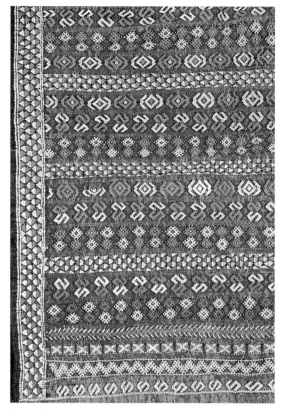

R-62 Soumak, geometric patterns in bands, Morocco

Ortaasya ve Semertkan

R-63 Diamond motifs on *zille*, Anatolian Turkey, 19th c.

R-64 Turkmen soumak, geometric pattern and border, Central Asia, 19th c.

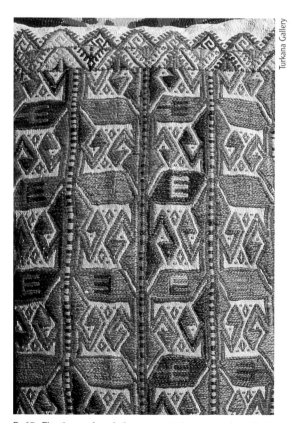

Turkana Gallery

R-65 Floating weft technique, geometric pattern, Anatolian Turkey, 19th c.

R-66 Braided oval rag rug

R-67 Crochet rag rug

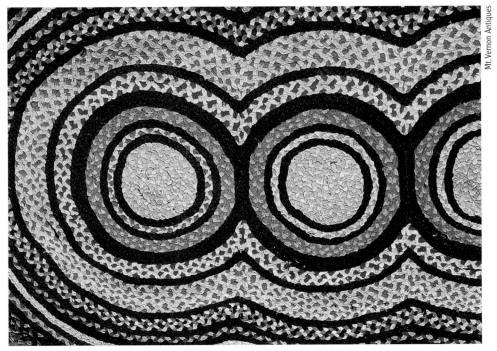

Mt. Vernon Antiques

R-68 Circle motifs in oval braided rug

R-69 Shirred rug from homespun fabrics, ca. 1840

R-70 Hooked rug, herringbone pattern, ca. 1860

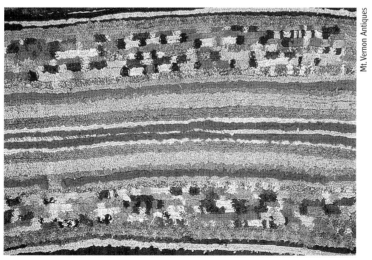

R-71 Hooked rug, multicolored confetti bands and stripes

Scott Bassoff-Sandy Jacobs, Antiques

R-72 Hooked rug, Masonic theme

Mt. Vernon Antiques

R-73 Hooked rug, owl and moon, ca. 1930

R-74 Hooked rug, dog scene

Bob Meltzer

R-75 Grenfell mat, dog sled scene, Labrador, ca. 1920–35

R-76 Hooked rug, grapes and vines

Mt. Vernon Antiques

R-77 Hooked rug, clamshell border around roses,
ca. 1930–40

Chuck Auerbach

R-78 Tree of Life hooked rug, ca. 1930

R-79 Amish hooked rug, block pattern

R-80 Hooked rug, multicolored scale pattern

Mt. Vernon Antiques

R-81 Hooked rug, multicolored squares in box layout

Mt. Vernon Antiques

R-82 Hooked rug, alternating stripes in box layout, ca. 1940

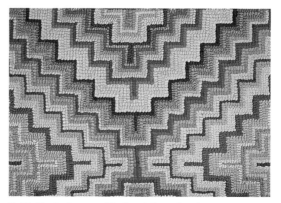

R-83 Hooked rug, multicolored zigzag bands

Ortaasya ve Semertkan

R-84 Central motif and border, Caucasus, 19th c.

R-85 Medallion design, Persia, 19th c.

Fardin's Oriental Rugs

R-86 Oriental rug, floral motif and border

John Murray

R-87 Pictorial rug, palace scene, Persia, 19th c.

R-88 Pile rug, animals, flowers, and stars

R-89 Pile mat, *boteh* motif, Persia, 19th c.

The Preservation Society of Newport/photo: David Bohl

R-90 Bakhshaish rug, landscape, Persia, 19th c.

R-91 Silk pile prayer rug, Ottoman design

R-92 Silk pile, medallion design

R-93 Turkmen pile rug, diamond motifs and border, Central Asia

R-94 Bands of chevron and floral motifs

R-95 Worn pile carpet, Persia

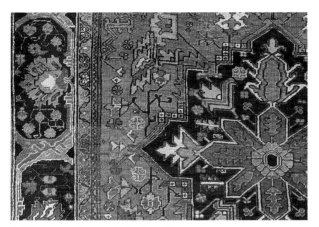

R-96 Serape pile carpet, floral motifs

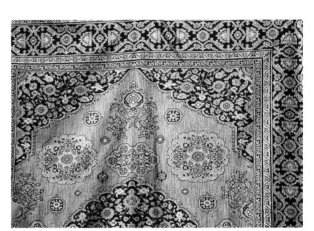

R-97 Floral motifs, medallions, and arabesque border, Persia

R-98 Shirvan pile rug, diamond motif, Caucasus, 19th c.

R-99 Lilihan rug, Persia, 1910

Fardin's Oriental Rugs

R-100 Shirvan pile rug, geometric motifs, Caucasus, 19th c.

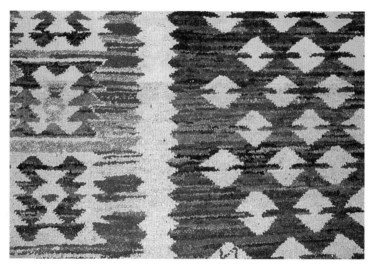

R-101 Boxed and diapered geometric motifs

R-102 Pile prayer rug, Caucasus, 19th c.

Chu's

R-103 *Ningxia* pile carpet, scale bands with cloud motifs, China

Tibet Carpet Center

R-104 *Metok* pile rug, flower pattern with interlocking border motif, Tibet

Tibet Carpet Center

R-105 *Penta chenden* pile rug, traditional floral motif, Tibet

Fardin's Oriental Carpets

R-106 Chinese art deco motif, ca. 1920

R-107 Flaming Jewel pattern (medallion, diaper, interlocking border), Tibet

Tibet Carpet Center

R-108 Antique *Khadi* diaper pattern with interlocking border, Tibet

Tibet Carpet Center

R-109 Saddle rugs, Tibet

Tibet Carpet Center

R-110 Contemporary *Khadi* diaper pattern, Tibet

Tibet Carpet Center

R-111 Stripe *Thigma* pattern, Tibet

Tibet Carpet Center

R-112 Abstract design, detail

Entree Libre/Marcel Zelmanovitch, designer

R-113 Abstract design, detail

Entree Libre/Marcel Zelmanovitch, designer

R-114 Bull's-eye and square motif, Tibet

Tibet Carpet Center

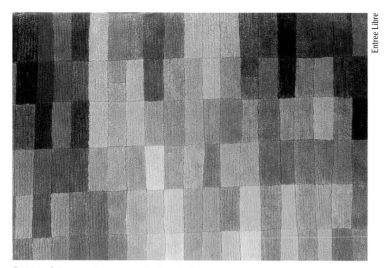

Entree Libre

R-115 Colorways for custom-designed pile rugs

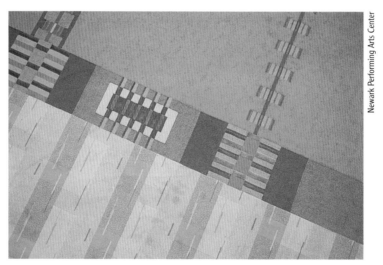

Newark Performing Arts Center

R-116 Broadloom carpeting, design based on African textiles

R-117 Broadloom carpeting, palm motif

R-118 Velvet-woven broadloom carpeting, rectangular grid motif

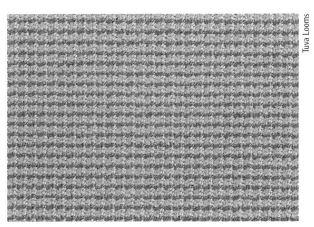

R-119 Velvet-woven broadloom carpeting, check motif

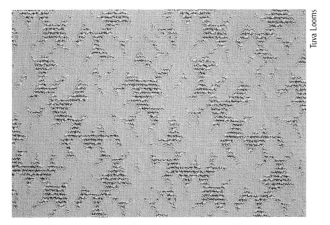

R-120 Wilton-woven broadloom carpeting, cut and looped pile, floral motif

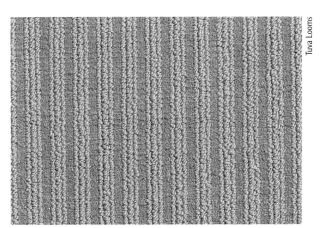

R-121 Velvet-woven broadloom carpeting, alternating cut and looped pile stripes

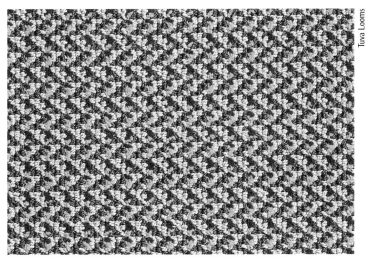

R-122 Wilton-woven broadloom carpeting, herringbone tweed

Tibet Carpet Center

R-123 *Penta chenden* pile rug, traditional floral pattern, Tibet

Tibet Carpet Center

R-124 *Halometo* pile rug, botanical motif, Tibet

© Helix Design Group, Folk Master Collection/photo: Helix

R-125 Red dog motif based on Bill Traylor artwork

Opposite: NW-0 Cast polyurethane laminated with holographic foil (Sommers Plastics)

Nonwovens

NW-1 Bull's head on curtain of interlocking plastic strips

NW-2 Carousel horse seen through clear vinyl curtain

NW-3 Soft plastic construction walls

NW-4 Geometric pattern incised on leather with fringe

NW-5 Draped plastic at construction site

NW-6 Carnival canopy with stars and stripes printed on vinyl

NW-7 Colored balloons

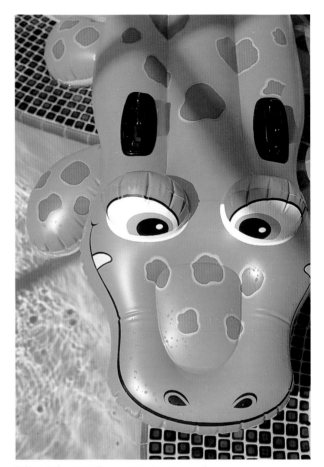

NW-8 Inflatable alligator in swimming pool

NW-9 Bar stools covered with vinyl-coated fabric, printed lettering

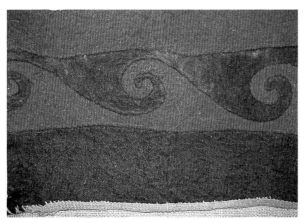

NW-10 Wave motif appliquéd on felt

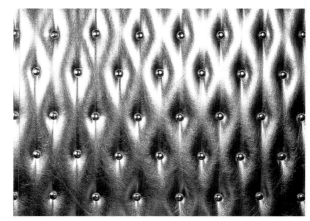

NW-11 Diamond-tufted metallic Naugahyde upholstery

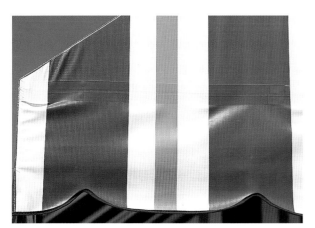

NW-12 Vinyl awning with printed stripes and scalloped edge

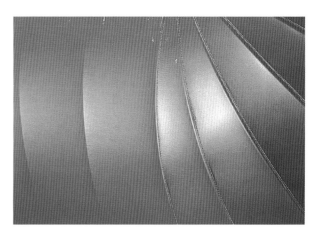

NW-13 Vinyl awning, top view

NW-14 Inflatable pool lounge

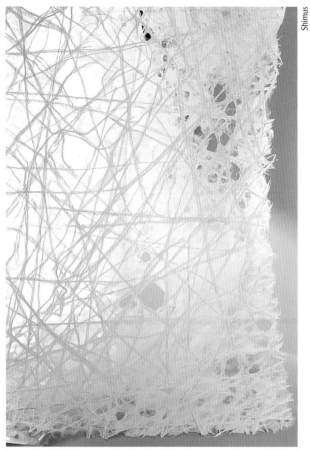

Shimus

NW-15 Washi

Ortaasya ve Semertkan

NW-16 Geometric pattern embroidered on felt *kali*

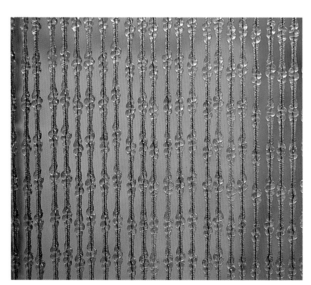

NW-17 Beaded curtain, cast vinyl beads, detail

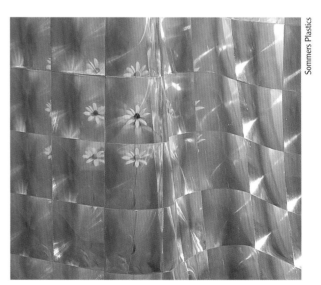

Sommers Plastics

NW-18 Flowers seen through square-calendered PVC fabric

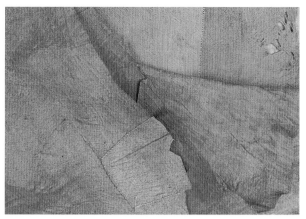

NW-19 Pieced bark cloth

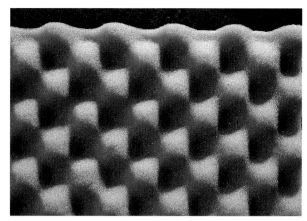

NW-20 Packaging, "egg carton" pattern, cast urethane foam

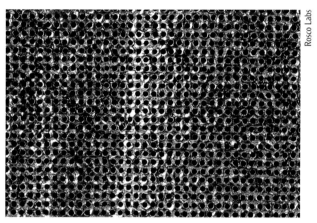

NW-21 Perforated silver mylar diffusion material

Rosco Labs

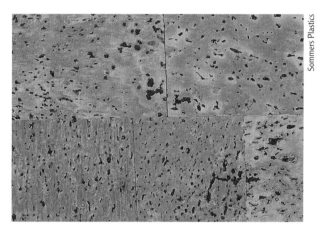

NW-22 Pieced cork wall covering

Sommers Plastics

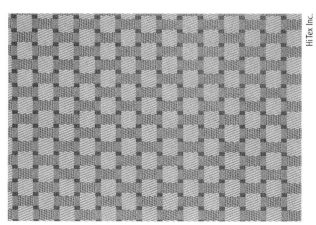

NW-23 Basket weave pattern on Crypton®, engineered upholstery fabric for heavy use

HiTex Inc.

NW-24 Fabric needlepunched and overprinted in herringbone pattern

Troy Mills, Inc.

NW-25 Geometric ethnic pattern printed on tapa cloth

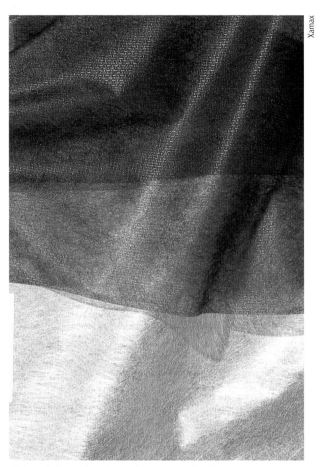

Xamax

NW-26 Industrial surface veil fabric, spunbonded polyester

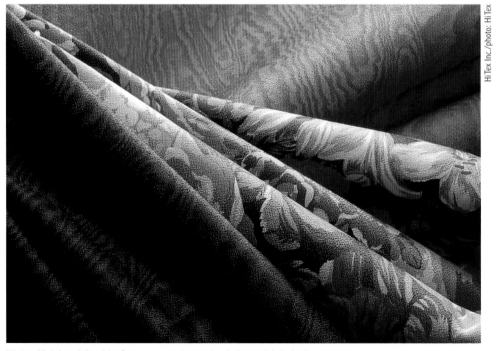

HiTex Inc./photo: HiTex

W-27 Moiré and floral in Crypton®, engineered upholstery fabric for heavy use

The Preservation Society of Newport

NW-28 Botanical, embossed and painted leather wall covering, Italy, 19th c.

Edelman Leather

NW-29 Leaf or feather pattern, embossed, dyed, and hand-antiqued calfskin

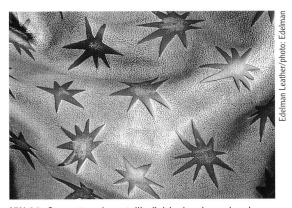

Edelman Leather/photo: Edelman

NW-30 Star pattern in metallic-finished embossed and dyed calfskin

Edelman Leather

NW-3I Art Deco pattern, embossed, dyed, and hand-antiqued calfskin

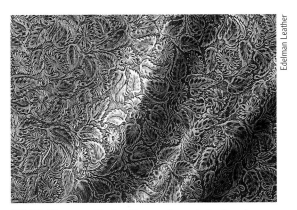

Edelman Leather

NW-32 Flower and leaf pattern, embossed, dyed, and hand-antiqued calfskin

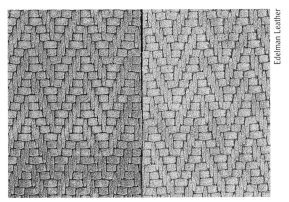

Edelman Leather

NW-33 Suede in two colorways, herringbone weave

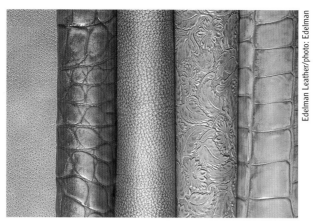

Edelman Leather/photo: Edelman

NW-34 "Old leather," embossed, dyed, and hand-antiqued calfskin

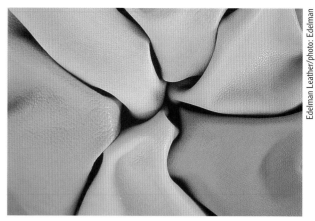

Edelman Leather/photo: Edelman

NW-35 Soft calfskin in colorways

NW-36 Pieced cowhide carpets

Edelman Leather/photo: Edelman

W-37 Perforated suede, small dot pattern

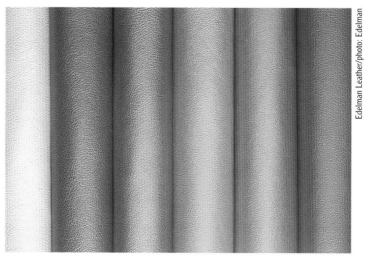

Edelman Leather/photo: Edelman

NW-38 Pearlized and metallic-finished cowhide in colorways

NW-39 Zebra pattern, hand-screened with dye on cowhide

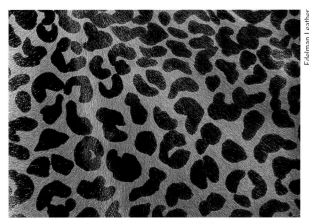

NW-40 Leopard pattern, hand-screened with dye on cowhide

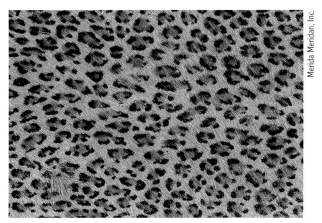

NW-41 Cheetah pattern, printed with dye on cowhide

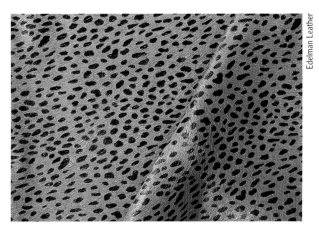

NW-42 Jaguar pattern, hand-screened with dye on cowhide

NW-43 Natural cowhides, pieced together

Shimus

NW-44 Dyed washi layered with gold metallic leaf

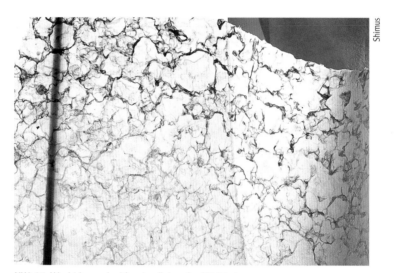

Shimus

NW-45 Washi layered with mica flakes, backlighted

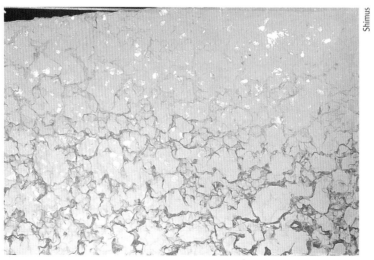

Shimus

NW-46 Washi layered with mica flakes, front-lighted

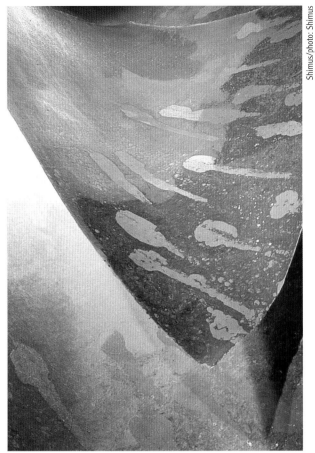

Shimus/photo: Shimus

Shimus/photo: Shimus

NW-47 Layers of dyed washi, laminated and shaped

NW-48 Construction from washi

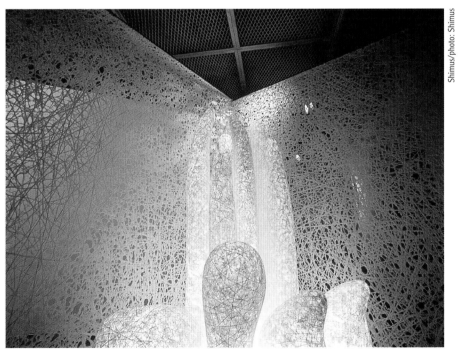

Shimus/photo: Shimus

NW-49 Cast washi

Maison Du Tapis D'Orient

NW-50 Cross and triangle motif, felt on felt

Turkana Gallery

NW-51 Scrollwork in dyed felt, Daghestan, Caucasus, 19th c.

Turkana Gallery

NW-52 Tribal motifs, felt on felt, Central Asia, 19th c.

NW-53 Square mesh PVC fencing

NW-54 Construction barrier fencing

NW-55 Construction barrier fencing

NW-56 Cotton tied net coated with clear flexible plastic

North Cloth

NW-57 Kevlar scrim sail material: (left) black adhesive; (right) natural adhesive

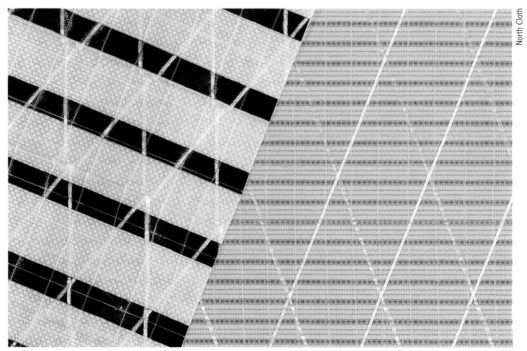

North Cloth

NW-58 Sail material: (left) Spectra Cloth® carbon; (right) Gatorback aramid and SpectraX®

NW-59 "Bubble" insulation, extruded polyethylene vacuformed and laminated

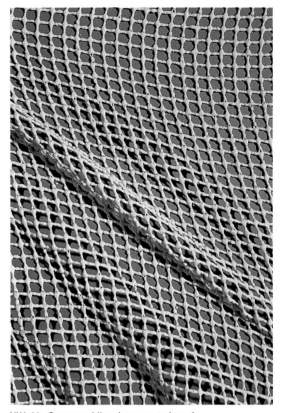

NW-60 Carpet padding, latex-coated mesh

North Cloth

NW-61 3DL® sail material, PBO (polybenzobisoxazole) and aramid

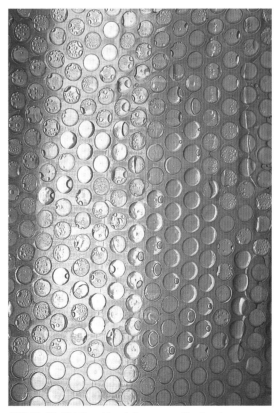

NW-62 "Bubble" pool insulation cover after longterm exposure to sun

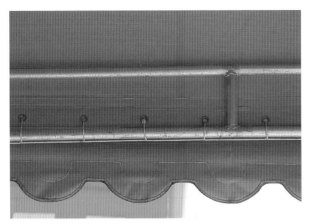

NW-63 Awning, scrim laminated between layers of vinyl

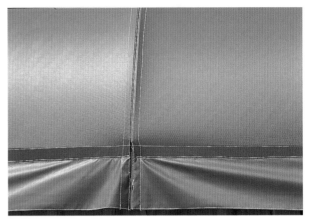

NW-64 Awning, scrim laminated between layers of vinyl

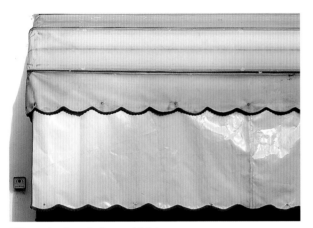

NW-65 Awning, vinyl-coated fabric

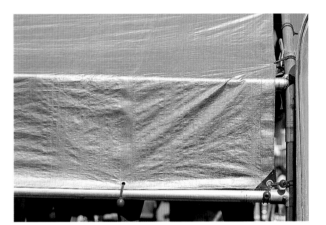

NW-66 Awning, scrim laminated between metallic vinyl layers

Groundworks-Lee Jofa

NW-67 Polyester mesh coated with clear and tinted polyamide

NW-68 PVC calendered with "basketball" texture

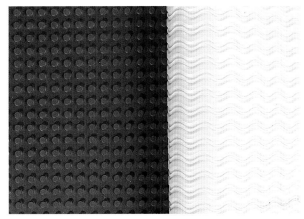

NW-69 Raised dot and zigzag patterns, cast vinyl matting

NW-70 Chevron and dot patterns, cast vinyl matting

NW-71 Ribbed, dot, and metal plate patterns, cast vinyl matting

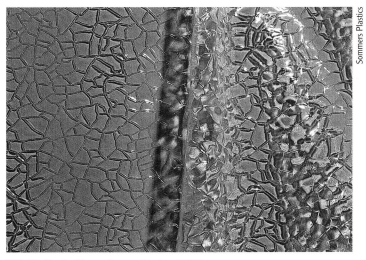

NW-72 Cracked ice pattern, calendered PVC

Sommers Plastics

NW-73 Serpentine texture in metallic-effect cast polyurethane

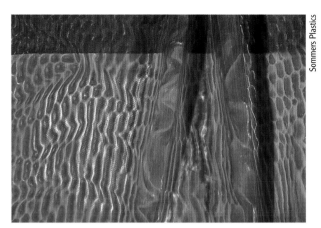

Sommers Plastics

NW-74 Water effect in clear texture, extruded PVC

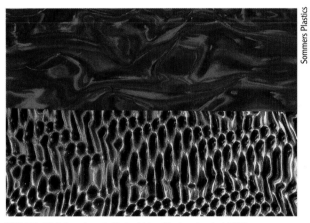

Sommers Plastics

NW-75 Moiré and metallic bubble effect, extruded PVC

Sommers Plastics

NW-76 Multicolored metallic grid, cast polyurethane laminated with hologram foil

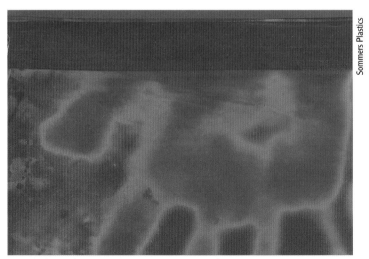

Sommers Plastics

NW-77 Heat color-reactive cast stretch polyurethane coated with vegetal cholesterol

Sommers Plastics

NW-78 Draped "stretch satin" cast polyurethane

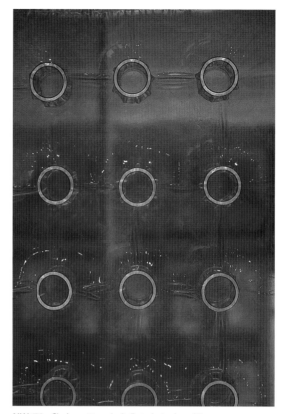

NW-79 Circle pattern in inflated vinyl cushion

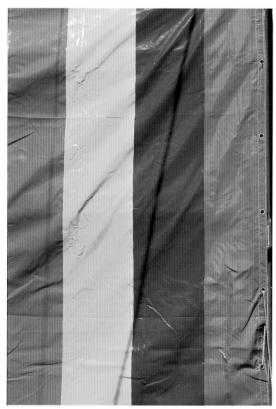

NW-80 Multicolored stripe tent

NW-81 Clear plastic sheeting

NW-82 Opaque plastic sheeting

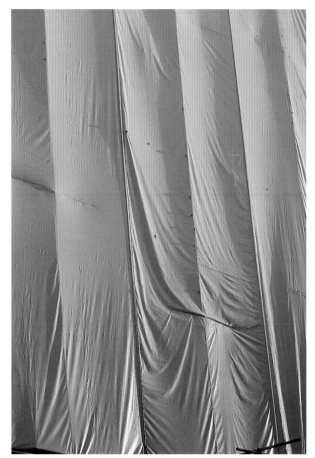

NW-83 Plastic material covering scaffold

NW-84 Clear vinyl restaurant entrance

NW-85 Clear plastic sheeting

NW-86 Plastic sheeting after exposure to weather

NW-87 Clear plastic sheeting and lattice

NW-88 Polypropylene tarpaulin on construction site

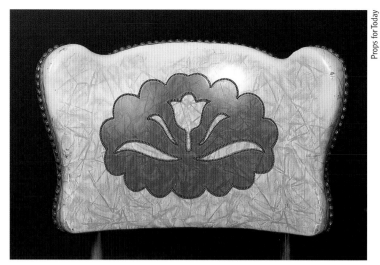

NW-89 Marble pattern and floral motif on kitchen chair back

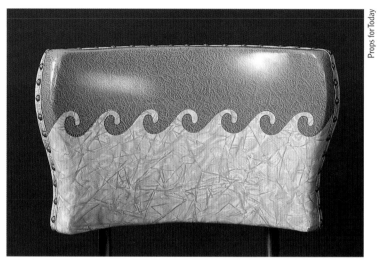

NW-90 Marble pattern and wave motif on kitchen chair back

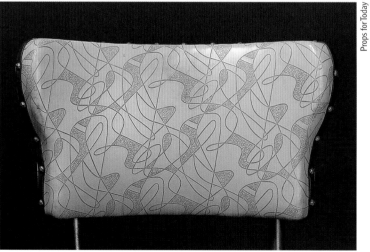

NW-91 Abstract motif on kitchen chair back

Furnishings & Structures

FS-1 Bolster on bench

FS-2 Damask pillows with tassels

FS-3 Rose motif chair upholstery and drapery, lace curtains

The Preservation Society of Newport

FS-4 Upholstered armchair, velvet, diamond tufting

FS-5 Armchair detail, matelassé upholstery and nailhead trim

FS-6 Leather and teak rocking chair

FS-7 Macaroons on floral print pleated skirt, ca. 1880

Chista

The Preservation Society of Newport

FS-8 Carnival game sign painted on vinyl

FS-9 Exterior view of curtains and oriental rug

FS-10 Curtains in window with stone frame

FS-11 Shop window with curtains

FS-12 Door window with lace panel

FS-13 Striped canvas shaped awning, side view

FS-14 Lace café curtains in restaurant window

FS-15 Austrian shades, sheer fabric

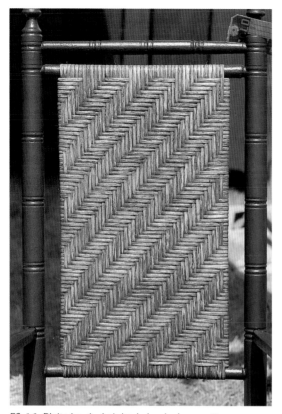

FS-16 Plaited rush chair back, herringbone pattern

FS-17 Hemp ropes around wood posts

FS-18 Knotted net used as guard on exterior stairs

FS-19 Rubber ducks in clear vinyl inflatable chair

FS-20 Burlap and rope baskets

FS-21 Sail cover, treated canvas

FS-22 Shop awning, Turkish lettering

FS-23 Matchstick bamboo fence

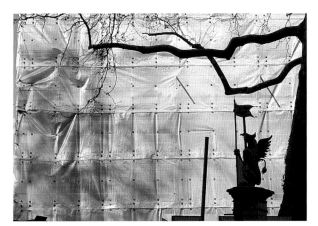

FS-24 Translucent woven slit-polypropylene yarn fence

FS-25 Umbrella with fringe

FS-26 Palm thatched roof, interior view

FS-27 Straw thatched roof, window and top details

FS-28 Bamboo over metal-framed roof

FS-29 Straw thatched roof

FS-30 Palm thatched roof

Photo: Guy Gurney

FS-31 Circular thatched roof, palm and wood, interior view

FS-32 Caned chair back, vinyl cord

FS-33 Chair back, interlaced hemp cord

Donghia

FS-34 Rattan side chair, basket weave

FS-35 Rattan chair back, basket weave

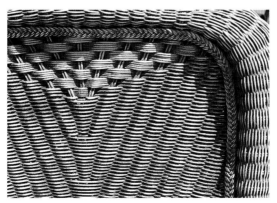

FS-36 Wicker chair back, chevron design

FS-37 Wicker chair back

FS-38 Leather chair back, nailhead trim and carved wood frame

The Preservation Society of Newport

FS-39 Velvet chair back, appliqué design

Brunschwig & Fils, Inc.

FS-40 Side chair with gilt frame, medallion motif, nailhead trim

FS-41 Upholstered chair back, polka-dot satin with nailhead trim

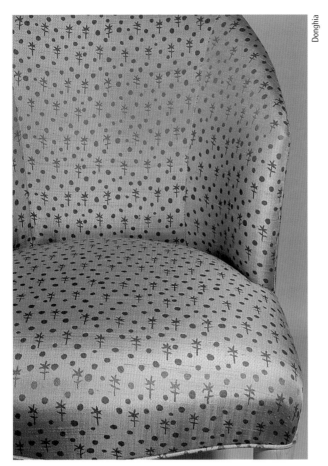

Donghia

FS-42 Matelassé upholstered chair, geometric pattern

Brunschwig & Fils, Inc.

FS-43 Antiqued leather chair, diamond-tufted back

FS-44 Upholstered sofa with carved gilt frame, floral design

Chista

FS-45 Leather and teak sofa

Courtesy of Calico Corners

FS-46 Upholstered wing-back chair, windowpane check

Randolph & Hein

FS-47 Leather sofa with nailhead trim, rolled arm detail

Courtesy of Calico Corners

FS-48 Upholstered bench, floral cut-velvet

Brunschwig & Fils, Inc.

FS-49 Upholstered chair with ruffled skirt, floral cotton print

The Preservation Society of Newport

FS-50 Armchair upholstered with 19th c. Sehna kilim, bullion fringe

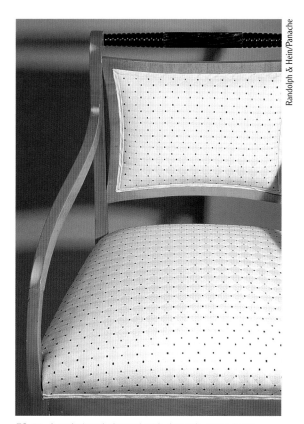

Randolph & Hein/Panache

FS-51 Armchair upholstered with damask, wood frame

The Preservation Society of Newport

FS-52 Armchair upholstered with needlepoint, Louis XIV style

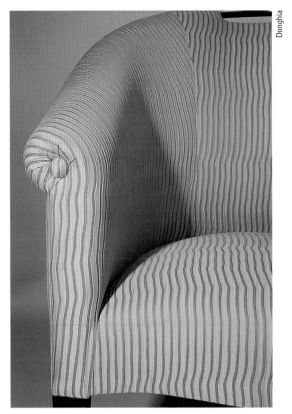

FS-53 Club chair upholstered with wavy twill

FS-54 18th c. easy chair upholstered with toile

FS-55 Ottoman upholstered with damask, tufted, with bullion fringe

FS-56 "Old leather" upholstered arm chair

FS-57 Ottoman upholstered with striped damask

FS-58 Striped upholstery on armchair, self-welt and nailhead trim

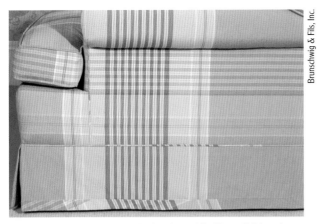

FS-59 Chair upholstered in plaid taffeta with skirt, self-bias trim, and self-welt

FS-60 Striped upholstery on armchair with self-welt

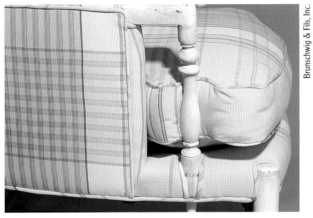

FS-61 Provincial armchair upholstered with plaid taffeta, self-welt, with painted frame

FS-62 Toile print slipcover, box-pleated skirt

FS-63 Tufting on floral upholstered footstool

FS-64 Upholstered sofa, velvet channel trim on patterned frisé or moquette

FS-65 Tassel fringe on silk brocatelle upholstered chair

FS-66 Scalloped design in nailhead trim

FS-67 Stripe frisé or moquette upholstered bench, satinwood frame

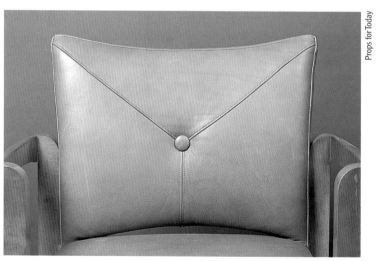

FS-68 Leather upholstered chair back

FS-69 Diamond-tufted floral upholstered chair back

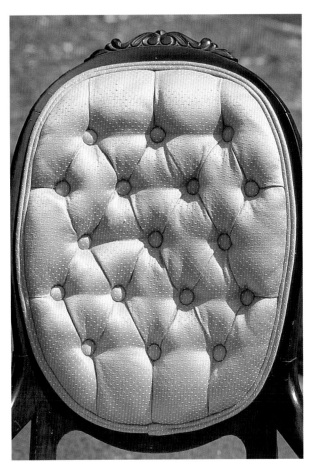

FS-70 Diamond-tufted upholstered chair back

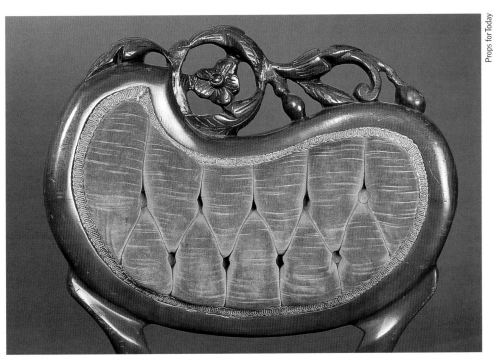

FS-71 Diamond-tufted velvet upholstered chair back with carved frame

Props for Today

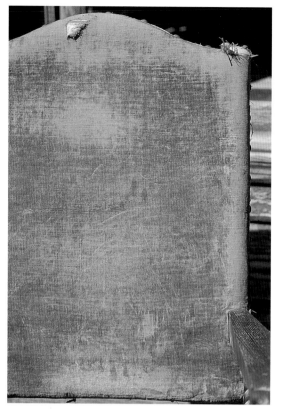

FS-72 Worn velvet chair back

FS-73 Worn upholstered chair

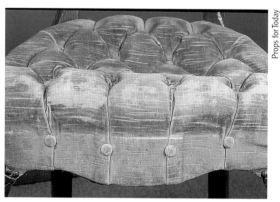

FS-74 Worn velvet tufted chair seat

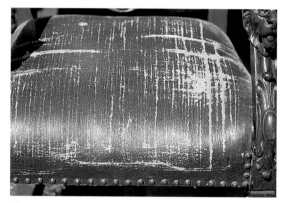

FS-75 Worn laminated leather chair seat

FS-76 Worn striped taffeta upholstered chair seat

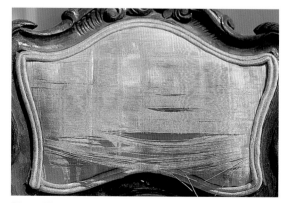

FS-77 Worn moiré upholstery on chair back

Props for Today

FS-78 Serpentine garland with floral stripes, damask

FS-79 Floral corner motif, silk damask, France, ca. 1900

The Preservation Society of Newport

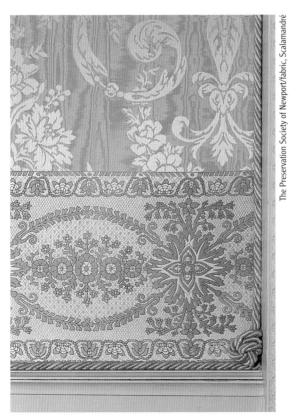

FS-80 Lampas, copy of 1900 French original

The Preservation Society of Newport/fabric, Scalamandré

FS-81 Boxed laurel wreath damask with rope trim

The Preservation Society of Newport/fabric, Scalamandré

Country Curtains

FS-82 Gingham curtains in window

The Preservation Society of Newport

FS-83 Cotton voile sheer curtains with ruffles

The Preservation Society of Newport

FS-84 Curtains in woven moiré pattern with wood blinds

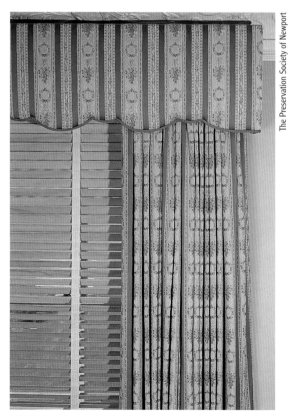

The Preservation Society of Newport

FS-85 Drapery and upholstered shaped valance, striped damask

The Preservation Society of Newport

FS-86 Silk velvet drapery and valance with appliqué over sheer curtains

The Preservation Society of Newport

FS-87 Satin fringed swag valance with jabots

The Preservation Society of Newport

FS-88 Bed canopy with swags and center tab

The Preservation Society of Newport/fabric, Scalamandré

FS-89 Silk brocatelle swag valance and draperies with sheers

The Preservation Society of Newport

FS-90 Damask and moiré swag valance and jabot

The Preservation Society of Newport

FS-91 Silk velvet portiere with Italian appliqué, 17th c.

The Preservation Society of Newport

FS-92 Austrian valance, jabot, and drapes, satin; voile
panels with Alencon lace borders

The Preservation Society of Newport

FS-93 Silk damask swag and jabot

FS-94 Lisere damask swag valance with macaroons and jabot

FS-95 Lampas swag bed canopy with Austrian treated back panel

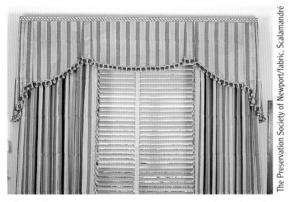

FS-96 Shaped valance and drapery in striped damask, with blinds

FS-97 Silk cut-velvet shaped valance with fringe, Prelle, Lyons

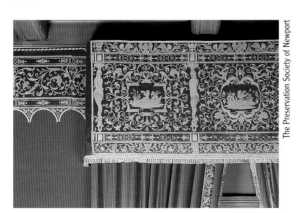

FS-98 Embroidered valance with matching cornice, Cuel, Paris

FS-99 Lampas swag and tab bed skirt with fringe, Pregaldini, Paris

The Preservation Society of Newport/fabric, Scalamandré

FS-100 Tassel tieback with drapery, lampas and cut velvet

The Preservation Society of Newport

FS-101 Damask drapery, valance, and jabot

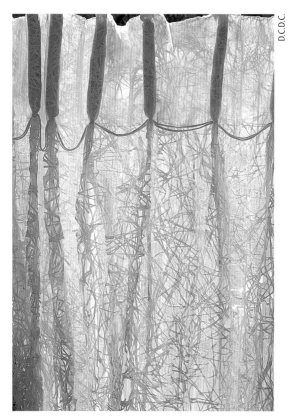

D.C.D.C.

FS-102 Pleated drapery, nonwoven backed with sheer fabric

The Preservation Society of Newport

FS-103 Tassels with glass insets in drapery tieback, France, 19th c.

The Preservation Society of Newport/fabric, Schumacher

FS-104 Toile bed valance and drapery

The Preservation Society of Newport

FS-105 Silk swag valance with cotton balloon shade

Country Curtains

FS-106 Lace curtains with heart motif, machine-made lace

Rigo Carden, Inc.

FS-107 Drapery woven with floral motif and trompe l'oeil fringe, France, 19th c.

FS-108 Sheer curtains in office building windows

FS-109 Ruffled curtain with wood window frame

FS-110 Tied-back sheer curtains

FS-111 Curtains in apartment-building windows

FS-112 Lace curtains and valance in window with shutters

FS-113 Café curtain and closed Austrian shade

FS-114 Floral motif on lace curtains

FS-115 Curtains in window with shutters

FS-116 Sheer hourglass curtain on glass door

FS-117 Striped cotton doorway curtain

FS-118 Chenille rope doorway curtains

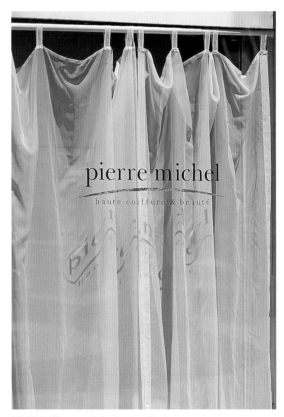

FS-119 Sheer curtains in storefront

FS-120 Sheer curtains in window with stone surround

FS-121 Lace curtains seen through leaded glass window

FS-122 Café curtains

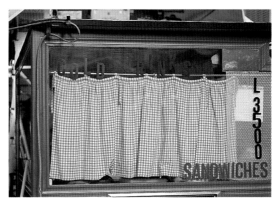

FS-123 Gingham café curtains in shop window

FS-124 Printed sheer and lace curtains

FS-125 Printed curtains in broken window

FS-126 Vinyl beaded curtain

FS-127 Lace curtains

FS-128 Sheer curtains in open window

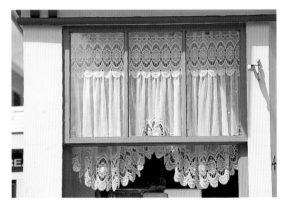

FS-129 Lace curtains in open window

FS-130 Sheer ruffled curtains in open window

FS-131 Muslin curtains in window

FS-132 Lettering on banner

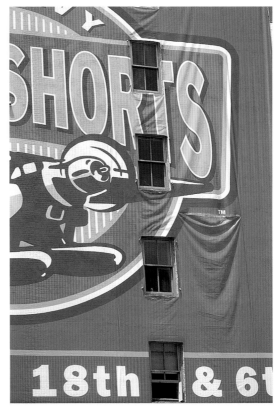

FS-133 Lettering and airplane on vinyl billboard

FS-134 Lettering on canvas banner

FS-135 Multicolored flags

FS-136 Banners with applied lettering

FS-137 Banners with Coca-Cola logo and Turkish lettering

FS-138 Striped canvas umbrella

FS-139 Umbrella

FS-140 Canvas patio umbrellas

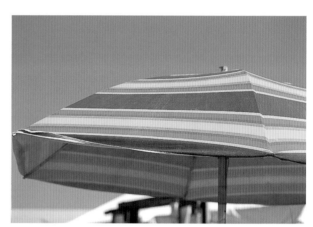

FS-141 Striped canvas umbrella

FS-142 Canvas patio umbrella

FS-143 Closed umbrella with printed lettering

Photo: Guy Gurney

FS-144 Dacron sail with rigging

Photo: Guy Gurney

FS-145 (foreground) Kevlar (yellow) and Dacron/mylar (white) sail; (background) nylon rip stop spinnakers

Photo: Guy Gurney

FS-146 Dacron sails

Photo: Guy Gurney

FS-147 Kevlar sails (yellow), nylon rip stop spinnakers (red, white, blue)

FS-148 Acrylic-treated canvas with lettering

FS-149 Vinyl/scrim laminate weathered awning

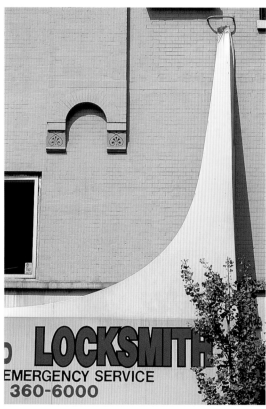

FS-150 Shaped vinyl with painted lettering

FS-151 Shaped treated canvas with applied lettering

FS-152 Vinyl/scrim laminate with scalloped trim and cast tassels

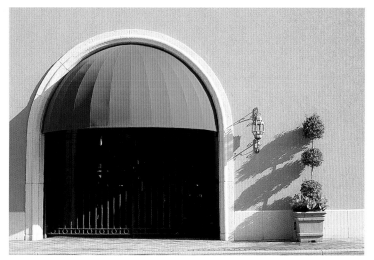

FS-153 Shaped treated canvas awning

FS-154 Treated canvas hotel awnings and umbrellas

FS-155 Vinyl delicatessen awning with lettering

FS-156 Weathered painted awning with Spanish lettering

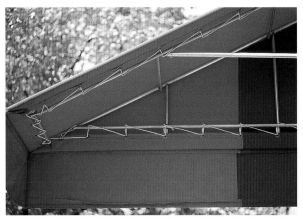

FS-157 Lacing and frame of canvas awning

FS-158 Canvas awning with painted Italian lettering

FS-159 Weathered awning with lettering

FS-160 Shaped awning with Spanish lettering

FS-161 Canvas awning with lettering

FS-162 Striped canvas awning

FS-163 Canvas awning with lettering

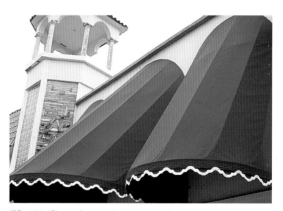

FS-164 Shaped treated canvas awnings

FS-165 Vinyl striped awning with Turkish lettering

FS-166 Multiple-striped acrylic treated canvas awning

FS-167 Shaped striped canvas awning with Italian lettering

FS-168 Closed canvas awning with Italian lettering

FS-169 Weathered canvas awning with Spanish lettering

FS-170 Weathered striped awning

FS-171 Canvas awning with Italian lettering

FS-172 Shaped vinyl awning with star border and lettering

FS-173 Vinyl laminate awning with English and Japanese lettering

FS-174 Striped canvas awning

FS-175 Striped canvas awnings

FS-176 Carnival tent

FS-177 Construction mesh fencing

FS-178 Tension tents

FS-179 Camping tent closure, detail

FS-180 Tensile structure arcade

FS-181 Striped events tent

FS-182 Carousel with fabric roof

FS-183 Lashed tent seam, detail

FS-184 Semipermanent pavilion with shaped roofs

FS-185 Tensile structure pavilion

FS-186 Cabana made from canvas canopy and old sails

FS-187 Temporary building with fabric and aluminum

FS-188 Scaffold covered with woven polypropylene fence

FS-189 Deteriorating construction tarpaulins and mesh fencing

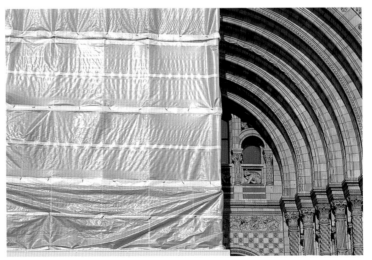

FS-190 Scaffold covered with woven polypropylene fence

FS-191 Vaulted arcade, treated canvas over metal frame

FS-192 Photovoltaic tensile structure

FS-193 Canopy over outdoor restaurant

FS-194 Tensile structure, pedestrian canopy and light source, detail

FS-195 Interior of large tent

FS-196 Inflated dome structure

FTL Happold

FS-197 Visitor center, tension tent

The following conversations are intended to give insight into the design, manufacturing, and uses of fabric. Here six professionals talk about their work in terms of the technical skills demanded of them, their sources of inspiration, their information and research needs, and the various ways they approach projects and solve problems. Art, architecture, textile design, conservation, scenic design, and manufacturing require

different training and preparation and have different objectives, but all of those interviewed have found themselves working with fabric. Their experiences give a multifaceted view of the world of fabric, and some of the ways art and design interact with research and technology.

(Note: The portions of text enclosed in square brackets are the interviewer's interpolations.)

INTERVIEW WITH CHRISTO AND JEANNE-CLAUDE
ARTISTS

Christo and Jeanne-Claude have been wrapping objects since 1958. As the scope and scale of their art have developed, they have worked with a broad range of fabrics, structural materials, manufacturing processes, and installation techniques. Their projects demand years of planning, and the careful orchestration of these elements with the specific aesthetic goal of each project.

Among the works mentioned in this interview are "Surrounded Islands, Biscayne Bay, Greater Miami, Florida, 1980–83," which floated six and a half million square feet of pink woven polypropylene; "The Pont Neuf Wrapped, Paris, 1975–85," the enveloping of a historic bridge with a polyamide textile that shimmered like silk; and "Wrapped Reichstag, Berlin, Germany, 1971–95," over a million square feet of aluminum-coated cloth cascading down the 131-foot (40m) tall building. Other works include: "Air Package" (1966), "Wrapped Coast, Little Bay, One Million Square Feet, Sydney, Australia, 1969," "Valley Curtain, Grand Hogback, Rifle, Colorado, 1970–72," "Running Fence, Sonoma and Marin Counties, California, 1972–76," "The Umbrellas, Japan/USA, 1984-91," "Wrapped Trees, Fondation Beyeler and Berower Park, Riehen, Switzerland, 1997–98." In progress at the time of the interview were "The Gates, Project for Central Park, New York City" and "Over the River, Project for the Arkansas River, Colorado."

Q You have created a diverse body of work with fabric as the common denominator. How would you describe your relationship with fabric?

A The interest in fabric began very early—in 1958—and we used many varieties of cloth, some very ordinary.

From the beginning, for all of the outdoor projects we have used synthetic fibers. Even the first outdoor project, in 1961, used tarpaulins treated against the rain. For the outdoor projects, natural fibers are not strong enough. Cotton and wool can't compare to nylon, Dacron, polyester, polypropylene.

Q How do you find the fabrics?

A We have to find something that is economical, and the most realistic for our needs. We shop around the industrial textile companies for a product that already exists, but sometimes it has to be altered. For example, for "Surrounded Islands, Biscayne Bay, Greater Miami, Florida, 1980–83," the fabric had to be buoyant. The fabric most appropriate was polypropylene, which will float, but miserably. We had to change the gravity ratio of the polypropylene to the water.

Q How was that achieved?

A The buoyancy of the fiber was increased by injecting air into the resin during extrusion. Then it was made into yarn and woven into fabric. Care had to be taken that not too much air was introduced, or it would be too brittle to be woven. We always use woven fabric, never film.

Another issue had to be solved. Miami light has a very high level of ultraviolet rays that breaks down colors, and pink is a very fragile color. The colorfastness was also accomplished in the extrusion steps. The resin wasn't pink when first extruded; the color happened when it was baked. The German manufacturer did a lot of research.

The fabric for "Wrapped Coast, Little Bay, One Million

Square Feet, Sydney, Australia, 1969" was bought off the shelf. It was an Australian erosion control agricultural product, and was the right straw color. Sometimes we find fabric that was a manufacturing mistake, but very good for our uses. For example, in 1972–73, General Motors was beginning research of air bags and had commissioned a rip-stop nylon. J. P. Stevens, the company that fabricated the nylon, made a mistake, and wove it much wider than GM had specified. We had been shopping around for "Running Fence, Sonoma and Marin Counties, California, 1972–76," and that mistake was exactly what we needed. We bought two million square feet.

Q Do you usually begin with the fabric when developing a project?

A It is only one part. "Running Fence" was designed to have fabric panels for several miles. The most difficult part was to find the place. When we found the location in California, we started to work with engineers and began requesting the permits. Then we shopped around for white fabric and began the life-sized tests with a variety of materials. We do this full-scale testing on every project in a place similar to the actual location.

For "Running Fence" we put up five different materials, and that night there was a big storm. When we returned to the site the next morning, the panel made of fiberglass was missing. We found the panel shattered on the ground—it couldn't resist the conditions. There are many complicated issues and requirements to test. But when working on the project, the materials we choose are truly the result of aesthetic decisions—we must find the most suitable material to give aesthetic satisfaction.

Q The fabric used for "Wrapped Reichstag, Berlin, Germany, 1971–95" made the building appear to be encased in falling water. How did you achieve that?

A First, we knew the scale of the building—massive, more than 130 feet tall. So we needed material of a heavy scale. As we shopped, we realized that to make the fabric fall properly over the building, it would take a support framework. We installed two hundred tons of steel on the building, reflecting its shape—shoulder pads, if you will. The building actually became 30 inches bigger in all directions, as if it had taken a deep breath. That was to allow the fabric the dynamic of sliding down the sides of the building. To test the design we used a friend's castle in Germany and later an office building where a scaffold was erected in the shape of a section of the Reichstag.

The fabric was manufactured in Germany for use as air and water filters. The original fabric was not silver, so it was sent to a factory that electroplated it with pulverized aluminum. Over a million square feet were coated with only four kilograms of aluminum. The fabric had to fit in the machine that applied the aluminum, so that determined the width of the woven fabric. This filter material is manufactured in white, black, and several shades of gray. Until all the colors were tested, we didn't know which would be the best base for the aluminum. The amount of aluminum applied also had to be decided. These choices were based on how it reflected the light when we hung it at the test sites and looked at it from various distances and times of day.

An interesting thing about the Reichstag project were the folds. They were 39 inches deep, so we were working with 100 percent fullness. But this was not a normal curtain; we had to move from vertical to horizontal, and control the direction of the folds. With the engineer, through scale models and tests, we found that a combination of metal structure and polypropylene ropes would allow the shaping of the fabric. The steel structure at the upper part of the building pushed the fabric away from the building, and the ropes pulled the fabric back. So we could sculpt the space.

Like an architect, we try to have a sense of how the material will act and what is physically possible. But the main consideration is always aesthetic. We are different from architects in that they tend to deprive the fabric of its basic quality as fabric: to be supple and capable of moving. Our fabric is meant to be fully dynamic and move all the time.

Q How did "The Umbrellas, Japan/USA, 1984–91" evolve?

A When we started to work with "The Umbrellas," our engineer had to find a way to attach the fabric to the structures. Aesthetically, we had to have an absolutely straight line of fabric where it met the rib. In most rain or shade umbrellas, the fabric is attached at points along the rib, but that made the fabric bubble along the rib (when the fabric moved). So we asked, "Who is working like this with fabric?" And we came up with sailmakers. These people are experienced in attaching fabric to a structure similar to the ribs of our umbrella-masts. They already had ways to make the connection. In a sail the fabric is attached to a channel in the mast. So that is how we fabricated the ribs.

Another problem with using beach umbrellas as a model is that they have separate fabric flaps on the top to accommodate the closing mechanism, and we wanted a clean triangle of fabric for each section. Our engineer designed a special spring mechanism to close the umbrella, and the structure allowed the fabric sections to move independently in the wind. We sent a full-size model of the aluminum structure to North Sails (a sailmaker) in Connecticut, and we spent six or eight months designing the pattern with them, using all the knowledge they had in sail making. The pattern was put together by North Sails, but the fabric was woven in Germany and sewn in southern California.

Q What other support structures have been designed for your projects?

A In "Surrounded Islands" the fabric was made to float well, but it was 17 feet wide and sewn into seventy-two sections that were laced together to form big shapes surrounding the islands. To energize the fabric and help it stay floating, a 5-inch-high foam rubber spine was sewn into the seams. It gave the shapes beautiful straight lines 70 feet long.

Because debris in the water would interfere with the fabric, we used a special boom in the shape of each island preceding the fabric. The booms were similar to the round booms used to contain oil spills, but ours were octagonal and straight, because that shape made the fabric better reflect the light.

When the prototype was tested in Key Largo, our marine engineer said that the floating fabric would not stay in the right shapes (because of tidal and wave action). What he did was marvelous. He put in radial lines that came out from the island, anchored to buoys and the boom and held in place with marine anchors. Not only did it hold the shapes, but the fabric could stay loose and float on top of the lines.

Q How do you approach fabric in a scale model?

A It is very difficult. We have tried very thin fabric, but it is not satisfying because the only thing really in that scale is film, not fiber, and it doesn't move to scale. When we did the Reichstag, our German engineers offered to do a computer model. But they could not make the computer model show how the fabric would move in the wind. A 1-to-16 model of "Over the River, Project for the Arkansas River, Colorado" was made with a research company that did the stress models for the Denver airport. They ran wind tunnel tests, but had no experience with fabric that was in motion and no data. While the full-scale tests are done, this company will take measurements of the real wind forces on the actual cables, hooks, and anchors. They can then compare the actual information with the wind tunnel results and get a better idea of predicting fabric movement in scale models.

Q Do you always work with the same engineers?

A We have a group we have worked with for the last thirty years, but we also work with local engineers in each country. For "Surrounded Islands" we had people from Colorado and Boston who had done the "Valley Curtain, Grand Hogback, Rifle, Colorado, 1970–76" and "Running Fence" with us, but they worked with a marine engineer from Florida.

Q How much does the site affect your basic design?

A We find a location suitable for the project. There are two different situations: the Reichstag is there, and there is no other. But with something like "Over the River" we have an idea to install fabric over a river. Then three years and fifteen thousand miles later, we find the river. We scouted eight or nine rivers, found six possible locations; the best was the Arkansas River in Colorado. At first the drawings are very fuzzy and simplistic, but once we have the site, the project begins to crystallize. We see that the fabric must allow the rafters moving under

it to see the sky, the mountains, and the clouds. So based on that vision, we found a company that would weave a very porous fabric that can be translucent when viewed from the water but opaque when viewed from the highway along the river.

When we do the tests, we want to see the fabric move like waves in the ocean. We use folds parallel to the river and controlled by hooks connected to the suspension cables. If the folds are too deep, there will be bubbles, not smooth waves. And if the fabric is too tight, it will be a trampoline. So we test different fabrics, different structures, some with the folds sewn in, and so forth. As with "Running Fence," we will know somewhat how the fabric moves, but there is always some surprise when we see the finished piece.

Q Are there basic differences between projects based on buildings and outdoor projects?

A Every design is particular to itself. The important thing is that the forms are simple. The "Running Fence" panels were taller than a normal fence but still built like a fence. Two poles with a panel between. We just used fabric rather than wood. The umbrellas were 20 feet tall, but umbrellas. The project grows within the space. At the beginning of "Running Fence" we planned to use big wooden poles. But many elements change as we go through the process and know more about the space, the light, and the engineering. The engineers asked if the big poles were an aesthetic choice. We said no, but we thought that was the size that was (structurally) necessary, and we had a good source for eucalyptus poles. But they explained that the weight of wood made them hard to install, and we could have the same strength with much thinner steel poles.

Q Do you keep records of each project?

A Each project has its own book, and everything is recorded. They are like recipes. But as each of our projects is completely different, we really don't use the information again. But if someone wants to know how to surround an island, the recipe is here.

One of the reasons we like to do what we do is that each project is a unique proposition. It is exciting because we explore different problems, discover new things. You might think that wrapping a bridge or the Reichstag is the same procedure. But not at all. "The Pont Neuf Wrapped, Paris, 1975–85" was above water; the fabric had to be brought in on barges and elevated when installed. With the Reichstag, fabric was dropped from the roof. Totally different demands on materials.

Q Looking at your preparatory drawings and collages, it is clear that the placement of ropes and cables is a part of the designs. How much of that is determined before the installation?

A In the first collages and drawings this element is not too specific, but if you look at the ones done closer to completion, the placement is exactly where we told the engineers it would go. This was not so for "Wrapped Trees, Fondation Beyeler and Berower Park, Riehen-Basel, Switzerland, 1997–98." Each one of the 178 trees demanded on-the-spot creativity because we could not determine the placement of the ropes in advance. The branches told us where the ropes should go.

Q How did you deal with fabric on trees?

A First we had to find fabric that was good for the trees. We had seen fabric used in Japan to protect trees from the heavy, wet snow that is common there. It is a polyester, woven to allow a great amount of air flow, while still strong and workable. For the project it was sewn into giant capes (specially tailored) for each tree and closed with a giant metal zipper. Once the zipper was closed, the excess length of fabric on the trunk was cut and finished with polypropylene rope—a larger diameter rope for the big trees than for the smaller ones.

Q How do you choose colors?

A Usually the color is easy. What other color would you choose for Miami than pink? But the first drawings were a very light and shy pink. It became more intense.

Q Why did you start to work with fabric?

A One of the most important parts of our work is its temporary character. It is the basic philosophy of the work. And that character is translated by the materials. Fabric has a fragility and a nomadic quality. The nomadic dimension of each project is extremely important. Like a nomadic tribe that builds a settlement with tents overnight, our intervention and transformation of the site is very immediate. Our projects are installed fast. They are fabricated off site, and fabric allows for the immediacy of transformation in the eye of the beholder. Within four days it is all there. All that energy of a collective effort is translated.

Fabric is so dynamic that it is very evocative. When we wrapped the Reichstag, we had rock climbers up in the Reichstag and thousands of people were watching through the see-through work fence surrounding the building. When the project was up and the fence was removed, millions of Germans and tourists came to the project for two weeks. You know what they were doing? They were touching the fabric, touching the rope. If you look at people around fabric, they always want to touch it. You usually don't see people touching buildings. That invitational and sensual quality is missing in other materials. The fragility of the fabric creates an urgency to be seen. Because everybody knows that in a few days it will be gone.

INTERVIEW WITH ROBERT BITTER
TEXTILE MANUFACTURER

Robert Bitter, President of the Products Division of Scalamandré, is also responsible for the Research and Archival Division, which houses an extensive collection of historical textiles and the private archives for the founders, Franco and Flora Scalamandré. Particularly interested in restoration and preservation of historic textiles, Mr. Bitter has lectured to many organizations and has served as a consultant for projects at The White House and The Treasury Building, Washington, DC; The Preservation Society of Newport; the New York Public Library and Metropolitan Museum of Art, New York; Prestwould Plantation, Clarksville, Virginia; the Missouri Governor's Mansion; Rockwood Museum, Wilmington, Delaware; and the Radio City Music Hall, New York City.

Q You are in charge of the Products Division for Scalamandré. What does that job involve?

A Wearing many hats. Scalamandré has evolved from a small studio where my mother (Adriana Scalamandré Bitter) and a head designer handled contract, residential, restoration, hospitality, and all the other business classifications that you can apply to this marketplace. Today most people in the com-

pany have a field of specialization. I oversee all the residential, contract, collection, and restoration groups. Half the work is done within our studios, and the rest of the work is sent to outside artists and studios. Probably what I do best is act as a bridge between work done here and what is done by the outside stylists, designers, and studios.

Q Do you ever get directly involved in a project?

A From time to time there are projects that demand my direct attention, for example, a wall covering going into the McKinley home in Canton, Ohio. The First Lady (Hillary Rodham Clinton) is involved, and Dr. Sheila Fisher, the Chairperson of Restoration and Acquisitions, was very interested in having it come from our mill studio and manufactured in the United States.

Q What are the steps in reproducing historical material?

A The wallpaper is actually an historical representation, rather than a reproduction or replica. We were given only a black-and-white photograph of the room taken in the late nineteenth century. First we had to figure out the scale of the motif based on the surrounding architectural elements and the decorative objects we could see in the picture. Those pieces that still existed were measured to determine the actual scale.

The paper could have been U.S. made or European, and we had to check both the block-printing and roller-relief techniques of the period. We referenced slide and book libraries, wallpaper designs from the Scalamandré archives and museums. We studied wallpaper collections in the States and in Europe to understand not only the pattern dimensions, but other details and the specific colors.

The most difficult part is color. The photograph only reveals the rough values of the design elements. You have to get a sense of the hues, the number of colors, the saturation aspects of each hue, and the light and dark characteristics.

Q Did you find documentation of the actual paper?

A No, but we found some papers that were similar. And we had a sense of the historical client. What colors Mrs. McKinley liked and what colors she didn't like.

Q How did you develop that sense?

A From letters, diaries, and other writings. Decorative objects and some original wallpapers in the house. There was enough information to develop a flow of color. We can't be sure how accurate it is, but it's the best we can do.

Once the paper is installed, who knows? Someone might come forth with a fragment from on old album that will show us how wrong we were. But this paper will complement the space, the objects, and the personality as best we can.

You have price parameters and a deadline. We were down to the hour: we received the screens seven days before the opening. Only because it was to be printed here could we depend on our own staff to create four different color strike-offs [test printings of each of the four component colors]. After seeing the strike-offs, we produced and shipped it on Monday night for a Tuesday morning delivery and installed it on Wednesday and Thursday for a Friday opening. If it had been a hot, humid day when we printed the paper [so the inks would not dry in time], we might not have been able to ship it out. Which means that I would have gotten on a plane to Canton with rolls of paper.

Q How do you reproduce a historical fabric?

A There are different degrees of reproduction. The first is done precisely the same way as the original. Someone has a hand-woven brocade; we can replicate that fabric using a hand loom and similar materials, but you have to keep in mind that the weavers are different. Even if you use all the same yarns and the same equipment, the result will vary slightly. But once installed, to most eyes it will appear the same. This is a replica—we use the same technique, keep the fabric the same width, scale, color, with all the details closely matched.

A fabric that has been copied from a hand-loomed fabric but machine-loomed is a reproduction. Instead of the original width of 24 inches, we might weave it at 48 inches. (We are capable technically of weaving the narrow width but rarely are asked to do so.) The result is double the width, but the visual characteristics are the same—the dimensions of the pattern, the weaves, content, and densities, the colors, hand, and luster. A reproduction captures the original integrity of the document.

We can reproduce textiles Scalamandré produced in the thirties or forties in precisely the same way, using just about the same dye stocks and the same machines.

Q What are the demands of the contract market?

A Specifications are quite different for each market. Within the contract field, generally we are working with architectural specifiers and purchasing agents. In industry you have to design fabrics that are specific to certain codes—tensile strength, abrasion, light-fastness, flammability. The testing is much more severe, and codes are often specific to particular regions.

Fifty percent of our line is conceived and produced for specific end uses, specific clients or sites. Custom upholstery, window treatment, or wall covering—all have specific requirements. If it is a wall covering, for example, we need to determine if it is a direct-wall application or an upholstered wall application, a fabric for a public arena or for a private executive office

Q Who is responsible for pulling this all together?

A It is generally a collaborative effort of the client, salesperson, studio head, and designer. We also act as a service, in that we have a great deal of pooled knowledge and experience. It is not just three generations of Bitters and Scalamandrés, but staff that has been with us in some cases for twenty, forty years. That staff networks with yarn companies, selects the right spinners, the appropriate dyers. Not all the work is done at the Scalamandré mills. In fact, a very small percentage of the fabric woven for the contract market is woven here. Generally, contracts demand large numbers and are more price sensitive. You need to be able to deal with a volume of fabric made from very specific yarns. Our mill is geared to natural fibers, and we don't necessarily have the finishing equipment needed for some synthetic fabrics. We look at every job in terms of yarn composition, time, cost, and the appropriate manufacturer. Then we get the client, architect, purchaser, and installer involved.

Q How long does it take to get a contract material from first discussion to the installation?

A Development of contract products for our stock collection averages about a year and a half to a year and three-quarters. Some take several years; some have to be turned around in three months. But the cycle time is shortening, and like most of the big studios, we have had to invest in CAD in a big way. It does a lot to reduce the number of mistakes. Because I can show you what you think you want in color, scale, and dimension—3D simulations. The detail is so great that I can show you the face, the back of the fabric, and the internal characteristics in cross-section. So we can narrow down your needs very quickly via CAD before we get to a loom and tie up people and production.

Q What is the biggest cost factor?

A It depends on the job, but generally labor. Sometimes it is the new machinery that should keep running three shifts, twenty-four hours a day. The timing is critical, and when samples go out we need immediate approvals.

Q How does the contract market differ from the restoration market?

A Contract likes to move very quickly. The restoration market tends to take much more time. There are executive directors, curators, outside consultants. Some projects can take five, seven years. A wallpaper project for the Hermitage, Andrew Jackson's home, took six to seven years. But there were many papers—side papers, borders, flocked papers—all of which were hand-block-printed by the traditional nineteenth-century technique.

Q From its beginning Scalamandré has focused on historic fabrics. How did that happen?

A One of my grandfather's first commissions was for Randolph Hearst, for San Simeon. It was a 7-yard, custom-woven, custom-colored, silk and linen streaky blue brocatelle. The original panel was submitted, and Scalamandré was asked to replicate it. They did what they thought was a wonderful job. It was yarn-dyed, and then they had to top-dye it to get exactly the right color. They put it on the roof to dry on an early spring day, and snows came and covered it. They thought it was ruined. They tried stretching and drying it, and between the soot of New York and the snow, the fabric streaked, shifted and shrank. But there was nothing to do but present it; my grandfather did. He was quite a salesman, and Mr. Hearst loved it. Because of all the irregularities, the fabric had a patina—it looked as if it had been there for years. From that, Scalamandré got other commissions.

Q Are there projects that demand: "It should look as if it has been hanging there for years"?

A Usually we are asked to bring things back. But when we make something with a visual richness and it is placed in an aged environment, it sometimes needs to be distressed, particularly with wall coverings. It is usually done on site by the installer, who brings down the colors by washing with colorants or fading agents, so that they get blended in. We may do some distressing off site, but because the lighting determines the colors you see—daylight, seasonal light changes, artificial light—you really have to have the material in place to see how it works into its environment.

A project for The Preservation Society of Newport, Rhode Island, involved reproducing an arts and crafts wall covering fabric that was seriously distressed, with horizontal banding. We had to create a woven match. So we used subtle weft color variations plus yarn-size variations in the different bands to create the effect of irregular banding.

Q Scalamandré designs and manufactures wall coverings, trim, and fabrics for upholstery and drapery. How do these products mesh within the company?

A They are quite different, but we manage our company like a cluster of workshops all orchestrated around the studio and customer service. The people in charge of the various departments basically run their own show within the company. What makes this facility unique is that it is not just a fabric mill producing a product for one market. We are dealing with over thirty markets—the custom market, drapery-weight fabric, upholstery-weight, thousands of different trimmings, a lot of which are hand-made.

Q Textiles have always reflected specific cultures. Do you think this is still true?

A Yes and no. There is still such a thing as an Italian style or an American style, but really anything goes today. Styles today come from personalities in interior design and architecture. Movements are going on from the formal to the very simple and everything in between. And then, as with all ages, fashion is shaped by social, economic, and political events. What affects design is also international. The most important shows are Milan, London, Como, Paris, New York, Chicago, and Los Angeles, and the top designers visit all the shows.

Q How does Scalamandré react to this arena?

A There was a period of time when our company only did what our clients wanted. As the company grew, it became more entrepreneurial in terms of design. Today we spend a lot of time, money, and effort with color groups, with focus groups, studying the trends and going to the shows. Ours is still very much a traditional house, so much of our line is based on classical design, and our clients expect us to maintain that. We have to be careful when we deviate from a classical look to something trendy. Those lines usually don't do well for us. People don't perceive us as the kind of house that presents those lines. It's a difficult mold to break. The simplest way might be to acquire a company with a different focus.

Q Is that why Scalamandré bought Boris Kroll, a textile company that was rooted in the Bauhaus style?

A Yes. We were quietly in the contract market for many years. We then acquired Boris Kroll and slowly integrated it into the Scalamandré contract line. BK was looked at as classic "nuts and bolts" contemporary design. We learned a great deal from it, and it influenced us in our residential as well as contract decisions. More than anything else, the durability and abrasion and wearability aspects of BK textiles have influenced many of our decisions.

Q What are the factors that affect durability of a fabric?

A The quality of the yarn, the twists in the yarn, the number of ends and picks, combined with the specific weave. You can make something that feels very soft, luxurious, and delicate as silk taffeta, of 100-percent silk, and it can withstand over 35,000 double rubs—that is, meet heavy-duty contract specifications.

Q How important are the technical aspects of manufacturing?

A Most people who get involved with Scalamandré do it not just for the aesthetics but because they appreciate the interior of the fabric. It is a blend of textile technology and design.

Q How were Scalamandré's extensive textile archives acquired?

A It started with regular seasonal visits to Europe. As importers, my grandparents, Franco and Flora Scalamandré, had to travel. My grandfather first dealt in decorative objects, and my grandmother was a designer for a stone and marble company. They bought textiles while in Europe. My grandmother did most of the selecting, although my grandfather received most of the credit because he was signing the invoices. She recognized quality and trends; he had taste, but he was more the engineer. She bought a great deal for her general collection as well as for design inspiration.

Through the years the company fell into the restoration field. People were not collecting as they are now, and many fine things were being thrown away. Pieces would be sent to Scalamandré to reproduce, and the client didn't want the old sample. So Scalamandré continued its collection, supplemented by material from auctions, individual dealers, private homes. We are pack-rats. My mother is an avid collector, and so am I.

Q What is in the collection?

A First, all the items that we have made—both reproductions and original products. Second, there are the period documents—wall coverings, fabric, trimmings, and costumes. Last, clothing, books, furniture, and machinery used and owned by the family and people associated with Scalamandré.

Q Are the museum-quality textiles in the general working archives?

A Absolutely. We look at them for study purposes, not so much for their monetary value. Occasionally I buy a collection, keep what I want, and sell the rest off at auction—basically paying for the pieces I purchased. I don't like to do that, but we don't have a lot of funds available for new purchases. A lot of the money for the archives over the last fifteen years has gone into acid-free storage materials, organizing, and photographing the collection.

We are now looking into digitally recording the images in order to have them available as computer data. Right now they are just not accessible enough. Sometimes it is easier to buy a new piece of research from a show or dealer than go through our own archives.

Q How do historical fabrics affect fabrics manufactured for the contemporary market?

A There is very little new under the sun. Whether it is a weave or motif or color, we reference earlier patterns. The majority of what we create is inspired to some degree by earlier textiles, some things very purely, some things very remotely. A strong part of our collection, primarily for the residential line, is a contemporary blend of classical textiles.

Even in the contract field, which is thought of as the most visually contemporary, we go back to various periods—the forties and fifties and 1890s. We research textures, weaves, and designs. The artists designing new textiles are creating montages of their inspirations—the documents, what they see at the industry shows, reactions to what they see on the street.

INTERVIEW WITH SUZANNE TICK
DESIGNER AND CONSULTANT

Suzanne Tick is a textile design consultant, serves as Creative Director for Knoll Textiles, and is a partner in Tuva Looms, which produces woven carpets. She re-engineers fabric constructions through development of new fibers and yarns for the contract and residential markets. She has been design director for contract companies such as Boris Kroll, Brickel Associates, and Unika Vaev, and developed a collection of residential drapery, upholstery, and wall coverings for Groundworks, a division of Lee Jofa. Ms. Tick has won numerous IIDA (International Interior Design Association) awards for her carpets and fabrics and received the Good Design Award from the Chicago Athenaeum for her work with Knoll. One of her experimental woven projects, which used a Japanese steel fiber, was included in "Structure and Surface: Contemporary Japanese Textiles" at the Museum of Modern Art in New York.

Q You are a textile designer and design consultant. What does that job involve?

A As a consultant at Knoll (an office systems and furniture manufacturing company), I am the creative director. I work with their staff, aesthetically direct the product, and manage the process of product development. Because of my knowledge of textile design and fabric manufacturing, I can train their people to develop and color yarn from blanketing to product introduction.

I advise on where the product should be manufactured and at what price point it should be. I work with the sales management team to find out what requests have been made by clients, particularly when they feel they are not getting the right type of product for the market, whether it is a styling issue or a price issue. Then I take all that information and figure out the direction the company needs to take.

What I do as a textile designer is to create material—beginning with the yarn and ending up with the final product of a fabric. A company will ask for a line of tapestries, upholsteries, drapery or wall coverings, and they let me come up with the collection and submit that to them for approval.

Q Do you manage those products through the system?

A No. Usually I design the product, develop the color palette, write the specification sheets, and provide information about product development—how much it costs, what the manufacturing minimums are, and other details about the collection.

Q What are the factors you take into account when designing a textile?

A My designs are generally determined by the end use and cost—whether it is wall covering, drapery, or upholstery. If it is going to be a wall covering in an executive office, it can be of a certain construction and a higher budget, which allows a higher end fabric. If it is for a hospitality area, the price point is different, the cleanability requirement is different, the fire codes are different. The context determines the design.

Take an upholstery meant for task seating (office seating): the fabric will need to be more modular in style. When the fabric is applied robotically to furniture, as it usually is in mass production, the requirements change. The fabric not only must be able to be applied quickly, but it has to have stretch and dimensional stability. And then there is always price and aesthetics. For a higher end upholstery fabric, the object is beauty and comfort, but I always try to find new yarns, or something

that is going to make it different from what is already in the marketplace.

Q You work a lot with new materials. How do those materials affect your designs?

A I look for new fibers and new ways of construction. Once I find them, we explore how to manipulate the material or process. Can the yarns be used in the warp or in the filling? How does a new finishing affect the fabric? If it is from the fashion industry, how can we adapt it to the furnishing market?

Q How do you find new products?

A I try to keep the studio open. If someone calls with new fibers or new types of materials, I will see them. I try to go to trade shows in different industries to see what is happening.

Q You have worked both within large textile corporations and as an independent designer. Can you compare those ways of working?

A When you work as a design director in-house for a company, you are juggling with all kinds of issues: questions from the sample maker, what gets sent out, proper testing of materials. It distracts from your ability to be creative. It is a great training ground running your own business. Now, as an independent consultant, I can step back and focus on the creative, and how to manage people and the design flow. The issues are clearer.

Q What factors have affected your designs?

A My design sense has always been modern. I have never been a traditionalist. That probably has as much to do with what I was exposed to as a child as what I was exposed to in the workplace. From the age of six on I was in art classes, being taken to museums, and I grew up in a very contemporary design and art environment.

I was educated as a printmaker. I always liked the process of making things—whether it was preparing the copper plates (for etching), or threading a loom. Because my prints looked like layers of fabric, it seemed like a good idea to take a weaving class, so I could acid-etch the fabric I wove into the copper plates. From then on I knew I wanted to create fabrics.

My first job was at Boris Kroll, a mill environment. Starting in the manufacturing end, I could see what it meant to take raw material, create a yarn, feed it into a loom, create a fabric, develop weaves to pass all the tests, and make it aesthetically pleasing at the same time. Then I went to Brickel, which was founded on Ward Bennett furniture designs—beautiful, handcrafted chairs. There I saw my fabric being applied to furniture. Later I worked for a boutique line that imported furniture from Italy and Scandinavia, and I tried to relate my designs to furniture designed by Alvar Aalto and Arne Jacobson. My experience at Knoll has led me to other design issues in our industry—for example, panel systems, and how you create products for task seating.

Q How do you create product for a panel system?

A I try to come up with a new look. My first project at Knoll was to create something inexpensive and environmentally friendly. I had to find a yarn that was responsible to the environment, new and interesting. Environmentally friendly panel fabrics were new to the market at that time. What we found was a yarn made from a solution-dyed fiber. We went to several mills before finding one that would do the weaving. The mill had to have looms capable of weaving wide widths with fine warp yarns.

I knew it would be different from anything else used for panel fabric in the industry, elegant and beautiful, which isn't something you think of when you think of office panels. I wanted a luster level that you can get from the weave, the finishing, by calendaring, or from the type of polyester. The fabric had to be beautiful for a certain price. We must have woven ten different designs before we found what looked and tested best.

Q Where were these trials made?

A On a handloom. At that time the trial samples were done at the mill's studio. Now we have a loom in our studio, and that production is done here.

Q Do you usually develop the design on the loom?

A If is for a dobby weave we will do it on the handloom ourselves, draft it out, and decide what the weaves are going to be. If it is for a Jacquard loom, we develop the patterns, get the yarn palettes from the mill, and do the layout on paper. We submit that to the mill, they scan in the patterns and provide the samples. Sometimes the mill will also do dobby samples.

Q What information do you give the mill?

A A design and the repeat with the weave structures and the colors. When we are starting from raw materials, we also give them the yarn. We lay out the color blankets, and anything else they need for the production process.

Q Besides price, what information did you get from Knoll before beginning this project?

A They gave me free rein. I asked to look at their history with this type of product, so I could see what sort of color range had worked in the past. Historically, you always have to have a good group of neutrals, and we went into some darker shades. Although the fabric was different from anything that had been used for panels, I knew this particular fabric was going to be on a dobby loom, and that it was a fine, tied warp construction, which meant that it had to be textural.

I knew that the color palette we had started developing was

going to be mostly filling-faced and I focused on how a limited color range would work. I tried to make it easy for everyone, so the manufacturer would do it, and so we could get it on the market quickly. From Knoll's purchasing side, they need to manage inventory. If the line took off, they would have to inventory twenty, twenty-five thousand yards at a pop for each color. The first palette came out to be fourteen colors.

Q What factors determine the cost?

A The yarn and manufacturing.

Q Once a product is in the manufacturing stage and sample books are out, what is your connection with the product?

A I am asked to promote it. The sales force wants to know the mission behind the development. I like that part of it. Being out with the sales force, seeing how people respond to the work, makes me a smarter designer, and I can get immediate feedback on what works and what doesn't.

Q Where do you find the code requirements for contract products?

A Everything has to pass ACT (the Association for Contract Textiles). They have published the standardized tests, so everyone is working from the same page. All the mills know the requirement, and the manufacturer is responsible for the testing. With a company like Knoll, we probably put three times the product development information into the system than a residential company. There are city and state codes as well. Not to mention codes for each type of furniture.

Q What are other differences when developing a line for a residential collection?

A I design for a division of Lee Jofa, Groundworks, and that work began with a strong desire to develop beautiful and elegant products that used unusual materials. They wanted a new collection—wall covering, drapery, and upholstery fabrics for a very contemporary market. The technical criteria are ACT standards, but residential codes require only 15,000 double rubs, not the contract abrasion standard of 30,000.

The color palette needed to be very fresh and alive. My object was to find the newest fibers and processes, and to push the envelope to develop a new look—one that was to be organic as well as technical.

Q How do you distinguish between a new look that will become a trend and a fad that will pass quickly?

A My work is not so much about trends as it is about unique interpretations with an old soul to them. Something new, but something that has a cultural or historical feeling.

Q Where do you get your ideas?

A One source is magazines like *View*, which talks about world trends, retail, and design influences. I try to learn what people are passionate about. This always surfaces, regardless of the subject. Whether it is about ceramics, jewelry, gardens, or whatever the passion is, it can be a good starting point. Another source are the kids you see on the street wearing things from thrift shops or clothes in the new fibers from skateboarding companies. Those companies always have the newest fibers and looks. Even the way they put color together is different. I am always looking at the younger generation; at what they wear and how they respond to what different markets offer them.

Q Do these observations affect both residential and contract designs?

A The residential market is all about the beauty of the product—the luster, the hand, or the dimension of the product. Whatever the product is, it has to be something that people emotionally respond to.

With a [contract] company I try to use what we see as high tech. For example, using iridescents and metallics gives a different look. You can have your flight of whimsy, but you have to have the sales numbers. You can push the envelope in terms of color. Colors are put together today that never would have coexisted five years ago. But you also have to remember that there may still be "dusty rose" finishes in an office interior, and you have to give them something that works for those interiors that are not being totally redefined. Sometimes it is the finish that drives the design.

Q Are any of your products designed for a specific user?

A What we have tried to do at Tuva Looms aesthetically is create clean classic woven carpet products for the commercial and residential design community. The color palette is neutral and tinted neutrals. This product was developed primarily for the architectural design firms that want carpet to be a canvas rather than a decorative element.

Q Is the residential market as cost-driven as the commercial market?

A No. But people are becoming more price conscious. I think you can do beautiful products at a lower price. That is the challenge.

Q What advice would you give a student interested in the textile business?

A They must really love textiles; there has to be a gut level of wanting to be in this field. They have to be open to whatever comes before them. They may not be designers, but they might be great marketing people. You can't have a set concept of what is going to happen. And you have to go through the trenches and constantly be educating yourself. The technical background is very important. If you can work at a mill level, I think that gives you a special edge.

Q Do you prefer residential or contract design?

A I like to design. To come up with things the markets haven't seen before. It makes them think about design and react to a product and say, "How can I use this?" "I love this." "I have never seen anything like this. What can I do with it?" It is working on an inspirational level.

INTERVIEW WITH NICHOLAS GOLDSMITH
ARCHITECT

Nicholas Goldsmith is a principal in FTL Happold Architects and Engineers, New York, a multidisciplinary design practice specializing in tensile structures. He was the partner in charge of design and production for such major and award-winning projects as the permanent structures of the Russell B. Aitken Seabird Aviary at the Bronx Zoo; the Hoboken Ferry Terminal at the World Financial Center; rehabilitation and renovation of the Donna Karan Corporation offices; the Carlos Moseley Music Pavilion, a portable performance space for the Metropolitan Opera and the New York Philharmonic; and many international projects. Mr. Goldsmith designed "Under the Sun: An Outdoor Exhibition of Light" at the Cooper-Hewitt National Design Museum. He has lectured widely on portable architecture and has taught as a visiting professor at the University of Stuttgart, the University of Pennsylvania, and Pratt Institute of Architecture.

Q You are an architect with a firm that specializes in tensile-membrane structures. What is a tensile structure, and how does it differ from a tent?

A Anything that is structurally in tension is a tensile structure. A tent is the primary name [for these structures]. We think of tents as relatively primitive in their technology—traditional dwellings of nomadic cultures, military structures, or circus or performance coverings. In the mid-twentieth century it became possible to further engineer those traditional structures and develop them to a higher technological level so they could be used as parts of permanent buildings or alone as permanent structures.

Computers enabled us to refine tensile systems structurally, and we now have fabrics that will last thirty years. The confluence of those elements—computers and high tech fabric—enabled uses different from those of the traditional tents.

Within the industry, a tent is designed to sustain sixty-five-mile-an-hour winds, is not up for longer than thirty days, uses lightweight rope and hardware and aluminum poles, and can easily be set up and taken down. A tensile structure is usually larger and has steel cables and a permanent foundation.

Q How do you approach designing tensile structures?

A I work in an integrated architectural and engineering practice, which is different from traditional architectural firms. In designing these special structures it is very important that the two disciplines go hand in hand. So rather than taking a project through design development and then bringing engineers aboard, we involve engineers early on.

Q How do you begin a design?

A The design process begins with thumbnail sketches, but you must define the needs of the project before you start the design, much like any other architectural project. If it is a concert facility, how many seats? Is it a facility that will be up for a short period of time? Does it need a hospitality facility or green room? All of those things affect the design. If the client has only a vague idea of the project, we try to determine their specific spatial and programmatic requirements in a predesign phase.

Q Would you describe the design process for a specific project?

A The Carlos Moseley Music Pavilion was a structure for summer performances by the Metropolitan Opera and the New York Philharmonic in New York's city parks. The program called for it to be set up in less than six hours, accommodate the lighting and acoustic demands of the performers, and respect the fragile locations of the city parks, and the unit had to be transported in standard semi-trailers on normal roads. There was a performance every twenty-four hours in a different park—fifteen parks in a season—and the performers had to be in the structure rehearsing by eleven o'clock in the morning. The trucks arrived at six a.m., so we had to get the set-up time down to under four hours.

Once we narrowed the possible solutions to these problems down to a couple of ideas, we went back to the client for the next phase of design development. They brought in a team of specialists—theater consultants to work on the sight lines and staging considerations, lighting and sound people.

Q How do you present designs to the client?

A The presentation depends on the project. In this case, we showed a model. The client came to us with an initial concept done by a theater designer, Peter Wexler, so we had an idea of what they visually wanted. It was a matter of taking that concept and developing it into something that would work for the situation.

Q What happened after the model was approved?

A We started developing the support structure—a tripod setup, using customized structures. The first idea was to rent, but crane companies who install rentals wouldn't get near this project. We immediately began discussions with the structural engineers in our company. A visually aesthetic tent structure, a sculptural form that is a lighting reflector and an acoustic blender, had to be balanced within a structural system that would change shape (from pieces in a truck to a performance space). To achieve the balance, we needed a dialogue of design and engineering. The result was a self-erecting tripod structure from which a taut, translucent fabric shell was deployed. This acted as a sound reflector for the music, as a screen for the computerized lighting system and video projections, and as rain protection for the stage.

Q How did you choose the fabric for the structure?

A It had to be a fabric that would fold easily, be waterproof, and meet the strength demands. There was no choice but some sort of coated polyester. For a permanent structure, you might use other materials, like Teflon-coated fiberglass fabric, as in the Denver Airport, or ETFE (Ethylene-TetraFluoroEthylene), a Teflon foil pillow system that looks like clear glass, or Tenara, a woven metal fabric.

Q What other choices were determined by the demands of a deployable structure?

A The fabric was the easiest element. The system of ropes and cables had to be very pliable. If metal plates, cables, and bolts had to be removed every time it came down, it would take a day to remove cables and hardware. The Moseley Pavilion fabric went up in about half an hour. It sat in a trough in the center of a truck with a roof that opens, and was pulled out with a hydraulic winch.

We designed adaptations to the trucks. Trailers were dismantled: concrete was poured in three trailers for foundations for the tripods (we had to carry our foundations) and other trailers were adapted for the lighting and sound. The trucks were the working components of the building. The hardest part was fitting everything into vehicles that complied with the maximum gross weight of 80,000 pounds to allow travel without a special permit. We were constantly working back and forth with specifications. The trucks are only a certain size and weight, so if things don't fit, the structure would have to shrink.

Q Are your construction drawings different from those for more conventional buildings?

A We do a set of fairly traditional working drawings. But we also do engineering work for the fabricators—like the cutting patterns for the fabric. The patterns can be generated in our office, and we can supply the fabricators with a computer disk that instructs the laser cutter. Because some smaller manufacturers don't have the expertise to do their own patterning, we get involved so we can use a broader group of fabricators.

Q Has FTL designed special software for patterning?

A Yes. Our sister engineering firm in England, Buro Happold, has, over the last ten or fifteen years, developed a program called Tensylsuite, a proprietary software that does form-finding, analysis, and patterning. We measure a few points off a physical model—some heights, a couple of perimeter locations—enough to define the boundaries, and then enter that information into the computer, which generates a mesh surface (the computer model). This is equivalent to a soap-film surface.

Q What is a soap-film surface?

A When designers worked without computers, they would build physical frame models of tensile structures and cover the open shapes with a soap film, forming a shaped bubble. If the bubble didn't burst, they had a minimal surface, which means that any point on the surface had equal tension. A minimal surface is the most efficient way to cover a shape. In fabric, wrinkles are eliminated, as are a lot of other fabrication problems. To translate the soap-film model, it was photographed, and from those pictures critical construction sections were determined.

Then, large-scale models of parts of the structure were built and covered with fabric. The fabric chosen for the model was scaled to approximate the way the actual construction fabric would react, but [the built model] couldn't begin to be as accurate or timely as a computer model. The modern industry of tensile structures depends completely on computer models.

Q Does that mean the physical model you show the client is only a presentation tool, no longer necessary in solving construction problems?

A No. The modeling techniques we use are based on structural modeling, and we still design our basic three-dimensional shapes by using physical models. It is not like taking a piece of paper and forcing it to render the computer model. It isn't eyewash. If you take a double-stretch knit fabric and pull it over supports in a scale model, you have a pretty good idea of the real curvature shapes.

The computer model optimizes the information. Exactly where the stresses will be, things like that, won't be clear from the stretch model, but there is a danger in working only with computer models. It is easy in computer modeling to make mediocre designs look very beautiful by adding lighting and shading. In presentation you wow the client, but when you actually build the structure, the design is kind of ordinary. That is something a physical model won't let you do.

Q What makes for a well-designed tensile structure?

A It is a marriage of poetry, art, and engineering. It has to be

an efficient working structure, but it has to have a shape that sings.

Q Your company develops rental systems for fabricators. How does the design of a product differ from designs done for a specific client?

A We design for manufacturers "off-the-shelf" products that use fabric in the construction of rental tent systems and tensile structures. Many of the basic demands are parallel [with those of custom projects]. The surfaces have to be balanced, there needs to be good drainage, and so on. Developing a product, however, is really designing the common denominator. You try to make something that will work reasonably well for a lot of different things. It is process of reduction, whereas designing for a specific client is more about understanding a specific site and needs.

One interesting thing. When we designed our first rental tent system in 1978, we used tensile structure technology. It worked like a rental tent, but it looked like a tensile structure. It had organic shapes and geometry; it didn't look like a traditional tent. Corporate clients using it for exhibition spaces liked the innovative look, but the largest market for tent rentals is more residential—weddings and parties. In that market it didn't rent at all. Those clients wanted a structure that looked like a traditional striped tent but functioned like a tensile structure (in that a tensile structure requires fewer vertical supports). We learned a marketing lesson, and made some design changes.

Q In more traditional architecture, site is a predominant issue. Is that also true with tensile structures?

A It depends on the project. If you are doing deployable or relocatable structures, a specific site is usually not a big issue. For a permanent structure, it is as primary as for any other building. The weather is also an influence. In a northern climate we may use ETFE, the Teflon foil pillow system. When inflated slightly, it has insulation values similar to glass. It allows for long, uninterrupted spans not possible with glass, and because there is a lot of direct light, there is solar gain. But this absorptive quality is not something you would recommend for a southern climate where you want to reflect light and heat.

Q Are there climates not suitable to fabric structures?

A Whether it is a heating or cooling issue, we can make double-skinned fabric roofs that, with proper insulation, have rating equivalent to thermal windows. There are also structures designed to look like fabric structures but built with rigid insulation.

Q You said that modern materials made these structures possible. How do you find new materials?

A The interesting thing is that although there are tons of new materials, the availability depends on manufacturers to turn a new material into a product. Because the market for architectural fabric structures is relatively small, there are not a lot of products available. Teflon glass fabric was first used in the space program, and then by the baking industry in conveyor belts for cookie ovens. It can go through very high temperature, and is nonstick. Only when it became a commercial product in another industry, did it become available as a material for tensile structures.

Q How do construction techniques affect tensile structures?

A The fact that we base our structures on tension rather than compression means there is a different technical vocabulary than that used for conventional constructions. There is also an architectural vocabulary that is different than that for accepted building concepts. People expect to walk through doorways and see certain elements—walls, vertical columns. But what happens when a column looks like a cocktail stick tapered on both ends and is sitting at a 30-degree angle? How does that affect us spatially? When a surface overhead is pulling in different directions, are you inside or outside? These are things that take a while to sift through.

Q Are the spaces created by tensile structures accepted as real buildings?

A I have been on building sites where the steel workers are setting up the frame and moaning and groaning about this strange thing. And then the skin goes up and they are wowed. They bring their families to the opening. This building type has been accepted for festival structures, pavilions, sport stadiums, and other public spaces. Many of our structures are elements of buildings that use conventional materials—for example, an atrium with glass walls and a fabric roof to give diffuse light. But when it comes to private living spaces, people are more conservative about the design and building of their own homes.

Q How do interior designers deal with these spaces?

A Most furniture and wall systems are based on square or rectangular structures, so if you are doing an environment based on curves, you are probably going to end up with custom-designed bookcases and wall systems. We do much of that design in-house.

Q Where are your structures manufactured?

A Well, for example, we did a leisure center in Saudi Arabia, and the whole building was prefabricated. The fabric roof was made in Buffalo, the glass walls were made in Texas, and the floor was local Saudi limestone and marble; the standard furniture was Italian, the custom furniture was made in Lebanon. All the cable fittings were German, and the steel supporting structure was British. This big puzzle showed up on site and then was assembled.

Q You and FTL were part of an exhibition at the Cooper-Hewitt Museum called "Under the Sun." Tell us something about that show.

A The purpose of the show was to highlight photovoltaic (PV) technology (a way of harnessing solar energy) as elements that could be incorporated into designs. We wanted to show that these systems are not just panels stuck on the roof of a house at 40 degrees angle to the sun. Rather, they can be thought of as part of the skin of the building, and it is now possible to incorporate PV cells into a range of industrial and consumer products.

We showed curtain-wall glass systems that were actually PV panels that could feed [solar power] directly into the building system or into a local power station. We developed a tensile structure with flexible PV cells integrated into the tensile membrane, which provided the power to operate the electronic and audio visual components of the exhibit. With tensile structures, the structure is in the skin, which also incorporates lighting and acoustics. Now that material can also be our power system.

Q Why do you design these sorts of structures?

A I find it interesting, just the way that designing airplanes in the early twentieth century must have been a wonderful challenge. Now the rules that are required in airplane design make it more of a step-by-step process. The fun thing about new materials and new technologies is that we don't know all the answers and haven't made a lot of rules.

The idea of developing emerging technologies as an integrated part of the building system is something that fascinates me and our firm. There is a tendency to design and build with the same materials and techniques and to try to make things more economical by using a thinner veneer. But rather than trying to save resources that way, how about designing more efficiently with less material or with materials that serve many purposes? In tensile structures we can use materials that are $\frac{1}{16}$ inch thick, can span 150 feet, and are held up by a few cables.

Right now we are using a lot more resources than we are making. If we are going to be able to pass on our standard of living to future generations, we must have different systems in place, use renewable energy systems and much less material. The evolution of architecture has been a movement of mass and membrane. Now we are going from heavy, massive materials to lighter, more efficient materials.

We started with tents, but civilization quickly went to Roman vaults. Our idea of architecture has been based on the Greek or Roman temple constructed of stone piles and lintels. As we moved into the twentieth century, design went into free-floating interior walls, and gained freedom of plan. One of the interesting things about fabric is that it frees architecture to become a shell—a basic shelter or skin to contain an ever-changing interior environment—a biological structure much like ourselves.

INTERVIEW WITH PATSY ORLOFSKY
PRESERVATION ADMINISTRATOR

Patsy Orlofsky is Executive Director of The Textile Conservation Workshop. The coauthor of *Quilts in America*, she has lectured widely on the history and care of textiles. She was program administrator of the New York State Conservation Consultancy and administrator of the New York State Council on the Arts field service program. Ms. Orlofsky has served on the board of directors of the National Institute for the Conservation of Cultural Property, the Advisory Panel of the Museum Program, New York State Council on the Arts, the Advisory Council of The Textile Museum, and the FAIC/Kress Conservation Publication Fellowship Review Panel.

Q You are director of the Textile Conservation Workshop. What sort of work is done here?

A We are a not-for-profit museum service, regional conservation laboratory. There are fourteen in the United States, and only two provide the full range of textile treatment services. Textiles are particularly subject to environmental abuses and to wear resulting from their original function. We combine the science of conservation with craftsmanship. The work is done in this laboratory, which includes cleaning and dyeing facilities, archival storage, various work areas, and a library.

Q What types of textiles do you restore?

A Absolutely everything—quilts, samplers, needlework, archeological and ethnographic textiles, Civil War uniforms, Chinese robes, hooked rugs, tapestries. The Workshop has been involved in projects that involve the conservation and restoration of historical sites with hundreds of textiles, including silk-covered walls, upholstery, and costumes.

Q How does one approach cleaning an important textile?

A When cleaning is necessary, a piece is vacuumed with a special vacuum. For many textiles, wet cleaning is the best method for removing acidic soils, which abrade the fibers and can accelerate deterioration. If wet cleaning is appropriate, the piece may spend the day soaking in a variety of baths in a large wash table. There is a series of soapings and rinsings in special detergents and purified water. An older textile is vulnerable when wet because of the additional weight and stress of handling. So it is not removed from the table until nearly dry after a series of drying steps: first sponging out excess water, then rolling in mattress pads and then in towels. Then it is spread out on a drying screen, and the warps and wefts are realigned. This reduces the need for further blocking. Finally it is covered with cheesecloth, which absorbs more moisture and prevents brown tide-line staining.

One of the greatest threats in cleaning any textile is the possibility that dyes may be fugitive. We have a suction table which is used for fabrics that are a problem when immersed. When localized cleaning is necessary, such as on a sampler where some of the embroidery thread might bleed, we use a suction disk under the object and draw the air through it. The stain can be gently cleaned, and the color won't move out by capillary action to the surrounding areas. This is particularly appropriate to silk. For pieces that demand more control, we use a suction disk the size of the tip of a dental vacuum.

We have also developed a technique called "contact cleaning" for pieces adorned with feathers and beads that are sensitive but cannot be suctioned. We isolate the areas from moisture with Mylar barriers and use other wet-dry methods to control capillary action. The technique wicks out dissolved soil while not saturating the textile. Dry cleaning may be recommended for some pieces.

Q What are the techniques used to restore various fabrics?

A In rare instances, when faced with something like a shattered silk [silk with disintegrating warp and weft], sewing is not the appropriate treatment. We will repair the fabric using a sheer fabric without much body and apply a very fine thermoplastic adhesive coating. When it is reheated with a small heating foot, it becomes tacky, and will hold the silk. It is a more gentle repair than poking holes with a needle.

In the case of a seventeenth-century Ukrainian icon, several different treatment techniques were required. The piece consisted of a silk ground with densely embroidered metallic threads, seed pearl outlines, and borders embroidered with Cyrillic inscriptions. As the ground fabric had deteriorated badly, we dyed silk patches to match the background area, and inserted those into the worn spots. Exposed weft threads were aligned and couched into place. A full Stabiltex lining was placed under the textile. The central portion was stitched to the textile. The edges of the embroidery were particularly deteriorated, so they were supported with a very thin layer of adhesive on the lining. The icon was then attached to a padded mounting panel and framed. The result was a visually coherent image safely housed in a period frame with archival materials.

Q What is the distinction between conservation and restoration?

A We are part of the larger field of museum conservation. All of the objects in a museum—paintings, paper, furniture, archeological pieces—have a distinct area of conservation and restoration. The field of textiles was the last one to become professionalized. Not so long ago, textile restoration was usually handled by the site manager, a seamstress, or anyone proficient with a needle. This was the case even in sophisticated historical societies and museums where a painting would never have been restored by anyone except a professional conservator.

By the time textile conservation was offered in graduate programs, it had become a tenet of the field to distance itself from its domestic roots. The upshot was the opinion that only strict conservation (meaning the stabilization of a damaged piece) should be done on textiles. This meant adding nothing to the original piece—no artistic sewing solutions. Whatever had to be introduced (backing fabric, for example) had to be very obvious. Restoration was thought to be falsification. There was a big gap between conservators and restorers, restorers being viewed as careless nonacademics who didn't keep documentation. What was done twenty years ago was often excessively obvious. The textile was structurally supported, but pretty it wasn't.

All that has changed. Now we use all of our skill to make things look beautiful. The trick is doing this without falsification. We have borrowed from other fields. For example, for centuries paintings have been restored or "inpainted" as they have been conserved. As we become more sophisticated, we are using restoration techniques in our conservation to make the structural work more beautiful. For example, when dealing with a severely distressed calico, we can use a solid-colored backing fabric and have an obvious patch. Or we can do the repair in a more subtle manner by reproducing the original pattern on the backing fabric with paints that don't fade, off-gas, or in any way affect the original fabric. We then apply the patch, and the fabric is basically untouched and the repair is hardly noticed. Now "restoration" and "conservation" are finally coming together.

Tapestries have always been restored. Tapestry is strong enough to withstand the rigors of conservation, but there is a tradition of pulling out old repairs, dyeing yarn, putting in new warps, because tapestries are valued for their pictorial aspect. They have always been expensive and thought of as fine art, and the bias of the marketplace demanded that they be pictorially complete.

Archeological and ethnographic pieces, however, are often not restored for a variety of reasons. There is an awe for past cultures, a sense that they are so terribly fragile that they won't bear intrusion, and restoration may interfere with scholarly information an anthropologist might be able to see. The wear patterns may be important. For example, a Guatemalan wrapped skirt would look like a rectangular textile to most people. But the way it was worn caused abrasions and dirt spots, and the scholar immediately recognizes that rectangle as a wrap skirt. Scholars don't want a conservator to come along and clean away clues to the cultural use.

Q What is the education of a textile conservator?

A I am actually a textile historian—the only person here who is not a bench conservator (trained in practical techniques.) My specific area of graduate study was conservation administration, because I wanted the point of view of collection management. We may be called in to deal with a collection of thousands of individual textiles, and one cannot spend many hours on a single object.

The accepted path is a combination of academic study and bench training. We have a National Endowment for the Arts internship for someone on the way to a formal graduate training program or with a master's degree in an adjunct field who wants to get practical training. But everyone here has a slightly different background. One started as a weaver, another is an anthropologist with an expertise in American Indian objects. Here a theater costumer may specialize in historical costume conservation. Another person is an expert in painted textiles. It takes a blend of history and practical skills, and a group of people to enable us to deal with the wide range of objects.

Q What are the steps in the conservation of a textile? Use, as an example, the shattered Chinese silk.

A That piece was on the wall in the client's house. Two of our conservators gave her an outline of what we would do, and returned with the piece. We examined the fabric and composed the treatment report. In that report we develop a context for working on the fabric. We want to know its provenance— where it is from, the date, its history. We were fortunate that the owner had some information. Then we look through our files for related pieces. Using extensive post-treatment reports done for previous projects, we have an insight into how many hours will be necessary for the work, and what techniques are effective on that sort of brittle silk. At this time, we also look for any necessary library research.

The conservator assigned to the project meets with a senior conservator and discusses how the work should be approached given the way it will be used by the owner. Then the conservator documents the object's condition and writes a step-by-step treatment report. All of this develops a certain intimacy between the conservator and the object. The report and cost are presented to the client. If all is agreed, the piece is photographed, and we proceed. We finish off with a post-treatment report which documents what was discovered when the piece was opened and the materials used during treatment. One of the reason that treatment report is so important is that the material included becomes research for future projects.

Q How do you choose restoration materials?

A For backings we prefer natural fabrics—cotton, silk, and linen. If the object is silk, we use silk, but otherwise cotton is chosen because it is very stable; linen is very reactive to humidity. If the piece is very reactive, we may want a support fabric that moves with the textile. We may dye fabric used as backing if it shows in the finished piece and must be a very specific color. There are special dyes safe for conservation use.

Q Are contemporary fabrics safer from deterioration than were the fabrics of the past?

A Not really. Synthetic fibers have their own set of potential problems. Pilling is very hard to remedy, and particular synthetics hold stains aggressively. They can also react to the environment, shrinking or stretching, and may not rebound.

Q How do you date a textile?

A Everything has different signposts. A nineteenth-century American quilt is dated by the printed fabric. I can place the decade of a printed fabric from 1750 to today. If it is an Indian paisley, the guide is the ways the *boteh* shapes (the teardrop floral motifs) developed.

Q What are the some of the more interesting textiles you have encountered?

A I really don't have any favorites, but the most thrilling to me are Coptic textiles. They are usually Egyptian, eighth to thirteenth centuries. And very eccentric objects come here. One piece I never quite got over was the little shirt that was found on the Lindbergh baby. A tangible artifact from that crime, it had been hand-sewn by the nurse. It was an amazing little object. The provenance of pieces like this these must always be taken into account when conservation begins to assure that the work can be done without eradicating the object's past.

Q You have a large quilt collection. How did that collection develop?

A Thirty-two years ago, while furnishing my house, I ended up going to a lot of flea markets, and at that time quilts were very reasonable and in large supply. I had always collected textiles and had fabric fragments around, and loved the idea that a quilt was just a larger version of all those textile pieces. When I looked at quilts, I realized I had been buying textiles from all over the world, and for the first time saw the wonderful history of American textiles. Little had been written specifically about American quilts, so to find out more I began to look at letters and diaries of women who made the quilts.

Women in the eighteenth or nineteenth century had very few avenues to pursue artistic and other talents, so a tremendous amount of creativity and skills went into those quilts. Quilts were originally made for warmth, but became creative outlets, and were made to commemorate weddings and births. The quilting bee became an important social event, and generally the quilt became an intimate part of the family. They were important enough to go from generation to generation, and so provide us with examples of textiles used in clothing and household furnishings from those periods, and are reflective of the different eras in this country's history. In a world where so much is disposable, we need these things.

INTERVIEW WITH SANTO LOQUASTO
THEATER AND FILM DESIGNER

A noted designer of sets and costumes for theater, film, opera, and ballet, Santo Loquasto has won Tony and Drama Desk awards for his set design for *Café Crown* (1989), and for costume design for *The Cherry Orchard* (1977) and *Grand Hotel* (1990), as well as Obie, Joseph Mararam, and Outer Critics Circle Awards. His costume designs for Woody Allen's *Zelig* and production designs for *Radio Days* and *Bullets Over Broadway* received Academy Award nominations; he has worked with Woody Allen on nineteen films. In the world of dance, Mr. Loquasto has collaborated with Mark Morris, Jerome Robbins, Glen Tetley, Helgi Tomasson, Agnes de Mille, James Kudelka, Mikhail Baryshnikov, Dana Reitz, Twyla Tharp, and Paul Taylor.

Q What are your responsibilities as a production designer?

A I really think of myself as a stage designer. The film work has had an enormous effect on how I work in the theater, and vice versa. Even the detail we achieve on film is not so different from what is required for the stage. Although the scale of some elements may be larger, the same use of variety and texture that pay off on film can be brought to the stage.

The production designer on films is responsible for everything the camera sees other than the actors. You must coordinate and collaborate with the costume designer and director of photography. There are times when you have an idea as to how the room will be populated, and how the color and shape of the room will be punctuated by the people, and you have to share this. For example, in a Woody Allen film there is a dinner party, and I spent a lot of time asking about busboy and waiters' uniforms, because that affected my choices. Particularly in a film with a modest budget, these subtle choices are very important—but regardless of the budget, they're important.

In a big-budget film, the designer can manipulate proportions, and may totally control and create the atmosphere. On a location-oriented film, even where the space has been totally reinterpreted, leaving only the shape of the room, all work is done within the format of that location. What is interesting about working on Woody's films is that he favors shooting a scene in one setup, so I often must find scenic devices that enable the camera to move effortlessly through the space.

Q Is your work on a location similar to the job of an interior designer?

A I walk in as both an interior designer and a storyteller, always trying to exploit the character within the location. When we did *Mighty Aphrodite*, a location was found for Mira Sorvino's apartment. The character is basically a hooker, but I still thought about what might be her aspirations, what sort of music she would like. We put together a visual profile of the character and then did her apartment. It was fun. The place had flamboyance and a good-natured vulgarity.

Later in the filming it was necessary to do an additional scene in this apartment. But the location was no longer available. We had started with an empty apartment, re-papered, painted, but all of that was gone. We found another apartment with a different and more surprising look to it. And while we were prepared to rebuild parts of the first location in the new one based on continuity photos and our production notes, it turned out that Woody really wanted to reshoot many scenes. So we started from scratch, and reshot all the scenes in this new location. And it was better. This apartment was more real and less of a cartoon. While still amusing, it was a better and more original take on this kind of woman.

Q How do you find the right things to reflect a character?

A By studying the characters, discussing them with my colleagues. You often worry about your sensibility being dated. Looking at a possible location, I was being taken around by the teenage children of the family. I said something complimentary about the house, and one girl turned to me and said "Oh, but it's so seventies." It was like a knife in my heart.

Often I'm not precise with the locations people and need to go out and scout with them. This approach is grounded in the reality of where people would live, and a good start is deciding which neighborhood is appropriate. But, then, often the exteriors are [shot] in one place, and the interiors another.

Q How is a sense of continuity maintained when a movie is shot like that?

A You work very hard at maintaining what is seen out the windows and staying consistent in the details in both locations. What is particularly difficult is shooting "day for night" [a night time scene shot during the day]. You are in an apartment with windows and light, and all the windows have to be blacked out. Nothing is more unrealistic than a completely black win-

dow, so window treatments become a constant concern. How do you layer a window so that it has depth and doesn't seem to be a dead spot? Sometimes the cinematographer will be able to put some light in back of the windows. Or the blackout material is reflective and has some life. You are constantly making mental notes about what people have done with windows—louvers, shutters, blinds, matchstick shades, sheers, drapes—trying to provide depth.

Q How do cinematographers affect your work?

A Entirely! You work with them in solving the problems of providing light on the set with variety and imagination—we try not to have every practical light lit in every room. There should be a differentiation of the character of the light and sources between sets, so that the film can be cut together with interest. Otherwise one scene melts into the next. We look at samples and research photos for ideas and use devices like various types of glass that partially obscure the view, but can still be a light source.

Some DPs [directors of photography] are very good with small cramped spaces; others demand very high ceilings so that they can hang lights overhead. So this affects location choices. Color can be important. For period films, there is a wonderful thick golden tone that lights beautifully. It instantly conjures up the thirties, because it looks like illustrations of that period. In *Bullets Over Broadway* I really pushed the look of Reginald Marsh—rather ripe, with a kind of zest and sensuousness of the time.

Q How do you realize that sort of research in the details of a room?

A If the film is mainly locations, we do a lot with paint and possibly the addition of telling period details. With *Radio Days* a building was found for a studio set that had beautiful Art Deco details and wood paneling. We put in speakers and baffles covered with the appropriate textured fabric, found the right recording-studio chairs and music stands, built a studio control panel, and it was done. The actual architecture was just waiting for us. In other cases, you may turn an apartment into a house with paint, paper, furniture, the works.

Q How do you make a room look lived in?

A Sometimes you get lucky. For *Crimes and Misdemeanors* there was an apartment in Chelsea [New York] that was perfect. It was cluttered and full of the right things. We changed the curtains, cleared a table, put a typewriter on it, and stepped back. In most instances you can find what you want if you are determined, and then it is just a matter of rearranging the furniture, or organizing the space differently.

If you do have to start from scratch, the hardest place to create is the routine household. For example, in *Everyone Says I Love You* we needed a big Park Avenue apartment with a staircase. The location was actually a house in Riverdale (just outside the city)—no one who lives in one of those Park Avenue apartments wants to rent to a film company. It was very tricky to create that feeling of a comfortable family home on the Upper East Side, even though all the rooms were basically right. It was a mix of family photographs, things the kids had brought in, stuff from the couples' previous marriages. Yes, there had been an interior decorator, but only in the living room. We reconstructed a family history so we could determine what the family chose in terms of color, what was found at a flea market, what the decorator introduced. The window treatments were actually the basis for a scene with the character of the interior decorator. That sort of normal—a seemingly random collection of visual information culminating in what appears to be a credible interesting mess—is time consuming and challenging.

Q Do you shop for props and set dressing or do you give instructions to the set decorator?

A Both. Some decorators are amazing shoppers, others have insights into services and manufacturers. This becomes important in a film with a number of restaurants and supper clubs—public spaces and social events. Normally the decorator and I split up the shopping or go out together. But as with locations, what is important is to be able to see what is available and to respond in a way that you begin accumulating set dressings that will reflect the characters. The reason I do so much of my own shopping is that choices are affected by what you see. I may say we have to have a red chair, and then find the perfect chair, but it is green.

I roam about New York City. You have places you go to repeatedly because you respond to the sensibility of the owners—their sense of humor or chic. I check out certain shopping neighborhoods. I know where to find flashy or restrained—but it's entirely subjective, of course.

Q Are your general design choices affected by prop shopping?

A Yes. I check out all those stores for the trends. In *Deconstructing Harry*, Kirstie Alley's apartment has a lot of beautiful fifties furniture that was just becoming popular when we shot the film. This particular choice of style had less to do with her character than with trying to portray a "spirit of New York" that is reflected in where those sorts of people live and shop.

Q How much input do you have in exterior shots?

A The fun of location films is that you get to introduce the director or writer to a place. The script calls for a scene to be in a coffee shop, but you can suggest a restaurant on Ninth Avenue and 21st Street with great light and a terrific view. They do not necessarily share your enthusiasm, of course.

The "walking and talking" scenes are often the most diffi-

cult. These scenes have to be plotted shot by shot, and the route has to be found in terms of what we see along the way: What time of day is it? Where is the sun? How do we see the actors? What are they responding to? Do you deal with the genuine traffic? You want to use all the variety within the city to visually support the story and still maintain geographical continuity.

Q How is fabric used in film?

A It is often the fastest and cheapest way to infuse color and texture into a set. For a film with a series of jazz clubs we bought bolts of really cheap fabrics for stage curtains, table cloths, and wall coverings, and it was amazing how perfectly the character of the textures registered on film. One fabric we found didn't seem particularly theatrical, but on film it read perfectly as old theater curtains. The other thing about altering locations this way is that you can get in and out of the location quickly. Often a major budget consideration is how fast the scenery can be dismantled and the space restored.

And then there is the statement made by upholstery and drapery choices. With contemporary furniture you may want the fabric smooth with no texture. Or you may use bold patterns for graphic effect.

Q Do you spend time on the set during the filming?

A It's a good idea to be around during the setups because you might find that one end of the room is not featured. So the important things can be moved closer to the camera. In some cases, I have flipped rooms (changing the furniture ground plan by turning it 180 degrees).

Q You also design scenery for the theater. What are the considerations here?

A Theater space is basically shaped by light, and the scenery channels the light. We sculpt the space with surfaces that reflect or absorb light, that are opaque, translucent, or transparent. Sometimes I would love to focus the audience on details with a camera lens. But we get the focus differently. In *Fosse*, which is a show about performance and the vocabulary of stage devices, we worked with different kinds of "nasty fabrics" that project the character of the theater—tawdry and glorious. Starting with the traditional front scrim, we then added travelers (stage draperies that move on tracks) and tabbed drapes made from a sleazy translucent black sequinned fabric that turned out to be chameleonlike. A friend who saw the show was talking about the wonderful red curtains. It was the black sequins under red light.

I wanted a wall of light bulbs to give off a flare of light similar to the effect of a star filter on a camera. An associate who specializes in resourcing fabric came up with a cheap white poly organza, which we seamed in two directions and stretched in front of the lights. It directed the light from the bulbs in different directions, creating a halo. So these visually crass fabrics turned out to be technically very flexible.

Q What are some of the fabrics used in the theater?

A Drops are now being painted on rear-projection screen (a vinyl film), which diffuses the light much more readily than muslin. Jennifer Tipton, a lighting designer I frequently work with, uses the RP screen in combination with a translucent muslin drop, and what results can be wonderful and easily toured.

In a production of *Swan Lake* we painted a drop on clear vinyl to hang in front of a black scrim. The scene emerges from behind the scrim. I first saw this material as a painted smoke drop in a John MacFarland production, and had no idea what was going on. It is an amazing product because it can also be cut into shapes without unraveling. Recently a production of *Twelfth Night* at Lincoln Center had curved drops made of cheap lace appliquéd onto scrim and then overpainted. The result was completely theatrical Moorish architecture with a true stage reality. I had no idea what the materials were. At intermission, like a novice, I had to go up and touch the scenery to see what things were made of.

Q Is color a primary element of stage design?

A Color is perhaps a more obvious tool for the stage. It is what the eye sees first, and the details are only seen after the impression has been made by the color, which is why the lighting is so important.

Q Do you work differently with a theater lighting designer than with a cinematographer?

A It is entirely different. In the theater, after the early production meetings the lighting designer usually doesn't arrive again until the set is on stage. I definitely design with light in mind, and anticipate things looking a certain way.

In discussing *Swan Lake* with the lighting designer, I described how I saw the opening of the third act with very specific color references. It was not a matter of dictating, but it had been designed with this image in mind—smoke and color in the atmosphere revealing cobalt blue costumes. It has a decadent and surprising feel when compared to the previous acts. You want the lighting designer's vision to be comparable or ideally to exceed yours. Also, I try to be aware of the designer's past work and draw on that.

Over the years I have collaborated with Jennifer Tipton, who brings quality, intelligence, and clarity to a variety of styles. One thing I have learned from her is that often the dancers are better seen when the stage is darker, and the boundaries of the space are lost.

Q What are some of the other specific design demands of dance?

A Usually to keep the scenery out of the way. But it depends. Years ago Jennifer Tipton and I did *The Catherine Wheel* for Twyla Tharp. It was a stage space delineated by a vertical pipe grid that the dancers had to dance through. At various moments Twyla wanted to use shadows of dancers projected on fabric. The size of the shadows was determined by the proximity of the dancer to the light source and the fabric. When the fabric was hung and stretched as the intended projection surface, the shadows were not particularly interesting. So we hung the fabric in drapes with extra fullness. When the shadows fell on the fabric, the images spilled into the folds, and became distortions of the figures. And as the fabric breathed with the dancers' movement, it became more fully integrated into the piece.

Q How would you compare designing for film and theater?

A Film is a faster and more immediate way of presenting individual images, and it is the cumulative effect of those images that provides the impact. On stage, the general view is presented immediately as the curtain opens, and the challenge is to keep it provocative. So you leave gaps for the audience to fill. For example, in an opera based on the play *A View from the Bridge*, the scenery is basically wet cobblestones and black-and-white projections, except when we see the sky, which has color, even dramatic color. We want the neorealist black-and-white film look of Visconti and Rossellini films to provide the atmosphere and detail, and the color to reinforce the emotional line of the text. Using projections of course brings a more fluid filmlike quality to the stage.

Look at the Bertolucci films designed by Fernando Scarfiotti. The two of them made visually spectacular films like *The Last Emperor*. They also did *Last Tango in Paris* and *The Conformist*, and both still affect how I, as a designer, look at any scene. The visuals are emotionally explored in a way that is credible. It is not just operatic lighting and the use of color; it is the complete reinforcing of the scene. True to the nature of the scene, but visually astounding either because of sumptuous beauty or delicate subtlety. This can be found in a scary little hovel or in an enormous marble hall with a desk at the end. It applies to both film and theater. It is all about what you see in a space, how the light enters, and how the people look.

GLOSSARY

Abaca. A long fiber derived from the abaca plant used for matting and ropes.

Acetate. Man-made cellulose-based fiber used for fabric of the same name.

Acrylic. Man-made, resin-based fiber used for fabrics and carpets. Acrylic has a soft hand, can be easily washed and dyed, and is thermoplastic. Acrylic fabric is resistant to wrinkles and does not deteriorate when exposed to sunlight.

Airbrushing. A method of applying dye or paint in which the medium is atomized into a fine spray.

Aniline dye. An organic colorant derived from coal tar or petroleum chemicals.

Animal fibers. Fibers harvested from animal fur and hair; for example, wool and mohair are staple fibers that are spun into yarn for fabrics and carpets.

Antimacassar. A protective cover for the arms and backs of furniture. The term usually refers to the crocheted doilies popular in the nineteenth century.

Antique satin. A fabric, made from a variety of fibers, that on the face shows yarn slubs in the filling and is satinlike on the reverse side. The intended effect is that of a seventeenth- or eighteenth-century silk. It is generally used for drapery.

Antique taffeta. Plain-woven fabric of fine, often filament yarns that resembles taffeta from the seventeenth or eighteenth centuries.

Appliqué. A separate piece of material that is sewn or bonded to an area of a base fabric.

Aquatic grass. A plant that grows in or around water whose fibers are used for plaiting, braiding, knotting, and weaving. Also known as sea grass, rush, aquatic rush.

Armure. A fabric usually with small geometric dobby patterns in one color. It was used during the eighteenth century, and the patterns resurfaced with an interest in that period of antique furniture during the early nineteenth century.

Arrowhead twill. *See* Herringbone twill.

Art silk. A 1920s term referring to a rayon-acetate blend that resembled silk. Originally "art. silk," an abbreviation for "artificial silk."

Asbestos. A mineral fiber that is inherently fireproof. It was widely used for theater curtains and in industry, but because it presents a health hazard it is no longer used in fabric manufacturing.

Aubusson. (1) A tapestry-woven textile, originally made in the French town of Aubusson. (2) A machine-made uncut-loop pile carpet made to imitate the handmade tapestries and carpets of Aubusson.

Austrian shade. A window covering with tightly controlled stitched vertical shirring that pulls up on vertical cords from the bottom. Also called Austrian pouf or Austrian valance.

Axminster. A cut-pile carpet made on a loom with a special tufting device that allows for a wide range of pile heights and colors. The weave is attributed to a factory in Axminster, England.

Balanced fabric. A textile constructed with warp and filling yarns of equal weight woven with an equal number of picks and ends per area. *See* figures G-1, G-15, and G-23.

Balloon shade. A soft fabric window covering that draws up from the bottom on vertical cords into full scallops, more voluminous and casual than an Austrian shade. Also called cloud or poufed shade.

Bark cloth. (1) A nonwoven material derived from tree bark soaked and then beaten into a coarse fabric. (2) Crepe fabric woven to resemble the texture of tree bark.

Basic weave. *See* Plain weave, Satin weave, Twill weave.

Basket weave. A variation of plain weave in which two or more yarns are woven together in both warp and filling directions. *See* figure G-1.

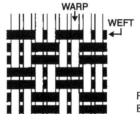

Figure G-1.
Basket weave

Bast fibers. Fibers derived from the inner bark, husks, and other parts of plants such as hemp, jute, or sisal.

Batik. A resist-dyeing process in which the design is drawn in wax drawn directly on the fabric. When the fabric is dyed, the waxed areas remain undyed. The wax is then removed.

Batiste. A fine, sheer, lightweight plain weave made of cotton, silk, wool, linen, or appropriate synthetic.

Batting. Fluffed fibers of wool, cotton, kapok, polyester, or other appropriate material formed into sheets and used as padding.

Bayadere. Originally a plain-woven fabric with bright contrasting horizontal stripes based on an Indian fabric. The term now refers to any horizontal pattern layout.

Beetling. A finishing technique in which damp material passes between a metal cylinder and mallets to increase the luster and give a harder surface to the fabric

Berber yarn. A thick, originally handspun, natural color yarn with very little twist.

Berlin work. Victorian needlework done from kits, produced in Berlin, Germany, that contained

canvas with printed color-coded patterns and matching yarn, called Berlin wool or zephyr.

Bird's eye. A woven pattern consisting of a dot surrounded by a diamond, found, for example, in dobby fabrics.

Blanket. Textile industry term for a sample piece of fabric woven in the various colors available in that line.

Blend. A yarn or fabric made from two or more types of fiber.

Blister cloth. Fabric with a pebbled surface made by a variety of techniques including crepe weave; weaving the cloth from a combination of yarn that shrinks and yarn that does not and finishing with a process to cause shrinkage; chemically causing areas on the fabric to react; varying the tension during the weaving.

Block printing. A process using blocks carved with a pattern to print a design.

Bobbinet. A lightweight hexagonal net fabric used for trim, curtains, and theatrical backdrops.

Bobbin lace. Handmade lace made by outlining the pattern on a cushion (or pillow) with straight pins and working the thread around the pins. Also called pillow lace.

Bonded fabric. A fabric made of two layers of cloth permanently joined with resin or an appropriate adhesive, sometimes to increase the structural integrity of the fabric. *See also* Laminate.

Bouclé. An irregular curly yarn made from heavy, pretwisted threads twisted around a fine core yarn.

Botanical. A design showing entire plant forms, often including the roots, rendered as in a botanical illustration.

Braid. (1) A narrow flat or round fabric constructed by diagonally intertwining sets of yarns. *See* figure G-2. (2) Any narrow fabric used for trimming.

Figure G-2. Braid

Braided rug. A rug made from strips of fabric that are braided together, wound into a spiral, and stitched together to form a round or oval mat.

Broad goods. Fabric wider than 18 inches (46cm).

Broadcloth. A fine plain-woven cloth of spun yarn woven on a loom wider than 27 inches (69cm).

Broadloom. Woven carpets wider than 12 feet (3.6m).

Brocade. (1) A compound fabric in which a supplementary warp or filling yarn (one that may be removed without affecting the base fabric) is inlaid into a base fabric during the weaving process to yield the appearance of embroidered motifs. In sections where the supplementary yarn is not visible on the face, it may float on the back of the fabric between the areas where it is woven; this is called continuous brocade. In discontinuous brocade, the supplementary yarn is only woven into the patterned areas. *See* figures G-3, G-4, and G-18. (2) Fabric constructed with a brocade weave.

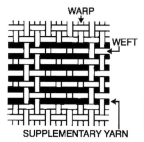

Figure G-3. Continuous brocade

Figure G-4. Discontinuous brocade

Brocatelle. A traditionally silk and linen fabric with a high-relief motif created with a stuffer pick. The motif, often in satin weave, is created with a supplementary warp in a color that contrasts with the ground.

Broché. Usually silk fabric with a small clipped brocade floral design.

Brushed fabric. Woven and knitted fabrics that have been napped and have a soft, pile-like hand.

Buckram. A coarse, open, plain-woven, heavily sized fabric used for stiffening.

Bullion fringe. (1) Fringe made from twisted yarn, 2 to 24 inches (5–61cm) long, used as upholstery and drapery trim. (2) Fringe made from metallic thread that is tightly coiled around a flexible cord.

Burlap. A plain-woven fabric made with jute yarn. Originally made for utilitarian purposes such as sacks, it is often dyed for decorative use.

Burn-out. The process of applying a pattern to a fabric by printing it with a substance that destroys one or more of the fiber types present, for example, voided velvet.

Calendering. Finishing process that uses heat and extreme pressure to produce fabric effects such as a luster, glaze, moiré, or embossed print, most commonly done on cotton or cotton-like fabrics.

Calico. Originally any cotton fabric imported from India with woven, painted, or printed colors and patterns. The term now refers to brightly colored printed plain-woven cotton fabrics with small-scale printed designs.

Cambric. *See* Handkerchief linen.

Candlewick. Fabric with a muslin base through which thick yarn (similar to that used for candle wicks) is pulled and either left looped or cut to give a tufted effect. This technique is now mechanized. *See also* Chenille spread.

Caning. Interlacing done with vertical, horizontal, and oblique elements, usually with woody plant material, resulting in a plaited fabric with a pattern of openings that are usually octagonal.

Canvas. A heavy, stiff, closely woven fabric, usually made of carded cotton or linen with no finish. Heavy canvas is called duck, but the terms are often used interchangeably.

Canvas work. See Needlepoint.

Carding. A method of preparing fibers for spinning in which the staple fiber is cleaned, straightened, and separated into single strands.

Carpet. (1) Fiber-based floor covering manufactured in a continuous length and designed to be laid wall-to-wall. (2) A sixteenth- or seventeenth-century term for table coverings. (3) A term often used interchangeably with "rug" to refer to pile woven floor coverings. *See* Rug.

Casement cloth. A fabric in which heavy yarns are spaced far enough apart to let light pass through. It is used for curtains and other window treatments.

Challis. Sheer, lightly napped, plain-woven fabric usually of fine wool or rayon.

Chandin. Lightweight cotton fabric from India used for drapery on ceilings.

Check. (1) A woven or printed pattern of squares on a fabric usually in two or three colors. When the warp and filling are the same layout, the fabric is a "true check." (2) Fabric with a check pattern.

Chenille. (1) A yarn that is not spun but made by a weaving and cutting process that results in a fuzzy yarn with an axial warp yarn. It resembles a caterpillar. (2) Fabric woven from chenille yarn.

Chenille bedspread. A common term used for spreads made with a tufted pattern but not with chenille yarn. *See also* Candlewick.

Chenille carpet. A machine-made pile carpet made from chenille yarn.

Chenille embroidery. Embroidery with chenille yarn, usually executed on velvet.

Chevron. *See* Herringbone twill.

China silk. A lightweight plain-woven silk made with irregular yarns. The term now is applied to machine-made silk made to resemble the original fabric that was handwoven in China.

Chiné. A warp-printed cloth usually in a French floral motif.

Chintz. A glazed plain-woven cotton that may be solid-colored, printed with floral designs or stripes, or embossed, originally imported from India in the seventeenth century. Unglazed chintz is called cretonne.

Ciré. A glossy finish, originally applied to satin, created by applying wax (or similar substances) and calendering or by applying heat to thermoplastic fabric.

Clipped. An effect created by cutting away the floating portions of supplementary yarns so that the remaining loose cut edges become part of the design. Motifs are usually isolated on a ground. Dotted Swiss is an example.

Cloth. A term applied to wovens, knits, felts, and other fiber-based, pliable materials, usually not including plastic films, rugs, carpets, or most paper. *See also* Fabric, Textile.

Coated fabric. Fabric finished by the application of a varnish, oil, vinyl, polymer, or similar substance, for example, oilcloth and Naugahyde.

Coir. Fiber derived from coconut husks. It is used for brushes but it can also be made into a yarn.

Colorfastness. *See* Fastness.

Colorways. The range of colors in which a specific fabric is available from the manufacturer.

Combed. (1) A term used to describe fibers that have been carded and then processed to remove the short fibers, and clean and straighten the others, resulting in smoother and stronger yarn. (2) Fabric made with combed fibers, such as combed cotton.

Compound fabric. Fabric woven with multiple sets of warp or filling yarn.

Conversational. A design that depicts a recognizable object or theme, such as a landscape, animal, or figurative motif. The term does not include floral or geometric motifs.

Copperplate printing. Technique by which a design is engraved on a flat copper plate to which printing ink is applied. The ink is wiped off the surface but remains in the incised lines and is transferred to fabric under pressure. The process, developed in 1765, allowed plates much larger than possible in block printing, resulting in the development of new printing styles, such as toile.

Cord. (1) A long, thin flexible material made of two or more yarns twisted together. (2) A rib on the surface of fabric.

Corduroy. A fabric with cut-filling pile vertical wales.

Cotton. (1) Fiber derived from the fruit of the plant of the same name, used to make yarn. Cotton fibers are classified as to length, strength, and geographical origin. (2) Fabric made of cotton.

Couching. An embroidery technique that involves laying thread on the surface of fabric, and attaching it with very fine, inconspicuous stitches.

Count. The number of warp and filling yarns per square unit of measure. The number of warp ends is mentioned first when referring to count, for example, 84 x 80, meaning one square unit contains 84 ends and 80 picks.

Counterpane. A bedcovering made of multiple layers, for example, a quilt.

Course. One row of loops in knitting.

Cramming. A weaving technique in which more yarns per unit of measurement are forced into a specific area than are used in other parts of the fabric.

Crepe. Fabric of crinkled appearance, usually as a result of the weave, yarn type, or finishing techniques.

Cretonne. *See* Chintz.

Crewelwork. Embroidery done with crewel yarn, a loosely twisted worsted wool, on a linen or cotton ground.

Crochet. A construction of interlocking loops made with a hooked needle.

Crushed pile. Pile fabrics finished by exposure to heat, moisture, crushing, calendering, and heat setting to flatten areas of the pile.

Cut pile. *See* Pile.

Cut work. A combination of appliqué and embroidery that involves removing areas of the ground fabric, sometimes filling the spaces with embroidery. The term is also applied to needle lace on a woven ground.

Damask. (1) A weave, named for its origin in Damascus, that produces a patterned reversible fabric by alternating patterned areas of satin (warp-faced) and sateen (filling-faced) weave. (2) Fabric of any construction with features characteristic of woven damask such as symmetrical layout or vase-and-plant motifs.

Denier. The mass in grams of 9,000 meters of a fiber, filament, or yarn. Higher denier indicates heavier material.

Denim. Heavy twill woven with dyed warp yarn, and white filling yarns. *See also* Twill.

Dhurrie. An Indian carpet woven from heavy cotton yarn, patterned with colored filling yarns.

Diaper. A design of small-scale geometric figures (originally diamond-shaped) in a usually diagonal layout of interlocking or closely aligned motifs.

Dimity. A sheer, plain-woven cotton with ribs of spaced yarns that produce a light corded effect.

Discharge printing. A technique in which chemicals are used to bleach out a design on a previously colored fabric, and then color is printed on the discharged areas. The result is a light design on a darker colored ground.

Discontinuous brocade. *See* Brocade.

Dobby. (1) An attachment to a loom used to facilitate the weaving of small geometric patterns. (2) The fabrics produced on a dobby loom. (3) Fabrics featuring a small, all-over geometric woven pattern.

Dotted Swiss. A sheer, traditionally cotton fabric, with a pattern of raised dots that may be created by weaving, embroidering, or flocking.

Double cloth. Fabric made by weaving two layers of cloth simultaneously on the same loom. Double sets of warp and filling yarns are joined together at regular points by binder yarns. *See* figure G-5.

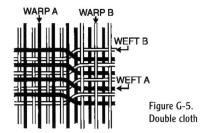

Figure G-5. Double cloth

Drape. Term used to describe how a fabric hangs.

Drapery. Pleated or gathered fabric hung in an architectural opening.

Drawn work. A type of needlework in which threads in a fabric are pulled aside according to a design and stitched together with a variety of decorative stitches using various kinds and colors of thread.

Duck. A very durable, plain-woven fabric, usually cotton or linen, available in a variety of weights.

Duvetyn. A satin or twill woven with a short raised nap. It is soft and drapes easily.

Dye. Colorant, either natural or synthetic, that chemically interacts with the fibers of a fabric. It may require various processes or substances, called mordants, to fix the color to the fiber.

Egyptian cloth. An open, plain-woven cotton made from long, fine staple fiber.

Embossing. A finishing process in which an appropriate thermoplastic fabric such as velvet and leather is calendered, usually with engraved rollers, to produce a dimensional design.

Embroidery. The decoration of fabric with needle-worked stitches.

End. An individual warp yarn.

End and end. Fabric woven with warp yarn of alternating colors.

Epingle. A fabric with short, uncut looped pile.

Eyelet embroidery. A needlework technique in which small areas are cut or burned out from a base fabric according to a design. The cut edges are surrounded by embroidery stitches.

Fabric. An inclusive term for textiles, plastic films, rugs and carpets, wire mesh, and other similar flexible materials.

Face. When applicable, the side of the fabric designed to be the front.

Faille. A plain-woven repp constructed with a fine, dense warp and a heavier filling. Often silklike, faille has a luster, crushes easily, and is used for moiré

Fastness. The property of dyed fabric to retain its color when exposed to sunlight, water, and other elements.

Felt. A nonwoven fabric made from loose natural or man-made fibers that are formed into a sheet by means of moisture and pressure. Cellulose and some synthetic fibers require a bonding agent.

Festoon. A fixed curtain at the top of a window or door hanging from two points and draped in a variety of styles. Also called swag.

Fiber. The chemically distinct primary unit of material used for the manufacturing of fabric. Fibers are spun into yarn for weaving, or formed into fabric by a nonwoven process.

Fiberglass. A man-made fiber made from extruded mineral filaments.

Figurative. A design using pictures of recognizable objects as motifs.

Figured weave. A fabric with a woven pattern or design.

Filament. A continuous fiber that occurs naturally, for example, silk and hair, or is man-made by extruding solutions and other processes. Filaments may be used in their entirety or chopped up into staple fibers and spun into yarn.

Filet. Handmade knotted net.

Filling. In a woven fabric, the yarn that runs horizontally, from selvage to selvage, crossing the warp. Also called weft. *See* figure G-15.

Filling-faced fabric. A textile with a greater number of picks (weft yarns) than ends (warp yarns) on the face, or in which the picks are heavier than the ends, causing the filling to dominate. *See* figure G-6.

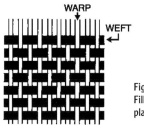

Figure G-6. Filling-faced plain weave

Film. A man-made fabric, manufactured directly from chemical solutions.

Finish. A process applied to constructed fabric to give it a desired final appearance or add performance features. Finishes include backing, beetling, calendering, embossing, napping, washing, waterproofing, and the application of stain-repellent.

Fishnet. A diagonally knotted net.

Flame stitch. An irregular chevron pattern resembling a stylized flame produced by weaving or printing.

Flannel. A light- to medium-weight plain- or twill-woven fabric that is lightly napped. It has a soft hand.

Fleece. A fabric, usually of knit construction, that is heavily napped.

Float. The portion of a yarn that passes over another yarn or yarns before it interlaces in the weaving process.

Flock. Very short fibers (.5–2mm) that are attached to a base fabric with some form of adhesive by the process called flocking.

Floss. Silk yarn that is barely twisted. It is used for embroidery.

Fortuny print. Originally, fabrics with a pattern in metallic or light color handprinted on a darker ground, designed by Mariano Fortuny. The patterns, which have an aged look and mottled colors within the motif, resemble those found in traditional brocades and damasks. Imitation Fortuny prints are now produced by machine printing.

Frisé. A woven-pile fabric of wool, mohair, or appropriate synthetic with short, uncut loops that may produce a pattern by varying the height or arrangement of the loops or shearing the loops at different heights. Frisé is used for upholstery.

Friezé, Friezette. Antiquated terms for frisé.

Fulling. A finishing process for wool or protein fiber in which the fabric is shrunk by exposure to moisture, soap, and agitation to give the fabric greater bulk and resilience.

Fusing. A process that uses heat or chemicals to join appropriate materials.

Gabardine. A fine twill-woven fabric with a dense sett made from plied worsted yarn. Gabardine is durable, drapes well, and has a hard surface, a slight luster, and a smooth hand.

Gauge. (1) The measure of thickness of plastics and similar fabrics. (2) The measuring unit for knitted stitches. The higher the number, the thinner the sheet and the finer the knit.

Gauze. A plain-woven, usually cotton, fabric, loosely woven from thin yarn. Also called scrim.

Ghiordes knot. See Knots, figure G-7.

Gingham. A plain-woven, lightweight fabric, usually woven in yarn-dyed checks.

Gimp. (1) A narrow woven band used for trimming. (2) A flexible core yarn wrapped with silk, plastic, or metal.

Glazing. A finishing process in which fabric is treated with a substance such as wax, shellac, or resin, often calendered, producing a polished surface.

Gobelin. (1) A handwoven tapestry from the Paris factory of that name. (2) The technique of weaving with discontinuous weft, creating a reversible design. It dates to the sixteenth century.

Graufrage. Embossed or stamped velvet made with heated metal cylinders etched with the design.

Grass cloth. A wall covering made with widely spaced warp threads and heavy bast fibers for the filling.

Gray goods. Fabrics that are woven but have not undergone any finishing processes. Also called greige or loomstate.

Greige. See Gray goods.

Grille. The bars spanning the open spaces between areas in lace.

Grosgrain. A narrow heavy ribbed fabric made with a warp of silk or a synthetic fiber with a similar luster, and a cotton filling. Often used for ribbons.

Gros-point, petit-point. Needlework made on a coarse canvas with the stitches at the intersections of the weave so the canvas is completely covered. Gros-point has 12 to 18 intersections, and therefore stitches, per inch (2.5cm); petit-point, 18 or more stitches per inch.

Gum. (1) An adhesive substance, called sericin, emitted by the silkworm along with silk filament to form its cocoon. (2) A group of natural, water-soluble substances used as adhesives, sizes, and glazes in the finishing of fabrics.

Haircloth. A stiff plain-woven fabric made from cotton and horsehair.

Hand. Term used to refer to the feel of a fabric.

Hand-blocked. Term describing fabric printed by hand using the technique of block printing.

Handkerchief linen. A calendered plain-woven cotton or linen. The finish ranges from soft and matte to stiff with a luster. Also called cambric.

Handloomed. See Handwoven.

Handspun. Yarn that is twisted on a hand-operated spinning wheel. It is more irregular than machine-spun yarn.

Handwoven. A term describing fabric made on a manually operated loom. Also called handloomed.

Harlequin. Any large diamond pattern, often in bright colors.

Harris tweed. A handwoven plain-woven or twill fabric made from handspun and hand-dyed wool yarn on the Hebrides, Scotland.

Heather mixture. A wool yarn that is a blend of tones and colors. The fibers are dyed before the yarn is spun. Also called stock-dyed.

Heat setting. A process applied to thermoplastic fabrics that stabilizes the material or forces it to retain a desired shape or effect.

Hemp. A long (up to 8 feet [2.44m]), strong bast fiber from the hemp plant. It is extremely resistant to rotting when exposed to water.

Herculon. A proprietary polypropylene fiber.

Herringbone twill. A variation of twill weave in which the diagonal lines of the weave occur in groups that alternate in direction. Also called chevron.

Homespun. A plain-woven fabric loosely woven from irregular, slubby yarn, sometimes with an uneven texture. Originally, fabric that was handwoven from handspun yarn.

Honeycomb. See Waffle weave.

Hooked rug. Rug made by pulling yarn or strips of fabric through a canvas or burlap ground with a hooked tool to form loops on the face.

Hopsack. A coarse, plain-woven fabric, sometimes a basket weave, constructed from burlap or similar fabric, used for sacking.

Houndstooth. The check pattern with pointed ends created by alternating blocks of light and dark yarn in both warp and filling in a twill weave.

Ikat. The Indonesian term for warp- or weft-resist dyeing. See also Kasuri.

Illusion. A lightweight, fine tulle or net.

Imberline stripe. A damask with a multicolor warp stripe.

Indian head. A plain-woven, preshrunk cotton fabric made with uneven yarn resulting in a slightly rough hand. It is used for table linens and draperies.

Indigo. A blue-black vegetable dye.

Interlacing. The crossing over and under of multiple sets of yarns to construct a fabric.

Jabot. An element of a window treatment that is a vertical hanging piece of fabric that comes to a point. Jabots are usually used in conjunction with a swag.

Jacquard. (1) A loom attachment that makes possible complicated woven patterns by utilizing a series of punched cards. Each punched hole directs the action of a warp yarn in relation to the passage of a filling yarn. There is a card for each pick. (2) A fabric patterned by means of a Jacquard loom.

Japanning. The finishing of fabric with Japan varnish, resulting in a hard, glossy face.

Jaspé. Yarn twisted of two different-colored plies. Also called marl.

Jersey. A fabric knitted entirely in a plain knit stitch.

Jute. A long (3–15 feet [.9–4.6m]) bast fiber used for twine and woven cloth. It deteriorates when exposed to moisture.

Kaitag. Intricate embroidery of silk on cotton or (rarely) silk from Daghestan in the Caucasus, believed to have spiritual and ritualistic significance. The motifs derive from Asian, Indo-Aryan, and Ottoman cultures.

Kali. An embroidered felt Persian floor covering. Also called Khali.

Kapok. A resilient, moisture-resistant fiber from the seed pods of the tree of the same name used for stuffing pillows, mattresses and life preservers.

Kasuri. Japanese term for warp- or weft-resist dying.

Khaki. (1) A light yellowish brown color. (2) A fabric, usually cotton, dyed a shade of khaki.

Kilim. A tapestry-woven textile often used for rugs. Also called khilim and kelim. See also Tapestry.

Knit. A fabric with a continuous interlocking loop construction made with a single continuous yarn, resulting in a fabric with some degree of elasticity. See figure G-12.

Knot. (1) A tied joining. (2) The means by which

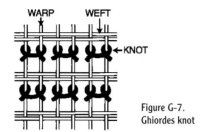

Figure G-7.
Ghiordes knot

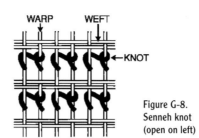

Figure G-8.
Senneh knot
(open on left)

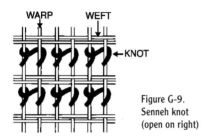

Figure G-9.
Senneh knot
(open on right)

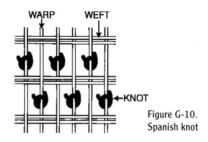

Figure G-10.
Spanish knot

each yarn is held in place in knotted pile carpets or fabric. The yarns are wrapped around the warp and held in place by the weft. Three basic types are the Ghiordes (Turkish), Senneh (Persian), and Spanish knots. *See* figures G-7, G-8, G-9, G-10.

Knotted pile. A technique of creating rugs or fabric by hand-tying looped yarn or strips through a base fabric, using a knot to secure the loop. *See* Knot.

Knotted lace. A fabric made by joining yarn with a series of knots, usually in a design. Examples are tatting and macramé.

Kobai. A Japanese corded fabric made with cotton or silk warp and silk filling.

Lace. A textile constructed by twisting, knotting, or intertwining threads to create an open fabric, either by hand or machine, by a variety of techniques. Most variations can be categorized as to the construction.

Lamé. A flat fabric made with a metallic yarn or yarn given a metallic finish or, by extension, fabric given a metallic finish after construction.

Laminate. A fabric composed of two or more layers of woven or nonwoven cloth joined by some adhesive process.

Lampas. Fabric woven with filling yarns of contrasting colors that surface in specific areas of the pattern like a brocade, but the yarns are not supplementary. When the filling color is not required on the face, it is woven inconspicuously on the back of the fabric. Lampas often refers to a brocade design and is not always descriptive of construction.

Lappet. A plain-woven fabric with extra warp threads that create the effect of a small embroidered pattern.

Lawn. A sheer plain-woven fabric, usually cotton or linen, that is constructed from carded or combed cotton. It has more body than gauze or voile

and may be stiffly finished as organdy.

Leno weave. A plain weave in which pairs of warp threads are alternately twisted between each insertion of filling yarn. The technique stabilizes yarns in an open construction. *See* figure G-11.

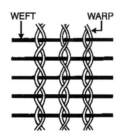

Figure G-11.
Leno weave

Lightfastness. *See* Fastness.

Linen. A bast fiber from the flax plant. Spun into yarn and woven, it makes a strong fabric.

Lisere. A silk fabric, usually ribbed, with brocaded flowers on a figured weave.

Loden. A naturally water-resistant wool fabric woven from fibers derived from the oily wool of mountain sheep.

Loft. Term used to describe the spring or bulk of a yarn or fabric.

Loomstate. *See* Gray goods.

Looped pile. *See* Pile.

Looping. Fabric constructed by yarn that crosses over itself and then forms the next loop. Variations include loop and twist, knits, crochet. *See* figure G-12.

G-12.
Looping

Lustering. A finishing process applied to yarn or fabric to produce a sheen, mainly by using friction but sometimes also heat or pressure.

Macaroon. An item of trim made from the same material as the piece to which it is applied. The fabric is made into a tube and than shaped into a rosette, coil, or other shape.

Madder. A vegetable dye that produces a red color. It was one of the earliest permanent colorants.

Madras. Originally a handwoven cotton of vegetable-dyed yarn, in woven plaids, checks, and stripes imported from India. The term now refers to a wide variety of woven cottons that fade easily.

Man-made. A general term for manufactured fibers and filaments synthesized from chemicals (for example, nylon, acrylic), cellulose-based fibers (for example, rayon), and fibers derived from minerals (for example, glass). Also called synthetic.

Marl. *See* Jaspé.

Marquisette. A leno-woven, net-like fabric that may be plain or patterned, and is used for curtains. *See* Leno.

Matelassé. A double cloth with a quilted or padded texture produced by inserting stuffer yarns between layers. Matelassé is usually jacquard-woven in solid or near solid colors.

Melton. A heavy woolen flannel, hardened, not napped or sheared, with a hard surface.

Memory. Term used to refer to a fabric's ability to return to its finished shape and character when stretched or manipulated.

Mercerization. A chemical process applied to cotton yarn or fabric that permanently increases its luster and receptivity to dye.

Mesh. A fabric that has regular openings between the yarns. It may be constructed by any appropriate method.

Metallic print. A process that applies a metal powder or other reflective material with a binder to a fabric.

Metallic thread or yarn. (1) A thin strip of metal used as a decorative element. (2) Yarn that has been coated with metal leaf or strips of plastic film that look metallic.

Microfiber. An extremely fine synthetic yarn with a count of one denier or less, used for woven or knit fabric. It produces a lightweight, dense fabric with a range of characteristics such as resistance to wind and water, while allowing the passage of moisture vapor. Fabrics of microfiber have a soft hand. They wash easily, drape well, and are good insulators.

Mineral fibers. Fibers derived from minerals, for example, asbestos and glass, that can be processed into yarn and fabric.

Mock leno. An open woven fabric that resembles a leno-woven fabric but does not have leno's characteristic twist in the filling.

Mohair. A long fiber, from the hair of the angora goat, that is spun into a soft, lustrous yarn. Commonly used for the pile in mohair "plush."

Moiré. (1) A process of calendering fabric with engraved rollers to produce a rippled surface resembling water marks. (2) Fabric produced by the moiré process fabric that has been printed to imitate the moiré effect.

Moleskin. A satin-weave fabric, tightly woven from cotton yarn, with a very short nap that produces a suede finish. Fabric with a similar effect is made from microfibers.

Monk's cloth. A heavy, usually cotton, fabric constructed in a loose basket weave.

Monofilament. A yarn made from a single man-made extruded filament.

Moquette. A short-pile upholstery fabric made from wool, mohair, or similar yarn. It may be cut or looped pile or a patterned combination. Also called Moquette velvet.

Mordant. A substance used to set dyes. It may be applied during different stages of the manufacturing process, depending on the dye, yarn, fabric, or desired effect.

Motif. The basic element repeated in a pattern or forming the theme of a design.

Multifilament. Yarn made from short man-made filaments that are spun together.

Muslin. A wide range of plain-woven cotton fabric that may be sheer or heavy, bleached or naturally colored.

Mylar. A plastic film, sometimes a laminate of highly reflective materials that appears to be metallic.

Napping. A finishing process in which the fabric is passed through abrasive rollers that disturb the surface, giving it a soft hand and a suede-like appearance.

Narrow goods. Fabric that is loomed no more than 27 inches (69cm) wide, formerly the maximum width available on commercial looms. Thus, narrow width may be an indicator of antique fabric.

Natural dyes. Colorants derived from animals, vegetables, or minerals, such as cochineal, indigo, madder, and aniline.

Natural fibers. Fibers derived from animals, vegetables, or minerals that can be spun into yarn.

Naugahyde. Proprietary name for a vinyl fabric meant to resemble leather.

Needle tapestry. A kind of needlework, done on a canvas base, that resembles woven tapestry.

Needlepoint. A type of needlework in which all stitches are worked through the spaces between the warp and weft of a piece of canvas, in contrast to surface embroidery, where the stitches are worked on the face of the fabric.

Needle punching. The mechanical process of joining a web of loose fibers to make a nonwoven fabric.

Net. An open fabric usually made by knotting yarns, threads, or rope in a square pattern.

Noils. Short fibers that are by-products of yarn production. They are spun into rough and novelty yarns or used as padding.

Nonwoven fabric. Cloth that is constructed by joining the constituent fibers or filaments by means of adhesives, pressure, or heat.

Novelty yarn. Yarn manufactured with a unique texture or other nonstandard qualities. See also Bouclé, Chenille.

Nub. A clump of fiber on a yarn intentionally introduced to give the yarn a specific texture.

Nylon. A chemically based man-made fiber. It is strong and durable but subject to pilling and static electricity.

Oilcloth. A waterproof fabric made by coating a base fabric (which may be napped) with a compound of oil, clay filler, and binders.

Olefin. See Polypropylene.

Olive drab. Dark, greenish khaki color. Also called OD.

Ombré. A woven or dyed effect in which different colors or tones gradually change, as from light to dark or red to blue.

Organdy. A sheer but closely woven plain-woven cotton muslin with a crisp finish.

Organza. A rayon, silk, or nylon fabric resembling organdy.

Orlon. A proprietary acrylic fiber.

Ottoman. A heavy plain-woven fabric with a prominent horizontal rib produced by using a filling yarn heavier than the warp.

Overprint. A process in which the design is printed over previously dyed or patterned fabric.

Overshot. A weave, typically used for coverlets, in which the pattern weft (usually supplementary) floats over a varying number of warp threads to form the design.

Oxford cloth. A fine cotton plain-woven fabric that employs a basket weave or variation, often using a white filling and yarn-dyed warp.

Paisley. A pattern of tear-drop shapes called *botehs* surrounded by floral designs, originally on painted and printed fabric produced in India, and copied on cashmere shawls first woven in Paisley, Scotland.

Panné velvet. A pile fabric made from silk or synthetic fibers with similar properties that is calendered in one direction to produce a high luster. It is lightweight and drapes well.

Passementerie. Trimmings and elaborate braids used for trim.

Paste-resist dyeing. A resist-dyeing process in which the resist is starch paste.

Patchwork. A technique in which pieces of cloth are stitched together to make one unit with no ground cloth. The pieces are typically small and of different colors or types of fabric.

Pattern. A design consisting of the repetition of one or more motifs arranged in a regular, continuous, or formal manner.

Peau de soie. A satin-weave fabric made from silk or synthetic fibers with similar properties that has a cross-rib and a slight luster.

Pelmet. A fabric-covered shaped valance.

Percale. A plain-woven fabric with a high thread count made from fine carded or combed cotton.

Persian knot. Senneh knot. See Knot, figures G-8 and G-9.

Petit-point. See Gros-point.

Pick. One filling yarn.

Pickage. Number of filling yarns or threads per inch.

Piece dyeing. Dyeing fabric after it has been constructed.

Pigment. An opaque colorant that does not chemically bond to the fiber as does dye. A chemical binder or binding process is necessary to adhere the color. Pigment may change the reflectiveness of the fiber or fabric, and may be used to create a matte effect.

Pigment printing. A printing process that employs pigments and binders rather than dye-based colorants.

Pile. Cut or uncut looped yarn on the surface of a textile produced by a variety of techniques including: (1) yarns knotted through a base fabric (see figures G-7, G-8, G-9, and G-10); (2) yarns woven over wires through a base fabric; the wires are slipped out to form a loop and may have a cutting edge which, when raised, produces cut pile (see figure G-13); (3) yarns woven through a double cloth and sliced to produce two pieces of cut-pile fabric (see figure G-14).

Figure G-13. Looped pile

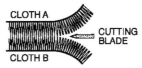

Figure G-14. Double cloth pile

Pilling. The formation of fuzzy balls on the surface of a fabric in reaction to abrasion.

Piqué. A woven fabric with raised areas, usually vertical cords or small geometric surface designs, created with heavy stuffer picks.

Plaid. A woven design formed by crossing warp and filling yarns of different colors. In a true plaid, the warp and filling are the same layout. Plaids may also be printed. See also Tartan.

Plain weave. The most basic of weaves, in which filling yarns alternately cross over and under warp yarns. Variations are produced by varying the character of the yarns used and the spacing and color of warp and filling. Basket weave and rib weave are variations of plain weave. *See* Figures G-1, G-6, G-11, G-15.

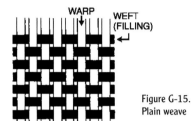

Figure G-15. Plain weave

Plaiting. A construction formed by interlacing two or more elements. Not usually applied to woven fabrics, the term refers to braids, mats, and baskets.

Pleat. Fold in a fabric fixed by stitching or heat.

Plissé. (1) Originally, a cotton fabric treated with caustic soda so as to shrink the fabric where the caustic soda is applied, producing a pleated effect. (2) Any fine lightweight pleated fabric.

Plush. A velvet with long pile, usually made of mohair, wool, or synthetic fiber.

Ply. (1) A single yarn element twisted with one or more others into a yarn or cord. (2) An individual layer of fabric in a product made of multiple layers, for example, flannel-backed vinyl.

Polished cotton. Cotton fabric with a sheen produced by a satin weave or finishing process.

Polka dot. A dot that forms a surface pattern; may be embroidered, printed, flocked, or woven.

Polyester. (1) A man-made fiber that is strong, washable, and abrasion resistant, but subject to pilling, static electricity, and staining. (2) Fabric made of polyester fiber.

Polypropylene. A man-made fiber that is bulky but lightweight and has a low melting temperature, which allows easy thermotexturing of the yarn. Polypropylene can only be solution dyed. Also called olefin.

Polyvinyl chloride (PVC). A widely used thermoplastic that can be extruded or molded and may be rigid or flexible. PVC film may be cut into strips and woven.

Pongee. Originally, plain-woven natural-colored silk, produced from uncultivated silk on handlooms, characteristically with slubs and irregularities. Also called tussah; however, pongee describes the fabric, tussah the yarn.

Poplin. Plain-woven fabric of cotton or man-made fiber with fine horizontal ribs produced by using a heavier filling yarn than warp and more picks than ends.

Portiere. A curtain that hangs in a doorway.

Prayer rug. An oriental rug with an arch design at one end used for kneeling during Muslim prayers.

Print. Fabric that has been printed.

Printing. A process in which a pattern or motif is applied to a fabric by means of rollers, wooden blocks, screens, stencils, or other techniques. *See* Block printing, Discharge printing, Resist printing, Roller printing, Screen printing.

Provençal prints. Country French textile designs derived from eighteenth-century wood-block prints, usually small-scale floral or geometric patterns in rich sunny colors.

Punched work. Openwork embroidery in which some threads of the base fabric are pulled aside and then stitched.

Quality. Term that categorizes fabric by fiber content, yarn size, and number of ends or picks per unit measurement without respect to weave construction, pattern, or finish.

Quill-work. A decorative technique used by Native Americans in which quills (from porcupines or birds) are dyed and woven into fabrics or skins.

Quilt. (1) A coverlet made by stitching through two layers of fabric that enclose a layer of padding. (2) To stitch through the layers of a quilt, usually in a predetermined pattern.

Raffia. A long fiber, usually less than 1 inch (2.5cm) wide, harvested from the raffia palm. Traditionally, the fiber is used to make mats and baskets but it may be woven into fabric.

Rag rug. A woven rug with a cotton warp and a filling made from cut strips of fabric.

Railroading. Applying fabric to furniture so that the filling runs vertically. Not all fabrics can be railroaded.

Raised embroidery. Needlework that creates a pattern by covering padding with stitching.

Ramie. Fiber made from the bark of the ramie plant. It is soft but strong and is used alone or blended with other fibers to make thread, twine, and yarn that can be woven or knitted.

Raw. The unprocessed state of a fiber.

Raw silk. Silk that has not been completely degummed and is stiff.

Rayon. A strong, easily dyed man-made fiber made from cellulose. It is used alone or blended with other fibers in a variety of textiles from carpeting to fabrics with a soft hand that drape well.

Repp. A fabric with a horizontal rib effect characterized by closely spaced warp yarns with ribs or cords in the filling. A slub yarn may be used in the filling for texture.

Repeat. (1) Term used to refer to a motif that, when duplicated in a regular manner, results in a pattern. It is applied to patterns that are woven, printed, embroidered, or created by other methods, and is also used to describe the spatial relationship between the motifs. For example, a pattern repeated every 24 inches is a 24-inch repeat. (2) The number of threads necessary to create the pattern in a weave.

Resin. A synthetic finishing substance applied to

fabric to give it stability or a specific luster or hand.

Resist dyeing. A process in which selected yarns or areas of fabric are colored while others are treated in a manner that prevents the acceptance of color. When the resist is removed, the design remains. The fabric may be over-dyed for additional effects. *See* Batik, Ikat, Kasuri, Paste-resist dyeing, Tie-dyeing, Tritik, Warp or weft-resist dyeing, Wax-resist dyeing.

Resist printing. A process similar to resist dyeing in which the resist is applied by means of a printing technique.

Rib. A straight raised ridge repeated across the length or width or diagonal of a fabric.

Rib weave. A plain weave with ridges produced by combining different weights of warp and filling yarns or by varying warp tension.

Ribbon. Narrow woven fabric used as trimming.

Rip stop. A lightweight fabric with additional yarns woven in to resist tears. Originally used for sails and parachutes.

Roller printing. The process of applying a design to fabric by means of engraved copper rollers.

Roman shade. A flat fabric shade that draws up from the bottom in accordion pleats.

Rows. (1) The average number of pile yarns per unit of measurement on the warp of carpet. (2) The stitches in knitting or crocheting that constitute one run from side to side.

Ruching. The gathering or close pleating of fabric within a confined area.

Rug. A floor covering of a specific size and design. Rugs may be flat- or pile-woven or both, but also may be made from nonwoven materials such as felt or animal skins. The term is often used interchangeably with carpet.

Sailcloth. Originally, cotton duck used for construction of boat sails, now a term that refers to a wide group of strong medium- or heavy-weight plain-woven fabrics of cotton, synthetic fibers, or a blend.

Sateen. A filling-faced satin weave. *See* figure G-16.

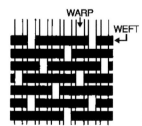

Figure G-16. Sateen (filling-faced satin weave)

Satin. A smooth, warp-faced fabric that is a product of the satin weave. *See* figure G-17.

Satin weave. A basic weave that produces a smooth surface by floating warp yarns over multiple picks (warped-faced) or floating filling yarns over multiple ends (filling-faced). The points of intersection of warp and filling are as widely spaced as possible. *See* figures G-16 and G-17.

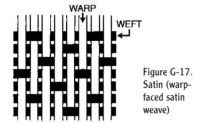

Figure G-17. Satin (warp-faced satin weave)

Screen printing. Technique of decoration developed from stenciling in which color in paste form is forced through the unblocked areas of a mesh onto the surface being decorated. The mesh may be woven fabric or metal screen, and may be flat and framed or on a cylinder.

Schiffli embroidery. A mechanical technique used to manufacture embroidered fabric. The decorative thread is attached to the fabric by stitches in the back of the fabric.

Scotchgard. A proprietary stain repellent applied to fabric and carpeting.

Scrim. Lightweight, loose, plain-woven cotton or linen fabric. Also called gauze.

Sculptured. Term used to describe the raised and depressed areas of a pile carpet design.

Seersucker. Fabric, usually cotton or blend, woven to create a permanent crinkled stripe in the warp produced by weaving alternating groups of warps slack and tight or by using warp yarns of different fibers, one that shrinks and one that does not when chemically treated.

Selvage or selvedge. Fabric edge parallel to the warp. The filling yarns are held by these end yarns, which usually are a stronger yarn than the rest of the warp.

Senneh (or Senna) knot. *See* Knot, figures G-8 and G-9.

Serge. Any smooth-faced regular twill fabric with a prominent diagonal.

Sett. Number of warp yarns or threads per unit of measurement.

Shantung. Plain-woven silk, originally made from uncultivated silk on handlooms in Shantung, China, with filling yarns of various thickness with slubs.

Sharkstooth scrim. A medium-weight cotton scrim used for theatrical drops. Woven with an open rectangular pattern, it is opaque when lighted from the front but translucent when objects behind it are lighted.

Shirred rug. A handmade rug with a pile made of fabric strips hooked through a canvas back.

Sheer. (1) Term used to describe lightweight, translucent fabric made from a variety of fibers in a variety of weaves. (2) Translucent curtains hung over glass windows, often behind drapes.

Shot fabric. Fabric woven with warp and filling yarns that reflect light differently, producing an iridescent effect.

Sign cloth. A medium-weight plain-woven fabric with the face filled with starch, clay, plastic, or vinyl, used for banners and outdoor signs.

Silk. (1) A continuous filament extruded by silkworms to form their cocoons, from which it is harvested. The raw silk filament is stiff from the gum called sericin that holds the cocoon together, and is removed by boiling. The cleaned filament is fine, supple, lustrous, and exceptionally strong. (2) Thread or fabric made from the silk filament.

Sisal. A long, durable, and flexible fiber from the leaves of the sisal plant. It ranges in color from light beige to yellow to olive and is used for twine, cord, mats, and carpets.

Size. Substance applied to yarn or as a finish to fabric that adds smoothness, stiffness, luster, body, or other surface qualities.

Slit tapestry. *See* Tapestry, figure G-19.

Slub. A thick twist or heavier part of a length of yarn.

Slub yarn. A novelty yarn spun with alternating thick and thin areas.

Solution-dyeing. The process of coloring synthetic fiber while it is still in the solution state, before it is extruded into filaments.

Soumak. A weaving technique that produces a patterned weft-faced textile, often used for rugs. The weft may be structural or supplementary, and is carried forward over four warp yarns and backward under two. The structural version uses no ground weft, and is called soumak wrapping. The supplementary version (also called soumak brocading) uses a ground weft and may be classified as an embroidery stitch.

Soutache. A round braid, usually with a herringbone pattern, used for trimming.

Spandex. An elastic, flexible, and abrasion-resistant proprietary fiber composed primarily of polyurethane.

Spanish knot. *See* Knot, figure G-10.

Spun-bond. A nonwoven process for producing fabric by randomly joining synthetic filaments. During the process, the filaments twist and loop, forming an irregular net.

Staple. Natural fiber or cut length of filaments spun into yarn.

Stencil printing. The technique of producing a design by means of applying ink or paint to fabric through a motif cut out of paper, plastic, or other appropriate material (for the stencil) that is laid on the surface to be printed.

Stitch resist. *See* Tritik.

Stretch yarn. Yarn that has been manufactured to have a permanent twist or crimp. It may be a continuous-filament synthetic yarn or contain elastic fiber.

Stuffer. An extra yarn that runs between the back and front of the fabric and gives weight or bulk or a relief effect. *See also* Brocatelle, Matelassé.

Striae (or strié). A fabric colored by irregular stripes that are a variation of the ground color, usually creating a mottled effect.

Suedecloth. Woven or knitted fabric that has been finished with a short nap to give a hand that resembles suede.

Supplementary yarn. A warp or filling yarn that may be removed without affecting the base fabric. *See* Brocade, figures G-3, G-4, and G-18.

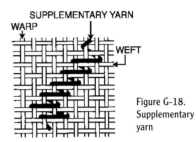

Figure G-18. Supplementary yarn

Suzani. Intricately embroidered covering or hanging from Central Asia.

Swatch. A small sample of fabric.

Swiss. Sheer, plain-woven cotton fabric with a hard finish that may have a variety of mechanical embellishments. The most common is dotted Swiss.

Swivel weave. A mechanical technique that produces novelty fabric that appears to have been embroidered, produced with a loom attachment that applies a separate yarn to the ground fabric without the necessity of floats between the motifs.

Synthetic. *See* Man-made.

Tabby. (1) Plain weave. *See* Plain weave, figure G-15. (2) Fabric made with a plain weave.

Taffeta. A very fine plain-woven fabric, usually made of silk, mercerized cotton, or a synthetic with similar characteristics, with a smooth face, and, usually, a luster.

Taffeta weave. Plain weave. *See* Plain weave, figure G-15.

Tambour work. An embroidery technique that uses chain stitches applied with a hooked needle, often found in machine lace.

Tapa cloth. A variety of bark cloth that may be made in a variety of weights and is highly receptive to paint and dye. It is one of the oldest nonwoven fabrics.

Tapestry. (1) A handwoven textile in which the design is created by discontinuous filling yarns worked over specific areas of warp and joined by a variety of interlocking methods including slit, dovetailed, interlocking, and eccentric. *See* figures G-19, G-20, G-21, and G-22. (2) The weaves used in these handwoven fabrics. (3) A jacquard fabric that is tightly woven, weft-faced, with multiple warps and fillings, often in patterns and textures that resemble handwoven tapestry.

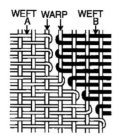

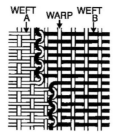

Figure G-19.
Slit tapestry

Figure G-20.
Interlocking
tapestry

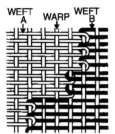

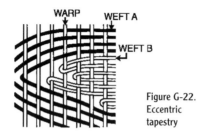

Figure G-21.
Dovetailed
tapestry

Figure G-22.
Eccentric
tapestry

Tartan. A plaid worsted twill or plain weave, usually symmetrical, true plaids, with distinct patterns that historically represent different Scottish clans. Today the term also refers to a variety of twill-woven plaids in many different yarns that resemble the originals. *See also* Plaid.

Tattersall. A large check, usually in multiple colors on a solid ground, creating a bold and gaudy effect.

Tentering. A finishing technique in which fabric is stretched to a desired size and heat set.

Tensile strength. The resistance of a yarn to breaking when stretched.

Tensile structure. A construction whose support system is based on a tension membrane between structural members, for example, a tent. In architecture, the term is usually applied to a construction with vertical supports, a foundation, boundary cables, and a fabric skin.

Terry cloth. A looped warp pile fabric woven with the pile on both sides, usually made of cotton or an absorbent synthetic.

Textile. A woven fabric.

Texture. The general description of a fiber, yarn, or fabric in terms of its structure, appearance, or hand.

Textured yarn. Filaments that have been processed to roughen their smooth appearance and yield a more handspun-like character.

Textures. Textiles that are woven with surface variations produced by the use of different yarns or loom techniques. These tactile variations are in the hand, character, and relief, but are not motif patterns.

Theatrical gauze. Plain-woven cotton or linen gauze, usually sized, used for theatrical scenery. It is available in broader widths than gauze manufactured for other purposes. Also called scrim.

Thermoplastic. The characteristic of a material to soften when exposed to heat.

Thermosetting. Process that uses heat to fix dyes and stabilize inks and paint, to produce finishes such as pleating, and to harden some synthetic fibers.

Thread. (1) A thin flexible cord, often plied and twisted, that is used for sewing and needlework. (2) A general term for yarn when used to refer to yarns in woven goods, as in "threads per inch."

Ticking. (1) A tightly woven textile usually used for making bedding. The weaves may be plain, satin, or twill. (2) Coarse, two-color stripes typically used for bedding fabric. Blue and white striped twill is the most common.

Tie-dyeing. A resist-dyeing process in which areas of fabric are stitched or tied into pleated wads before the material is dyed. The tied areas are protected from the dye. The fabric may be over-dyed. The technique may be applied to the yarns before weaving.

Toile de Jouy. A printed linen, cotton, or silk fabric characterized by floral designs and genre scenes printed in a single color on a light ground, usually finely drawn in the style of engravings. The French town of Jouy was the site of the first western factory to produce these copper-engraved prints of designs that originated in India for the European market. Commonly abbreviated to toile.

Trapunto. A quilting technique that produces a raised design by outlining the design with stitching, and then stuffing the defined areas with batting or cord.

Tricot. A durable knitted fabric with vertical wales on the face, usually made of acetate, nylon, or rayon.

True check, true plaid. *See* Check, Plaid.

Tritik. A resist-dyeing technique that employs a drawn-up stitch as the resist method. It allows for intricate designs. Also called stitch resist.

Tuft. Yarns or strips of pliable material pulled

through a base fabric so that either both ends of the material are on the face of the fabric or a group of long loops is formed. Tufts may be tied or fastened, as in the case of quilts where they hold layers in place, or they may be secured with a backing, as in a tufted carpet, or they may serve purely for decoration.

Tufted. (1) Carpet produced by a tufting machine rather than a loom. The tufts are secured to the base by latex or a similar substance. (2) Fabric with tufting in lines or patterns. The tufting may be done by hand or a mechanized method. *See also* Candlewick, Chenille bedspread. (3) In upholstery, the use of buttons, pleats, or tucks to hold fabric and padding in place, producing raised patterns, typically diamond or rectangular (biscuit) shaped.

Turkish knot. Ghiordes knot *See* Knot, figure G-7.

Tussah. A coarse, light brown silk yarn made from cocoons of uncultivated silk worms.

Tweed. A broad group of woolen fabrics and yarns. The yarn is often multicolored or the fabric may be woven from several colors of yarns, in plain or twill weaves. The hand ranges from rough to soft, but varieties are distinguished by a speckled, nubby quality derived from the yarn. Some specific tweeds are Harris and Donegal, named for the place made.

Twill. A basic weave in which the filling yarns pass over one or more and under two or more warp yarns in successive, offset progression to create the appearance of diagonal lines. Denim is the ubiquitous twill fabric. Some variations of the weave are herringbone and bird's eye. *See* figure G-23.

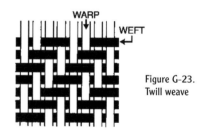

Figure G-23.
Twill weave

Twill damask. A twill-woven fabric in which combinations of warp- and filling-face weave mix to create an intentional pattern.

Twining. A construction in which groups of two or more yarns or similar materials twist around each other as they are interlaced with elements in the opposite direction. *See* figure G-24.

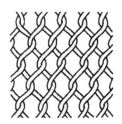

Figure G-24.
Twining

Twist. The rotation of a group of fibers or filaments about its axis either to the left or right. Direction of twist is the angle of inclination of the group relative to the axis, and is designated S-twist (left) or Z-twist (right).

Tyvek. Proprietary spun-bonded fabric made of olefin.

Unbleached muslin. Lightweight plain-woven cotton fabric left in its distinctive cream natural color.

Urethane. A group of chemical compounds based on isocyanates that are mixed so as to produce a wide variety of foam materials that range from soft to rigid to brittle.

Valance. A rectangular border usually used at the top of a window. It may also refer to a bed canopy or similar decorative use.

Vegetable dyes. Dyes derived from botanical sources, for example, madder and indigo.

Velour. (1) A pile fabric constructed in a plain or satin weave, usually cotton, with a dense, short cut pile that lies in one direction. (2) A napped, often knitted, fabric made to imitate velvet. (3) A general term for velvet and plush.

Velvet. A warp-pile fabric with a short, dense cut pile. It has a soft hand and may be constructed as a double cloth or by means of cutting wires.

Velveteen. A filling-pile fabric constructed similarly to velvet, usually of cotton.

Viscose rayon. See Rayon.

Vinyl. A nonwoven water-repellent film that may be used alone or laminated to a backing fabric.

Voided velvet. A patterned fabric in which the pattern is made by the contrast between pile and a non-pile ground. It may be made by a burn-out process.

Voile. A sheer, plain-woven fabric with a low thread count made from a variety of fibers. It has a crisp hand.

Waffle weave. A group of fabrics woven on a dobby loom that have dimensional, square ridges forming a waffle-like texture.

Wale. (1) One of the ribs or cords in a woven fabric with prominent ribbing, such as corduroy. (2) A lengthwise row of stitches in knitted fabric.

Warp. The yarn elements that run lengthwise on a loom. The warp yarns are in place before the weft or filling yarns are woven over and under them. Individual warp yarns are called ends. See figure G-15.

Warp dyeing. A process in which the warp is dyed before the fabric is woven. See also Warp-resist dyeing.

Warp-faced. Fabric that has a greater number of ends (warp yarns) than picks (filling yarns) on the face, or in which the ends are heavier than the picks, causing the warp to dominate.

Warp print. A process in which the warp yarns are printed before the fabric is woven. The filling yarns are usually solid-colored. During weaving, the warp yarns shift slightly, resulting in a slightly blurred pattern.

Warp or weft resist dyeing. A resist-dyeing technique in which the warp or weft or both are tie-dyed before the cloth is woven.

Washi. Handmade Japanese paper often used in furnishings such as shoji screens and decorative wall hangings. Used since ancient times, it is manufactured in many thicknesses and may be laminated.

Watered fabric. See Moiré.

Wax-resist dyeing. A resist-dyeing process that uses hot wax as the resist.

Weave. The process of interlacing warp and filling materials at right angles. The basic weaves are plain, twill, and satin; other weaves are based on these. See Figures G-15, G-17, and G-23.

Weft. The yarn elements in a fabric that run horizontally or from selvage to selvage, crossing and interlacing with the warp, commonly called filling today. Also called woof. See figure G-15.

Wool. Fiber derived from the fleece of sheep. The fibers are resilient, and may be blended with other natural or man-made fibers.

Woolen. Yarn spun from short, crimped wool fibers and the fabric woven from that yarn, for example, tweed. See also Worsted.

Worsted. Yarn spun from long, combed wool fibers, and the fabric woven from that yarn. It has a smoother, finer, more even character than woolen yarn. Gabardine and serge are worsted fabrics. See also Woolen.

Yarn. A strand made from spun fibers or continuous filament that is used in weaving, knitting, and other similar processes.

Yarn dyed. Term that describes fabric made from yarn dyed before the construction of the fabric.

Zephyr. See Berlin yarn.

ANNOTATED BIBLIOGRAPHY AND RESEARCH SOURCES

BOOKS AND PAMPHLETS

AF Encyclopedia of Textiles. 3rd ed. American Fabrics and Fashion Magazine Editors. Englewood Cliffs, NJ: Prentice-Hall, 1980. Information on textile fibers, history and origins, design, manufacturing process, fabric finishing, and definitions. Illustrated with photographs and drawings.

All New York: The Source Guide. David Armory Lown and Patricia Twohill Lown. New York: W. W. Norton, 1997. Guide to over 5,000 suppliers and manufacturers of furnishings, design centers, and related services in New York.

Basic Guidelines for the Care of Special Collections. Nancy Davis, Pamela Hatchfield, Jane Hutchins. Washington: American Institute for Conservation of Historic and Artistic Works, 1973. Pamphlet from the AIC. See entry under Associations and Libraries.

The Book of Silk. Philippa Scott. London: Thames & Hudson, 1993.

The Care and Preservation of Textiles. Karen Finch and Greta Putnam. Berkeley, CA: Lacis, 1991. General reference for the nonspecialist written by a textile conservator. Photographs and illustrations.

Caring for Your Collections. The National Committee to Save America's Cultural Collections. Washington, DC: National Institute for Conservation, 1992. Conservators have contributed topical chapters to this practical guide to maintenance of textiles, furniture, and other objects.

The Collector's Dictionary of Quilt Names and Patterns. Yvonne M. Khin. Washington, DC: Acropolis Books, Ltd., 1980. Drawings of 2,400 quilt patterns organized by category with an index of specific pattern names.

The Connoisseur's Guide to Oriental Carpets. E. Gans Ruedin. Rutland, VT: Charles E. Tuttle, 1971. General classifications are detailed, countries of origin listed with maps, and line drawings of identifying features.

Considerations for the Care of Textile and Costumes: A Handbook for the Non-Specialist. Harold F. Mailand. Indianapolis, IN: Indianapolis Museum of Art, 1980. Pamphlet with instructions for textile maintenance, list of supplies.

The Curtain Book: A Sourcebook for Distinctive Curtains, Drapes and Shades for Your Home. Caroline Clifton-Mogg and Melanie Paine. New York: Bulfinch Press Book, Little, Brown, 1997. Pictorial survey of selected modern and historical window treatments. Glossary, source section.

Designing and Painting for the Theatre. Lynn Pecktal. New York: Holt, Rinehart and Winston, 1975. A reference guide to the production of theater scenery. Techniques and materials are explained with text, charts of theatrical fabrics and their applications, lists of formulas, and step-by-step explanations of processes. Illustrated with line drawings and photographs. Bibliography and glossary.

Dictionary of Fiber and Textile Terminology. Hoechst Celanese Corporation, 1990. A reference for textile terminology with emphasis on man-made fibers. Includes line drawings, an appendix of weaving guides and other technical tables, and is regularly updated. Available only from Hoechst Celanese Corporation, PO Box 32414, Charlotte, NC 28232. 704-554-3081.

A Dictionary of Lace. Pat Earnshaw. Buckinghamshire, UK: Shire Publications, 1982. Dictionary of lace types and terminology with photographs, drawings, and bibliography.

The Dictionary of Needlework. Sophia Caulfeild and Blanche Saward. New York: Arno Press, 1972. Reprint of the 1882 edition, which defines terms with text and engravings of general types of needlework, with detail drawings of stitches, patterns and techniques used in embroidery, lace, macramé, knitting, tatting, and other needlework.

A Dictionary of Textile Terms. 14th ed. Dan River. Danville, VA: Dan River Inc., 1992. A pocket-sized textile and fashion industry lexicon, regularly updated. Available only from Dictionary Department, Dan River Inc., 1325 Avenue of the Americas, New York, NY 10019.

Encyclopedia of Textiles. Judith Jerde. New York: Facts on File, 1992. Alphabetically arranged reference of textile terms, construction and maintenance techniques, manufacturing processes, people and topics.

Elements of Weaving: A Complete Introduction to the Art and Techniques. Jack Lenor Larsen and Azalea Stuart Thorpe. Garden City, New York: Doubleday, 1967. A practical overview of weaving technique, materials, and equipment. Bibliography and glossary.

Fabrics. 8th ed. Grace Denny. Philadelphia: J. B. Lippincott, 1962. Fabric names and definitions, with photographs and additional technical information. Bibliography.

Fabrics for Interiors: A Guide for Architects, Designers, and Consumers. Jack Lenor Larsen and Jeanne Weeks. New York: Van Nostrand Reinhold, 1975. A practical study of fabrics and their applications that explains textile constructions, finishing and coloring techniques, and industry terms and requirements. Illustrated with line drawings and photographs. Bibliography and glossary-index.

Fairchild's Dictionary of Textiles. 7th ed. Phyllis G. Tortora, Robert S. Merkel, ed. New York: Fairchild Publications, 1996. A reference for terms, with overview of textile industry, listing of synonyms, trade associations, professional and educational organizations, bibliography.

A History of Dyed Textiles. Stuart Robinson. Cambridge, MA: The MIT Press, 1969. A general study of dye techniques, materials, and explanations of terminology. Chart details geographical distribution of techniques. Appendices include international listing of textile museums, collections, and libraries. Bibliography.

A History of Printed Textiles. Stuart Robinson. Cambridge, MA: The MIT Press, 1969. A general study of print techniques and explanations of terminology with special emphasis on Great Britain. International listing of textile museums, collections, and libraries. Bibliography.

The Identification of Lace. Pat Earnshaw. Buckinghamshire, UK: Shire Publications, 1994. Study of the identifying characteristics of types of lace.

Interlacing: The Elemental Fabric. Jack Lenor Larsen with Betty Freudenheim. Tokyo: Kodansha International, 1979. A view of fabric's basic structures. Extensively illustrated with line drawings and photographs. Bibliography and combined glossary-index.

The Illustrated Dictionary of Lace. Judyth L. Gwynne. Berkeley, CA: Lacis, 1997. Entries are accompanied by a photograph, date, material content, construction, application, and museum sources. Glossary.

Kilim: The Complete Guide. Alastair Hull and José Luczyc-Wyhowska. London: Thames & Hudson; San Francisco: Chronicle, 1993.

Know Your Fabrics: Standard Decorative Textiles and Their Uses. Lucy Taylor. New York: John Wiley & Sons, London: Chapman & Hall, 1951. A study of types, uses, and history of decorative fabrics. Listing of fabrics includes definitions and decorator terms used prior to 1960. Photographs and line drawings illustrate text.

Lace. Virginia Churchill Bath. Chicago: Henry Regnery, 1974. A study of types and of historical and modern laces and construction techniques. Illustrated with general photographs, and close-up shots and line drawings of techniques and structures. Bibliography.

Lace: History and Fashion. Anne Krantz. New York: Rizzoli, 1989. A survey of lace used in furnishings and fashions from the sixteenth century to the present. Includes photographs, a short glossary, bibliography.

Metallic Fabrics for Architecture-GKD Design Guide. 2/97 ed. Dueren, Germany: GKD-Gebr. Kufferath, GmbH. KG, Metallweberstrasse 46, D-52348 Dueren, Germany. Product catalog with wide range of woven metal fabrics, with applications, and structural information. Illustrated with drawings and photographs.

The National Trust Manual of Housekeeping. Hermione Sandwith and Sheila Stainton. London: Viking Penguin Books, 1988. The traditional maintenance methods as applied to collections in England's National Trust homes.

Needlework in America. History, Design, and Techniques. Virginia Churchill Bath. New York: A Studio Book, Viking Press, 1979. Overview of the history and techniques of needlework. Photographs and detailed drawings of motifs and techniques helpful in identification. Bibliography.

The Needleworker's Dictionary. Pamela Clabburn. New York: William Morrow, 1976. Dictionary format of terms, tools, and styles of needlework in fashion and furnishings. Illustrated with photographs and line drawings. International listing of collections and museums, and bibliography.

Nonwoven Fabric Primer and Reference Sampler. E. A. Vaughn. Cary, NC: Association of the Nonwoven Fabrics Industry, 1992.

Oriental Carpet Design: A Guide to Traditional Motifs, Patterns and Symbols. P. R. J. Ford. London: Thames & Hudson, 1992.

Oriental Carpets: A Complete Guide. Murray L. Eiland Jr. and Murray L. Eiland III. New York: Bulfinch Press, Little, Brown, 1998. Identification and survey, organized by geographical origin. General definitions in text.

The Oriental Rug Lexicon. Peter Stone. London: Thames & Hudson; Seattle: University of Washington Press, 1997.

Plain and Fancy: American Women and Their Needlework, 1700–1850. Susan Burrows Swan. New York: A Rutledge Book, Holt, Rinehart and Winston, 1977. A survey of needlework. Glossary of stitches and techniques is illustrated with line drawings and photographs. Bibliography.

The Primary Structures of Fabrics. Irene Emery. Washington, DC: The Textile Museum; London: Thames & Hudson, 1994. A basic text classifying textile structures. Extensively illustrated with close-up photographs.

The Quilt Encyclopedia Illustrated. Carter Houck. New York: Harry N. Abrams, with the Museum of American Folk Art, 1991. Information about quilting history, terms, techniques, tools, patterns, and care, with photographs.

Quilts in America. Patsy Orlofsky and Myron Orlofsky. New York: Abbeville Press, 1992. A survey of quilt history, techniques, patterns, and styles. Includes guidelines for determining age, instructions for care, photographs, and bibliography.

Rio Grande Textiles. Nora Fisher, ed. Santa Fe: Museum of New Mexico, 1994. A survey of southwestern textiles including history and techniques of dyeing, weaving, and needlework. Illustrated with photographs, line drawings, maps, and tables. Glossary, bibliography.

Rugs and Carpets of the World. Ian Bennett, ed. New York: A & W, 1977. Rugs and carpets categorized by period, type, and geography, weaving techniques and materials. Photographs and line illustrations, information regarding purchase and maintenance, glossary, bibliography, maps of major weaving areas.

Silk. Jacques Anquetil. Paris: Flammarion, 1995. An illustrated history of silk weaving and applications in furnishings and fashions. Bibliography and glossary.

Softness and Movement of Light. Robert Kronenburg. Architectural Monographs No. 48, FTL Todd Dalland and Nicholas Goldsmith. London: Academy Editions, 1997. A review of the work of two architects who design tensile structures with an overview of tensile design, materials, and techniques. Photographs and line drawings, bibliography.

The Story of Silk. Dr. John Feltwell. New York: St. Martin's Press. 1991. An overview of the history of silk making and the silk trade. Appendices list silk weavers, museums, societies, and associations. Bibliography and glossary.

Style Sourcebook: The Definitive Illustrated Dictionary of Fabrics, Paints, Wallpaper, Tiles, Flooring. Judith Miller. New York: Stewart, Tabori and Chang, 1998. A survey of period styles organized chronologically. Photographs show 2,300 samples with purchasing details.

Tapestry. Barty Phillips. London: Phaidon Press, 1994. A broad survey of tapestries from many cultures and periods. Includes photographs, illustrations, information regarding purchase and maintenance, lists of collections, bibliography, and glossary.

Techno Textiles: Revolutionary Fabrics for Fashion and Design. Sarah E. Braddock and Marie O'Mahony. London: Thames and Hudson, 1998. Contemporary textile technology and applications in fashion, furnishings, industry and art. Photographs, bibliography, glossary, directory of suppliers, museum and exhibition information.

Tensile Architecture. Philip Drew. Boulder, CO: Westview Press, 1979. Survey from nomadic tent cultures to the late 1960s' work of Frei Otto. Extensive bibliography.

The Tent Book. E. M. Hatton. Boston: Houghton-Mifflin, 1979. Illustrated text covers the general history, architectural constructions, artistic and consumer uses. Includes a source guide and bibliography.

Textile Art. Michel Thomas, Christine Mainguy, and Sophie Pommier. New York: Skira/Rizzoli, 1985. Illustrated history of textile art including archeological fabrics, tapestries, and contemporary fabric art. Bibliography.

The Textile Art in Interior Design. Melanie Paine. Photography by Bill Batten. New York: Simon and Schuster, 1990. A decorator's view of textiles and applications. Extensive source directory, bibliography, glossary.

The Textile Arts: A Handbook of Weaving, Printing, and Other Textile Techniques. Vera Birrell. New York: Schocken Books, 1973. An overview of textile constructions, techniques, and materials. Illustrated with photographs and drawings. Bibliography and glossary.

Textile Collections of the World. Cecil Lubell, ed. New York: Van Nostrand Reinhold, Vol. I (United States and Canada) and Vol. II (United Kingdom and Ireland), 1976; Vol. III (France) 1977. Guides to textile collections by city. Photographs and maps.

Textile Designs: Two Hundred Years of European and American Patterns. Susan Meller and Joost Elffers. New York: Harry N. Abrams; London: Thames & Hudson, 1991. A visual encyclopedia in color of 1,823 printed designs, organized by motifs with captions indicating date, print technique, usage, and scale of reproduction.

Textiles: A Handbook for Designers. Rev. ed. Marypaul Yates. New York: W. W. Norton, 1996. A study of the textile industry for the professional and student, emphasizing the processes and practices of textile design. Illustrated with photographs and drawings. Bibliography and glossary.

Textiles, 5000 Years. Jennifer Harris, ed. New York: Harry N. Abrams, 1991. A comprehensive survey of a wide range of textiles and applications by twenty-four experts. Illustrated with photographs and line drawings. Extensive bibliography, glossary.

Textile Terms and Definitions. Manchester, England: Textile Institute. Quadrennial publication compiled by the Terms and Definitions Committee of the Textile Institute. See entry under Associations and Libraries.

Thomas Register of American Manufacturers. 88th ed. New York: Thomas Publishing, 1999. Published in thirty-four volumes, this resource lists products and services alphabetically, with company contact information, and cross-references. Products are by type and application, geographical locale, and specific supplier. Updated annually and available on line. 5 Penn Plaza, New York, NY 10001.

Traditional Indian Textiles. John Gillow and Nicholas Barnard. London: Thames & Hudson, 1991.

Traditional Indonesian Textiles. John Gillow. London: Thames & Hudson, 1993.

Traditional Textiles of Central Asia. Janet Harvey. London: Thames & Hudson, 1996. Illustrated overview of costume and decorative textiles with museum source section.

The Tribal Eye: Antique Kilims of Anatolia. Peter Davies. New York: Rizzoli International, 1993. An illustrated view of Anatolian kilims, including general information about wool processing, dyeing, weaving techniques, patterns and motifs, and the cultural role of kilims. Bibliography.

Window Treatments. Karla J. Nielson. New York: Van Nostrand Reinhold, 1990. A survey of fabric and other window treatments with historical and technical notes. Illustrated with line drawings. Bibliography and glossaries for window, contract, and fabric terms,

World Textiles: A Visual Guide to Traditional Techniques. John Gillow and Brian Sentance. London: Thames & Hudson; New York: Bulfinch Press, Little Brown, 1999. An overview of handmade textiles. Glossary, bibliography, and information on collections with public access.

PERIODICALS

Architectural Digest. Condé Nast Publications, 6300 Wilshire Boulevard, Suite 1100, Los Angeles, CA 90048. Monthly publication with color photographs and topical features. Of particular interest are departments covering international shopping sources.

Crafts. Crafts Council, 44A Pentonville Rd., London N1 9BY, England.

Fabrics and Architecture. Bimonthly magazine of the Industrial Fabrics Association. Provides design and specifying information on industrial fabrics used in architecture. See entry under Associations and Libraries.

Hali: The International Magazine of Antique Carpet and Textile Art. Hali Publications, St. Giles House, 50 Poland Street, London W1V 4AX, England. Monthly publication with color photographs that includes topical articles, book and exhibit reviews, and an extensive international calendar of auctions, exhibitions, fairs, and conferences.

Industrial Fabric Product Review. Monthly publication of Industrial Fabrics Association. Articles on developing technology, publications, and market trends, calendar of events and listings of new products and publications. Annual directory issue, *Industrial Fabric Product Review Buyer's Guide*, lists companies, products, and trade names. See entry under Associations and Libraries.

Interior Design. 345 Hudson St., New York, NY 10014. Monthly publication with color photographs, topical features, book reviews, calendar of events and exhibits.

Interiors. BPI Communications, Inc., 1515 Broadway, New York, NY 10036. Monthly publication with color photographs and topical features. Calendar of industry events and exhibits.

International Textiles. Benjamin Dent & Co., 23 Bloomsbury Sq., London WC1A 2PJ, England.

Rowan Journal. Rowan Yarns, Green Lane Mill, Holmfirth, West Yorkshire HD7 1RW, England.

Surface Design. The Journal of the Surface Design Association, Inc. PO Box 360, Sebastopol, CA 95473-0360. Quarterly publication with color photographs, articles about fabric design and technology, reviews of books and exhibits, and educational notes.

Surface Newsletter. Quarterly newsletter of the Surface Design Association. News of association, calendar of topical events, book reviews, industry health and safety information. See entry under Associations and Libraries.

Textile Forum. English edition of Textilforum. Textil-Forum-Service/B. Sterk Friedenstr. 5, PO Box 5944, D-30059 Hannover, Germany. Quarterly publication with color photographs, articles about textiles in furnishings and fashion, construction techniques, a calendar of international topical events, reviews, and listings of textile libraries, publications, and Internet publications.

Textile History. W. S. Maney & Son, Hudson Road, Leeds LS9 7DL, England. Biannual journal that covers design, conservation, and textile applications in articles by specialists. Also includes reviews of books and exhibitions.

The Textile Museum Journal. The Textile Museum, Washington, DC. Annual compilations of articles by scholars and specialists in textile fields. The Journals no longer in print are available as photocopied volumes. See entry under Associations and Libraries.

The Textile Museum Book List. Semi-annual catalog of books available for purchase. Many are difficult to find elsewhere. See entry under Associations and Libraries.

The World of Interiors. Condé Nast Publications, Vogue House, 1 Hanover Square, London W1R 0AD, England. Monthly publication with color photographs, features about interior design and antiques, reviews of books and exhibits, and calendars of industry events, exhibitions, antique fairs, and auctions.

ASSOCIATIONS AND LIBRARIES

American Institute of Architects, 1735 New York Ave. NW, Washington, DC. 20006-5292

American Institute for Conservation of Historic and Artistic Works (AIC). 1717 K St., NW, Ste. 301, Washington, DC 20006.

American Fiber Manufacturers Association (AFMA). 1150 17th St. NW, Ste. 310, Washington, DC 20036.

American Textile History Museum. 491 Dutton St. Lowell, MA 01845-4221. Collection and library, by appointment.

American Society of Interior Designers (ASID). 608 Massachusetts Ave. NE, Washington DC 20002

Association of the Nonwoven Fabrics Industry (INDA). 1001 Winstead Dr., Ste. 460, Cary, NC 27513.

Cooper-Hewitt National Design Museum, Smithsonian Institution, 2 E. 91 St., New York, NY 10128-0669. Textile and wall coverings study collections: Design Resource Center (by appointment); Library: The Doris and Henry Dreyfuss Memorial Study Center (by appointment).

Fashion Institute of Technology. 227 W. 27th St., New York, NY 10001. The Museum at the Fashion Institute of Technology

Textile Collection. Membership necessary for nonstudent use of collection; appointment necessary for nonstudent use of library.

Industrial Fabrics Association (IFAI). 1801 Country Rd. BW., Roseville, MN 55113-4061.

Institute for Textile Technology. PO Box 391, Charlottesville, VA 22902.

International Institute for Conservation of Historic and Artistic Works (IIC). 6 Buckingham St. London WC2N 6BA, England.

Interior Design Society (IDS). PO Box 2396, High Point, NC 27261.

International Interior Design Association (IIDA). 341 Merchandise Mart, Chicago, IL 60654-1104.

International Society of Interior Designers (ISID). 1933 S. Broadway, Suite 138, Los Angeles, CA 90007

Material Connexion. 4 Columbus Circle, New York, NY, 10019. Membership necessary for use of collection of furnishings and construction materials, information services, data bank.

Metropolitan Museum of Art, Antonio Ratti Textile Center. 5th Ave. and 82nd St., New York, NY 10021. Textile study collection (by appointment).

Musée Historique des Tissus (Textile History Museum). 34 rue de la Charité, F-69002 Lyon France

Musée des Themes et de l'Hôtel de Cluny (Cluny Museum), 6 Place Paul-Painleve, F-75005 Cluny France.

Musée du Louvre (The Louvre), Palais du Louvre, F-75041 Paris France

National Institute for Conservation. (NIC) 3299 K Street NW, Suite 403, Washington, DC 20007.

Philadelphia College of Textiles and Science. Henry Ave. and Schoolhouse Lane, Philadelphia, PA 19144. Textile study collection, Paley Design Center, 4200 Henry Ave. (by appointment); Gutman Library open during scheduled hours.

Surface Design Association. PO Box 360, Sebastol, CA 95473-0360.

Textile Institute. 10 Blackfriars St., Manchester M3 5DR, England.

The Textile Museum. 2330 S Street NW, Washington, DC 20008. Textile study collection (by appointment). Library open during scheduled hours.

Textile Society of America. PO Box 70, Earleville, MD 21919-0070.

Victoria & Albert Museum, Department of Textile and Dress. Cromwell Rd. SW7 2RL, London, England. Textile collection: Over 5,000 textiles accessible in study rooms, additional sections by appointment. National Art Library: prearranged pass is necessary.

Whitworth Art Gallery. The University of Manchester, Oxford Rd. M15 6ER, Manchester, England. Textile study collection (by appointment).

FABRIC SOURCES

(Note: Information given is as provided by the suppliers. Country codes precede phone numbers outside the United States. The country code for the U. S. is +1)

American Silk Mills Corp
41 Madison Ave., 41st floor
New York, NY 10010-2202
212-213-1919

Chuck Auerbach
557 Letchworth Dr.
Akron, Ohio 44303
330-867-5515

Auntie Macassar Ltd.
PO Box 636
New Rochelle, NY 10802
212-459-4217

Joh. Backhausen & Son
Karntner Strasse 33
A-1010 Vienna
Austria
43-1-514-04-62

Baker Furniture
1661 Monroe Ave NW
Grand Rapids, MI 49505
616-361-7321

Scott Bassoff-Sandy Jacobs,
    Antiques
200 Robbins Road
Rindge, NH 03461
603-899-3373

Bernhardt Textiles
1839 Morganton Blvd. SW
Lenoir, NC 28645
212-888-8664

James W. Blackmon, Antique Textile
    Art
2140 Bush St., #1
San Francisco, CA 94115
415-922-1859 (by appointment)

Joan R. Brownstein, Art &
    Antiques
2068 Ellis Hollow Road
Ithaca, NY 14850
607-539-6507 (by appointment)

Brunschwig & Fils, Inc.
979 Third Ave.
New York, NY 10022
212-838-7878

Marcy Burns American Indian Arts
PO Box 181
Glenside, PA 19038
215-576-1559

Calico Corners, Everfast, Inc.
203 Gale Lane
Kennett Square, PA 19348
610-444-9700

Rigo Carden, Inc.
40 W. 25th St., Gallery 214
New York, NY 10001
212-924-5754

Phyllis Carlson
3390 Rt. 30
On the Village Green
Dorset, VT 05251
802-867-4510

Lolly Chase Antiques
26 Cedar St.
Millis, MA 02054
508-376-8805

Chista
537 Greenwich St.
New York, NY 10013
212-924-0394

Chu's
1 Hollywood Road
Central, Hong Kong

Cocoon International Trade Co.
Arista Bazaar #93 3440
Sultanahmet-Istanbul, Turkey
90-212-638-3330

Teresa Coleman Fine Arts, Ltd.
79 Wyndham St.
Central, Hong Kong
852-2526-2450

Country Curtains
Main St., Dept. 5158
Stockbridge, MA 01262
800-456-0321

The Country Gallery Antiques
Rt. 315
Rupert, VT 05768
802-394-7753

Country Repeats
Southbury, CT 06488

Robert Coviello
44 Main St.
Essex, MA 01929
508-768-7039

Craftex Mills, Inc. of Penna.
450 Sentry Parkway East
Blue Bell, PA 19422-0795
610-941-1212

Crezana
134 D Mariner Dr.
Southampton, NY 11968
516-283-3101

D.C.D.C
30 W. 70th St.
New York, NY 10023

Marie Despres
15 Cannon Rd.
Norwalk, CT 06851

Nikki & Tom Deupree
American Furniture and Fine Arts
    of the Eighteenth and
    Nineteenth Centuries
480 North Main St.
Suffield, CT 06078
860-668-7262

Doblin Fabrics
2 Park Ave., Suite 1606
New York, NY 10016
212-578-1233

Rick Dodge
Antiques, Decorations, Prints,
    Books
Box D16
Montague, MA 01351
413-367-9676

Donghia
485 Broadway
New York, NY 10013
212-935-3713

Teddy & Arthur Edelman, Ltd.
28 Hawley Road, PO Box 110
Hawleyville, CT 06440-0110
212-751-3339

Entree Libre
110 Wooster St.
New York, NY 10012
212-431-5279

Exquisite Kimono
724 West Knoll Dr., #110
West Hollywood, CA 90069
310-657-5014

FTL Happold Architects and
    Engineers
157 Chambers St.
New York, NY 10007
212-732-4691

Fardin's Oriental Rugs
2490 Black Rock Turnpike,
    Box 327
Fairfield, CT 06430
203-335-1157

Fonthill Ltd.
979 Third Ave.
New York, NY 10022
212-755-6700

Franetta Fabrics, Inc.
1460 Broadway
New York, NY 10036
212-354-1727

Carolyn Forbes, Textiles, Antique
    Clothing and Accessories
Hollis, NH 03049
603-889-1494

GA Peach Designs
185 E. 85th St., 20F
New York, NY 10028
212-722-2765

Gallery Shirvan
Haliclar St. 50/52/54
Grand Bazaar
Beyazit-Istanbul, Turkey
90-212-522-4986

Gillian Hine Antiques
PO Box 127
Lancaster, PA 17608-0217
717-397-4152

G. P. & J. Baker Limited (U.S.
    sales, Lee Jofa)
P. O. Box 30
West End Rd.
High Wycombe
Bucks HP11 2QD England

Ewa Grabowski
Bloemgracht 17
Amsterdam 1016KB Holland
31-20-6225614 (April through
    November)

Grey Watkins, Ltd.
979 Third Ave.
New York, NY 10022
212-755-6700

Renate Halpern Galleries, Inc.
325 E. 79th St.
New York, NY 10021
212-988-9316 (by appointment)

William & Connie Hayes, Antiques
    and Textiles
90 Heide Farm Lane
Belleville, PA 17004
717-935-5125

Helix Design Group L.L.C.
244 Fifth Ave., Suite 2181
New York, NY 10001
800-564-2885

Historic Offerings
PO Box 12W
W. Townsend, MA 01474
978-597-6935

HiTex, Inc.
32813 Middlebelt Road
Farmington, MI 48334
248-855-6000

Istanbul Bazaar
Kapalicarsi, Cevahir Bedesten
Serif Aga Sok. 15-20-44-47
Istanbul, Turkey
90-212-5122-25-51

Karavan Art
Klodfarer Cd. Dr. Sevkibey Sk.
Ortaklan Han 6/2
Sultanahmet-Istanbul, Turkey
90-212-638-52

Joe & Mary Koval, Antiques
Box 97
Schellsburg, PA 15559
814-733-0092

La Belle Epoque
Piazza S. Francesco 18
52100 Arezzo, Italy
39-575-35-5495

Patricia Lea
77 Inchcliff Dr.
Gales Ferry, CT 06335
860-464-0466

Lee Jofa
201 Central Ave. South
Bethpage, NY 11714
516-752-7600

Louis Lawrence, Fine Artwork,
   Japanese Antiques
2124 Broadway, Suite 142
New York, NY 10023

Main Street Antiques
Kent, CT 06757
860-927-4916

Maison Du Tapis D'Orient
Arasta Çarsisi #151
Sultanahmet-Istanbul, Turkey
90-212-517-6808

M&J Decor
983 Third Ave.
New York, NY 10022
212-391-6200

Malden Mills Industries, Inc.
46 Stafford St.
Lawrence, MA 01841
978-659-5127

Manuel Canovas, Inc.
136 E. 57th St.
New York, NY 10022
212-752-9588

Maverick Group
Yates Weisgal, Inc.
185 E. 85th St., Suite 20F
New York, NY 10028
212-722-2765

Bob Meltzer
245 E. 58th St.
New York, NY 10022
212-644-8267

Merida Meridian, Inc.
643 Summer St.
Boston, MA 02210
800-345-2200

Kay Mertens, Vintage Textiles,
   Linens
1788 Everett Place
East Meadow, NY 11554

Marie Miller, American Quilts
Route 30
Dorset, VT 05251
802-867-5969

Monkwell Limited (U.S. sales, Lee
   Jofa)
10-12 Wharfdale Rd.
Bournemouth
Dorset BH4 9BT England
44-1202-752944

Diana de Mori
Piazza Grande 10
52100 Arezzo, Italy
39-575-27-505

Mt. Vernon Antiques
PO Box 66
Rockport MA 01966
978-546-2434

Mulberry at Home (U. S. sales,
   Lee Jofa)
219 King's Rd.
London SW3 5EJ England
44-171-8233886

John Murray
140 Horseshoe Dr.
Williamsburg, VA 23185
757-220-2114

Thomas Murray, Asiatica-
   Ethnographica
PO Box 1177
Mill Valley, CA 94942
415-679-4940

Jeffery Myers, Primitive and Fine
   Arts
12 E. 86th St.
New York, NY 10028
212-472-0115 (by appointment)

Myrna Myers, Arts d'Extrême
   Orient
11, rue de Beaune
Paris, France
33-1-4261-1108

Newark Performing Arts Center
1 Center St.
Newark, NJ 07102

North Cloth
189 Pepe's Farm Road
Milford, CT 06460
203-877-7638

Norwalk Museum
141 East Ave.
Norwalk, CT 06851
203-866-0202

Nuno Corporation
B1F AXIS Bldg., 5-17-1
Roppongi, Minato-ku
Tokyo, Japan 106-0032
81-3-3582-7997
212-421-9114 (NY showroom)

Orientations Gallery
802 Madison Ave.
New York, NY 10021
212-722-7705

Susan E. Oostdyk, Antiques
201-472-4435

Ortaasya ve Semertkan
Beyazit Meydani Devlet
Kütüphenses Unu, 3
Beyazit-Istanbul, Turkey
90-212-5829338

Panache
8445 Melrose Ave.
Los Angeles, CA 90069

Susan Parrish
Antique Quilts, Folk Art, American
   Indian Art
390 Bleecker St.
New York, NY 10014
212-645-5020

Passamaneria Valmar
Via Porta Rossa, 53/r
50123 Florence, Italy
39-55-284493

Payne Fabrics Inc.
979 Third Ave.
New York, NY 10022
800-527-2517

P. M. Vintage
Pretty Miss, Inc.
142 Stuyvesant Ave.
Lyndhurst, NJ 07071
201-804-8979

Pollack & Associates
150 Varick St.
New York, NY 10013
212-421-8755

The Preservation Society of
   Newport
424 Bellevue Ave.
Newport, RI 02840
401-847-1000

Props for Today
330 W. 34th St.
New York, NY 10001
212-244-9600

Randolph & Hein
232 E. 59th St., 3rd floor
New York, NY 10022
212-826-9898

Rich Beau Tiques
716-658-4334

Jon Eric Riis, Antique Textiles
875 Piedmont Ave. NE
Atlanta, GA 30309
404-881-9847

R. Jones & Associates, Inc.
3054 Irving Blvd.
Dallas, TX 75247

Robert Allen Fabrics
55 Cabbott Blvd.
Mansfield, MA 02048
212-696-0535

Rodolph, Inc.
999 West Spain St.
Sonoma, CA 95476
707-935-0316

Rohleder GmbH
Hofer Strasse 25
D-95176 Konradsreuth, Germany
49-92-92-590

Rosco Labs
52 Harborview Ave.
Stamford, CT 06902
800-767-2669

Trudi Roth, Antique Textiles
Canaan, NY
518-392-3463

Stella Rubin
12300 Glen Road
Potomac, MD 20854
301-948-4187

Sherryl Sachs, Antique Textiles
75 Summit Ave.
Sea Cliff, NY 11579-1142
516-671-3767

Scalamandré
37-24 24th St.
Long Island City, NY 11101
718-361-8500

Denise Schmidt
68 Riverside Dr.
Fairfield, CT 06430
203-254-3264

Shimus
City Shijo Karasuma 105
Shinmachi-nishiiru, Nishikikoji-dori
Nakagyo-ku
Kyoto 604 Japan
81-75-211-336

Susan Simon, Antique Textiles &
    Decorative Arts
New York, NY
212-663-5318 (by appointment)

Sivasli Istanbul Yazmacisi
Necdet Danis
Kapalicarsi, Yaglikcilar, 57
Istanbul, Turkey
90-212-526-77-48

Snow Leopard Antiques
Susan Curran
Lexington, VA 24450
540-464-8147

Sommers Plastics
81 Kuller Road
Clifton, NJ 07015
800-225-7677

Spink
Indian and Islamic Works of Art
5 King St., St. James's
London SW1Y 6QS England
44-171-930-7888

Stock in Trade
4 Calhoun St.
PO Box 336
Washington Depot, CT 06794
860-868-5090

Sunbury Textile Mills, Inc.
460 Broome St.
New York, NY 10013
212-925-4600

Swan Antiques
Rocky Hill
125 Apple St.
Essex, MA 10929
508-768-6878

Swede Tech, Inc.
4031 NE 17th Terrace
Ft. Lauderdale, FL 33334
800-737-7059

Swiss Net
World Textile Network
421 Seventh Ave., Suite 1006
New York, NY 10001

Synthetic Industries, Inc.
4019 Industry Dr.
PO Box 22788
Chattanooga, TN 37422
423-892-8080

Tech in Tex
Obernosterer-Strickstoff® GmbH
6850 Dornbirn, PO Box 10
Mitteldorfgasse 1, Austria
49-5572-20664 0

Textile Artifacts
12589 Crenshaw Blvd.
Hawthorne, CA 90250
310-676-2424

Textile Arts
1571 Canyon Road
Sante Fe, NM 87501
505-983-9780

Textillery
PO Box 3190
Bloomington, IN 47402
800-223-7673

Thomas Dare (Headquarters)
11-12 Saxon Business Centre
Windsor Ave.
London SW19 2RR England
44-181-542-1160
U. S.: 979 Third Ave.
New York, NY 10022
212-371-2358

Threads Of Life
Ethnographic Art—Textiles from
    Indonesia
Jalan Bisma #3
Ubud, Bali, Indonesia 80571
62-361-976583 (Fax)

Tibet Carpet Center
127 Madison Ave.
New York, NY 10016-7036
212-686-7661

Tinsel Trading Co.
47 W. 38th St.
New York, NY 10018
212-730-1030

Toltec Fabrics
437 Fifth Ave.
New York, New York 10016
212-684-2380

Troy Mills, Inc.
18 Monadnock St.
Troy, New Hampshire 03465
603-242-7711

Turkana Gallery
125 Cedar St., PH
New York, NY 10006
212-732-0273

Turkey Mountain Traders
7008 Main St.
Scottsdale, AZ 85251
602-423-8777

Tuva Looms
636 Broadway Room 1200
New York, NY 10012
212-598-1021

Unika Vaev USA
920 Broadway
New York, NY 10013
212-388-1000

Valdese Weavers
1000 Perkins Road SE
Valdese, NC 28690
828-874-2181

The Webb-Deane-Stevens
    Museum
211 Main Street
Wethersfield, CT 06109
860-529-0612

Charles Wibel
Antiques, Collectibles, Ephemera,
    Books
PO Box 546
Farmington, NH 03835-0546
603-755-4568

Wilton Historical Society
249 Danbury Rd.
Wilton, CT 06897
203-762-7257

Wren & Thistle Antiques
111 Tauton Ave., Rt. 44
Seekonk, MA 02771
508-336-0824

Linda Wrigglesworth
34 Brook St.
London WIYA England
44-171-408-0177

Xamax Industries, Inc.
63 Silvermine Rd.
Seymour, CT 06483
203-888-7200

Zee Stone Gallery
G/F, Yu Yuet Lai Building
43-55 Wyndham St.
Central, Hong Kong
852-2810-5895

PHOTO CREDITS

David Bohl
Museum Photographer
1046 Nantasket Ave.
Hull, MA 02045
781-925-5212

Michael Lent
421 Madison St.
Hoboken, NJ 07030
201-789-4866

Guy Gurney
PO Box 7206
Wilton, CT 06897
203-761-1021

ABOUT THE CD-ROM

The accompanying CD-ROM contains screen resolution TIFF files for all of the images in the book.

With the appropriate graphics software, the CD images can be used by artists and designers in developing concepts, preparing presentations for clients, and communicating visual information to others. Although the images are primarily intended for on-screen display, they can also be printed on either a black and white or color printer.

Further information about the image formats can be found on the readme.txt file on the CD.

Note: All images credited in this book to manufacturers or individuals are their property, and the designs may not be used for any commercial application without permission. Addresses are listed in Fabric Sources on page 324.

Original images can be obtained from the author. Write to P. O. Box 7206, Wilton CT 06897.